# A
# BEAUTIFUL
# CONSTRAINT

# A
# BEAUTIFUL
# CONSTRAINT

How To Transform Your Limitations Into Advantages, and Why It's Everyone's Business

**ADAM MORGAN & MARK BARDEN**

WILEY

For Cleo, Josie, Will, and Louis

# CONTENTS

# INTRODUCTION

## The beauty in constraint, and why it matters

**A few years ago,** the Internet meme "Do Your Best Jagger" sprung from the game of the same name. The rules were not complicated: players could challenge each other, at any time, in any place, in any medium they liked, to do an impression of Mick Jagger of the Rolling Stones performing on stage.

As soon as you received the challenge, you were obliged to do your impression. There was no waiting until you were somewhere a bit more private, or until you had taken your coat off, or finished your falafel. You had to channel your inner Mick there and then, in front of whatever audience you found yourself—and in the consequent video lay the success of the meme.

The interesting question is not so much why one would ever start on this kind of madness, but why the game worked so well. How was it that, even when imitated poorly by a reluctant amateur at the counter in Subway, the audience understood that Sir Michael Philip Jagger was briefly in their midst? How did the veteran rocker come to create an onstage routine recognizable to anyone with even the briefest acquaintance with a Rolling Stones concert?

The answer lies in the beneficial effect of a constraint.

In Keith Richards' autobiography, *Life*, Jagger's fellow Stone explains how this distinctively flamboyant style came about. When the Stones started, he says, they played very, very small venues, and by the time the equipment was set up and the audience in place the singer often had a space no bigger than the size of a table to perform in. But as the front man of a band ambitious to break through, Jagger learned to work it, even in such a confined area, and it was from this combination of desire and restriction that his unique moves evolved.

At some point, consciously or unconsciously, the young singer made a decision about how to respond to the space constraint. It could have led him to be static, restricted, somehow less; instead he used it as stimulus to be more dramatic, engaging, distinctive, compelling. He used it to make him more.[1]

## Beauty or the beast?

Constraints have a bad rap. Constraint is, by definition, a negative thing. Its imposition prevents us from acting as we would like to, because it restricts us in some important way. Constraints hold us down, knock us back, make us fail. "Don't fence me in," the old song says: if you want me to show what I can do, then leave me unconstrained.

This book's aim is to show how and why the opposite is true. How constraints can be fertile, enabling, desirable. Why they are catalytic forces that stimulate exciting new approaches and possibilities. How they can, in fact, make us more than we were, rather than less than we could be. Why we should see in them beauty, rather than the beast, and why that is more important now than ever.

## The invisible gift

The beneficial power of constraint is all around us, whether we recognize it or not. In lifelong relationships, we commit to one partner to the exclusion of others; the constraint we put on ourselves allows us to focus our emotional energy on building a life with that person, and gives us a deeper level of intimacy and security in return. In play, we understand that the limitations our favorite game's rules impose also give that game its unique character, energy, and pleasure; to relax those parameters means less of each. And a critical part of good parenting lies in understanding what limits are beneficial both to our children and to our family life—and then staying true to them, whether they are welcomed by our adorable little digital natives or not.

In business, the forced but delicious fruits of constraint are all around us, their starting impetus now all but forgotten. Google's home page is as simple as it is because that was the limit of Larry Page's coding ability at the time. He couldn't afford external resources, and all he knew how to do was create a search box and a logo—so while the rest of the search brands visually cluttered their home pages, Google's simplicity stood out for its understated respect for the user. Mario, the most famous character in the world's largest entertainment business, is as colorful as he is because of the challenges of eight-bit technology: to compensate for poor pixilation definition, designer Shigeru Miyamoto gave the character a large nose to emphasize his humanity, a mustache to obviate the need for a mouth and facial expressions, overalls to make it easier to see his arms in relation to his body, and a cap to free him from the problems of animating hair; the most recognizable character in video game history was born of technical constraints. Basketball owes much of its relentless energy to the introduction of the 24-second shot clock in 1954. And Twitter—well, we all know about Twitter. Which of us would be using Twitter at all today, if it had a limit of 14,000 characters rather than 140?

While the benefits differ, each of these constraints prompted a kind of enhancement. The people working with them made their constraints beautiful.

## New realities that call for a renewed inventiveness

Any good business has always worked within clear parameters. The whole concept of a brand, for instance, is in effect a beautiful constraint. It is the clarity on what that brand is not, as much as what it is, that allows a team to focus on finding fresh, relevant, and inventive ways to be true to what it stands for. When a brand stops respecting those limits and tries to become something it is not, it becomes weaker.

As authors and practitioners, we have spent most of our professional lives thinking about strategy and constraint. Our company specializes in challenger brands and businesses, for whom an ability to turn constraints to their advantage is particularly important. Challengers always have ambitions larger than their resources, and often lack what conventional wisdom would consider to be critical: a marketing budget, an R&D department, or a certain kind of functionality, for instance. They have to work with their constraints, reframing the conversation, creating a different marketing or business model. Indeed, how a challenger can make constraints beautiful often lies, for them, at the heart of a successful strategy.

In the sixteen years since we started eatbigfish, there has been a broader shift toward thinking like a challenger. It has become common to hear established market leaders talking about the need to maintain a challenger mindset as they seek to keep pace with a changing world, alert to insurgents keen to eat their lunch. Forced to compete for growth with ever-leaner headcount, resources and time, the injunction to "do more with less" has entered the mainstream—albeit without any real definition of what that means or how to do it. Regardless of the nature or size of the business, constraints of time, resources, and people are here to stay. One of the leadership challenges of today, like it or not, is the requirement to grow within constraints.

There is no shortage of stimuli here. All around us we see a new generation of inventiveness with constraint at its heart. Cars that go faster while using less fuel, fast food that's healthier, farming methods that create greater yields while using less water.

Sometimes these businesses are responding to constraints imposed on them. A new beer company, launched in the recession, lacked a marketing budget and was denied a bank loan. So instead they shared equity for cash, multiplying customer loyalty and advocacy, and became the fastest growing food-and-drink brand in the UK. Four California schools found a way to catch students up three grade levels in a year while biting down on a reduced budget. An unloved, long-struggling detergent brand, denied access to superior cleaning ingredients, found a different way to create value, and became Unilever's fastest-growing global brand.

Often, though, they are businesses that look to create breakthroughs and competitive advantages by imposing challenging constraints upon themselves. A new boutique hotel chain created a high-end yet affordable experience by denying itself many of the givens of a great hotel, such as the reception desk and restaurant. A seventy-year-old furniture

## The injunction to "do more with less" has entered the mainstream—albeit without any real definition of what that means or how to do it.

company set itself the target of producing a coffee table for just twice the price of a latte to put on it, and found an entirely new way to make a table. The ruling body of a motor sport precipitated a clutch of new innovations by requiring every competing team to produce engines that were 30 percent more fuel efficient, while maintaining the speeds that keep audiences excited.

We are living in an era of extraordinary people rewriting our sense of what is possible. They make an unarguable case that a constraint should be regarded as a stimulus for positive change—we can choose to use it as an impetus to explore something new and arrive at a breakthrough. Not in spite of the constraint, but because of it.

### The Age of Scarcity, The Age of Abundance

We sit at a nexus between an abundance of possibilities on one hand, and the reality of scarcities on the other. As business people, there is so much insight and opportunity available to us today. If we care to, we can learn how dynamic companies are breaking through, anywhere on earth. We have unprecedented opportunities to connect with our customers. Scores of potential partners could help us rethink, retool, manufacture, source, create, connect, and grow. And we can access the knowledge of everybody in our business, 24/7, if they would only take the time to reply to us. Which is where scarcity, the other reality, kicks in. Because, like us, they are all under pressure to do more with less, to manage an abundance of choices with tight budgets and lean teams. And these are only the current constraints. Fluctuating raw-material costs, retailers looking to recoup their own reversals in fortune from us, changes in the regulatory landscape, emerging new competitors from unexpected sources—every year offers a fresh series of constraints that will shape our trajectory forward, for better or worse.

Our personal and social lives are defined by the same dynamic of expanded opportunity and keenly felt limitation. We have access to more entertainment, knowledge, and personal development options than we will ever have time to use. Technology puts us in touch with an ever-expanding number of people. The ability to explore and share what we are passionate about is exponentially greater than it was even fifteen years ago. And yet we also feel short of time, energy, and attention. As Arianna Huffington has put it: "A world of too much data, too many choices, too many possibilities and too little time is forcing us to decide what we value."[2]

And as global citizens, we participate in a world of finite natural resources, with an increasing global population and increased demands from a new wave of ambitious economies. Potential new sources of abundance—cheap energy from solar, or more ideas from greater access to knowledge, for example—have yet to fully answer the challenges. We will need to learn to live with new kinds of constraints if we want the planet to support the next generation in the way it has supported ours.

So are things getting better, or are they getting worse? The answer, we have to believe, lies in our own hands. It hinges on how we choose to approach these new and emerging constraints, and whether we have the confidence to choose the path toward stimulating new possibilities. We are the stories we tell ourselves, according to psychologist Timothy Wilson; if we believe constraints only limit us, then they will. But Wilson also notes our remarkable capacity to redirect our narrative by taking small steps in a new direction, which become self-sustaining when they pay off. Our hope is to provide those steps, and start to change the narrative, so we can all grow to make constraints beautiful.[3]

### What is a constraint? And what do we mean by making it beautiful?

So where do we begin? It is striking that, while the world is full of encouragement in this regard (most cultures have an expression equivalent to "every cloud has a silver lining"), it's harder to find practical ways to translate that encouragement into action. The first version of the old American expression "When life gives you lemons, make lemonade" dates back to 1915; yet in the intervening hundred years of human experience nobody seems to have sat down to write a second part to the saying: what the recipe for making lemonade might actually be.

There is a body of influential work on the modern relevance of lean,[4] frugal innovation,[5] Jugaad,[6] and even the value of dyslexia to entrepreneurs.[7] Each of these offers insights into a different part of what it means to thrive within a particular set of constraints. Where substantive work has been done specifically about constraints in business, its focus is different from ours. *The Theory of Constraints* (known as TOC), first introduced in 1984, differs significantly from our ambition, both in its narrow definition of a constraint and in the type of response it proposes. It defines a constraint in terms of a performance-limiting restriction on a system, and specifically the one that is most limiting—the organization's weakest link. TOC proposes solutions for restructuring the organization, or key processes within it, in order to manage that constraint, eliminating its negative effect. Once this weakest link has been removed, what now becomes the new weakest link in the system becomes the next constraint on which to focus.[8]

TOC is a successful approach for some situations and businesses. Our interest, though, is not in eliminating constraints, but in positively leveraging them. We are proposing broader definitions of constraints and the situations in which we encounter them, and describing methods that can unlock a constraint's transformative benefits to make it a beautiful source of possibility and opportunity.

It will help to define first what we mean by a constraint, and what we mean by making it beautiful.

**In this book, a constraint is a limitation,** imposed by outside circumstances or by ourselves, that materially affects our ability to do something. Constraints fall into four different groups: constraints of foundation (where we are limited in something that is usually seen as a foundational element for success); constraints of resource (where we are limited in an important resource, such as money or people); constraints of time (where we are limited in the amount of time we have to do something); and constraints of method (where we are limited by having to do something in a certain way). An example of a constraint of foundation would be starting a shoe store without being able to let customers try shoes on before purchase (because you are an online retailer). A constraint of resource might be an airline having to fly a four-plane route, but having only three planes to do it with. Constraints of time need the least explanation here; we will all recognize these in our lives. And an example of a constraint of method might be making a hospital apply the systems of serving fast food to the way it performs life-changing eye surgeries.

**By making a constraint beautiful,** we mean seeing it as an opportunity, not a punitive restriction, and using it as a stimulus to see a new or better way of achieving our ambition. You will probably be familiar with the examples we have used above to illustrate the point.

The first example, the shoe store that wasn't able to offer customers the chance to try before buying, was, of course, Zappos. That limitation spurred them to introduce two important dimensions to the Zappos experience: first, a "we'll pay all shipping and make it really easy for you to return" process and, second, what they famously call "wow" customer service: warm, friendly interactions that have made customers not only comfortable buying shoes in this way, but evangelists for Zappos, with Net Promoter Scores typically in the early 1990s. CEO Tony Hsieh now describes Zappos as a customer service business that happens to be selling shoes. They could, he says, just as well go into the airline business.

The second example, a constraint of resource, is about Southwest Airlines. In the 1970s, they had to sell one of their four planes, but were determined not to lose any of the routes they had acquired. To keep them, they were forced to find a way to fly four routes with three planes. This led them to a different constraint, one of time: they worked out that they could fly a four-plane route with three planes only if they could hit a ten-minute turnaround time. They had to get all the arriving passengers and luggage off, clean the plane, and get the departing passengers and luggage on within ten minutes—when the average U.S. domestic airline turnaround time was an hour. The ways they found to do this (introducing the then unfamiliar concept of unallocated seating, for example), allowed them to maintain their four routes and even bring in new customers, who loved not sitting around on the tarmac as they did on other airlines.[9] New practices became parts of their longer-term model as a low-cost airline and the record years of profitability that followed. And the moment defined for the company what made them special: a few years ago when we interviewed Colleen Barrett, then President of Southwest, and asked her what best captured the spirit of Southwest for her, this was the story she told—a story of constraint-driven inventiveness some thirty years before.

The third example, of a constraint around method, is about Aravind eye hospitals. Their founder set himself the ambition of delivering mass-market, high-quality eye surgery for poor Indians at a fraction of what a comparable operation would cost in the West. His obsession with efficiency famously led him to emulate the assembly-line discipline he saw at McDonald's Hamburger University. Now Aravind can carry out 60 percent as many eye operations as Britain's NHS every year, at a thousandth of the cost, and with half the rate of surgical complications experienced in eye surgeries in the UK.[10]

In each of these long-established businesses, constraint linked to ambition has spurred better practices or even transformations. In each case, the people involved accepted the constraint and found a new opportunity in it.

We are not suggesting that all constraints have the potential to be beneficial. The latest research into the psychology of scarcity, which we will explore later, has shown the disabling effect of extreme poverty, creating a kind of tunnel vision that prevents people from being able to focus on anything else, or have any real insight on how to improve their situation. Extreme constraints like this, so fully dominating a life, are not constraints with a potential beauty, and this book does not attempt to encompass them. But most of us are fortunate not to be in this position; it is the broader set of constraints in our lives that we will focus on.

## The learning journey: Five groups for whom constraint means more

Are the people behind cases like the ones above just a few brilliant individuals, or is there an underlying approach we can all learn from? We weren't expecting to find a formula, but we thought we could, at least, establish whether the ability to make constraints transformative was an intuitive process—the unique gift of an exceptional individual—that could not be transferred, or whether we could uncover and develop just enough process to be useful to a broader group. Three years of research took us to five different sources of learning:

### 1. Creative and problem-solving professionals

For engineers, designers and other creative problem-solvers, a formal definition of the constraints within which they must work is essential to channel energies and expand creativity. It was David Ogilvy, eponymous founder of the iconic advertising agency, who celebrated this relationship with the remark, "Give me the freedom of a tight brief." We went to talk to some of the most admired in their field: Michael Bierut, a principal of the design firm Pentagram, whose clients include Saks Fifth Avenue and the *New York Times*; Dan Wieden, the adman who created Nike's advertising; and Yves Behar, the product designer behind One Laptop Per Child and Jawbone. Alongside this group of "creatives" we added the likes of Farm Input Promotions Africa (FIPS-Africa), who are finding ways to increase productivity for smallholder farmers in Kenya, and the principals of Stanford University's Design for Extreme Affordability course, who teach students to develop products and services for the world's poor.

### 2. Challengers in Business who indeed do more with less

We drew on our own research over the last sixteen years for the Challenger Project, a study in which we have interviewed over two hundred brand owners and business leaders who achieved significant growth in the face of different kinds of constraints. Over the same period, our consultancy has also worked with many different types of companies and challenges; our experience is hands-on and practical, not simply that of the ivory tower; it was this very experience, in fact, that drew us to this subject in the first place.[11]

### 3. Academic research

There are over 70 academic studies relating to the effects of constraints on creativity. Janina Marguc at the University of Amsterdam helped us explore them all. Several of these were illuminating, and we have referenced them where they added insights, or helped more fully explain some of our own findings or beliefs.[12]

## 4. Cultures and ideas explicitly linked to overcoming constraints

There are interesting subcultures that deal with constraints. In computer science, the concept of kludging (finding a quick and dirty solution because you have no other option) is related to the hacker ethic, and the French have the related concept of Système D. Some countries have similar, farming-led cultures around a "can-do" attitude towards constraints—South Africa's Afrikaans expression "a farmer makes a plan"(essentially working one's way round an obstacle or setback) is not far from the Indian culture of Jugaad, and finding a solution to a challenge with whatever you have at your disposal. Each of these is a way of thinking about tackling a problem, rather than a process, but provided useful learnings nonetheless.

## 5. Old dogs learning new tricks

We also looked at large companies that had learned to use constraints productively in different areas of their businesses. From these we gained confidence that something like the "just enough process" we were seeking to define could also be learned and applied within large organizations that had not always behaved in this way.

Our journey took us to San Francisco and to New York University to talk to leaders of some of the most influential studies on the effects of constraints on creativity, to Johannesburg to learn how the South African mining industry communicates critical safety messages to audiences with limited common language, and to Mumbai to understand how a retailer made a success of a western franchise whose products neither its consumers nor its staff understood. We looked at the invention of the aircraft carrier, the transformation of healthcare in Alaska, and the creation of human capital in Taiwan. We learned from people who had sudden epiphanies and people whose breakthroughs came one step at a time over twenty years. We visited corporate cultures that routinely ask employees to tackle questions they have no idea how to answer, and succeed. We met supply-chain directors, pit stop mechanics, marketers, bakers, entrepreneurs, educators, start-up founders, scientists, designers, agronomists, and engineers, all of whom were ambitious and determined enough to have found ways to use constraints to their advantage, and from whom we learned what we needed to develop tools and frameworks for applying the learning to other situations.

**Ten years from now, we would like to search Google for a definition of constraint and see it include this:** *a limitation or defining parameter, often the stimulus to find a better way of doing something.*

Because inspiration, stories, and principles will only get us so far, we needed to be able to translate this way of seeing into a way of doing, of applying, of leading. The book offers six tools to help work through how to turn our own constraints into sources of possibility and advantage. And it offers a simple overachieving process to frame those tools, not because there is a formula for success, but because if we want to apply this to our organizations as well as ourselves, we will need to bring others along with a common understanding.

With this book, we want to make the questions "Where is the beauty in this constraint?" or "How can we make this constraint beautiful?" both natural to ask and reflective of a new way of seeing constraints— one that is alight to their possibilities rather than shadowed by their threat. To capture the capability to realize that potential, we hope to reclaim the word and the idea of *inventiveness*, and make it a concept that's more accessible for more people, in more domains. In the business world, innovation seems to have become a little elitist, something for special departments in corporations, or those whiz kids in Silicon Valley, all of whom work on Big Ideas. We are proposing that inventiveness can sit alongside that, but as a generalist rather than specialist capability, one brought into the activities of every one of us around constraints. While we will focus primarily on the application of this inventiveness to constraints in business and enterprise, we will also have half an eye on a more personal application, and a perspective on how it relates to some of the bigger issues we face as global citizens.

The structure of the book, and how to use it

## PART ONE: The process of making constraints beautiful

The first part of the book unpacks the mindset, method, and motivation needed to find the beauty in a constraint. These six steps define the ABC approach.

In Chapters One and Two we explore how to understand and create the right mindset about constraints: what is blocking us from having that open, optimistic sense of possibility, and how we can become unblocked. We begin in **Chapter One: Transformers, Neutralizers, and Victims** by looking at three different perspectives on the impact of a constraint on an ambition, and whether they are personality types or just perceptual stages that we can actually move between. **Chapter Two: Path Dependence** explores how our habitual ways of behaving prevent us from finding new ways to solve new problems, and how we often remain blind to these habits, making it harder to break them.

The section on method in **Chapter Three: Propelling Questions** begins with an exploration of the most productive kinds of questions we can ask, and what makes them so powerful in addressing constraints. In **Chapter Four: Can-If** we look at how to answer those questions in a way that keeps optimism, as well as sustained creative thinking, alive in the solution phase. This group of chapters concludes with **Chapter Five: Creating Abundance**, an exploration of what it really means to be resourceful in a business culture that has largely forgotten what resourcefulness is, and offers a tool for seeing afresh our real potential here.

**Chapter Six: Activating Emotions** looks at the third of our key elements, motivation, and in particular at the theory and practice of engagement with constraints: why emotions are so important, which we should be focusing on, and why.

*Figure 0: Chapters One through Six—The six steps that define the ABC Approach*

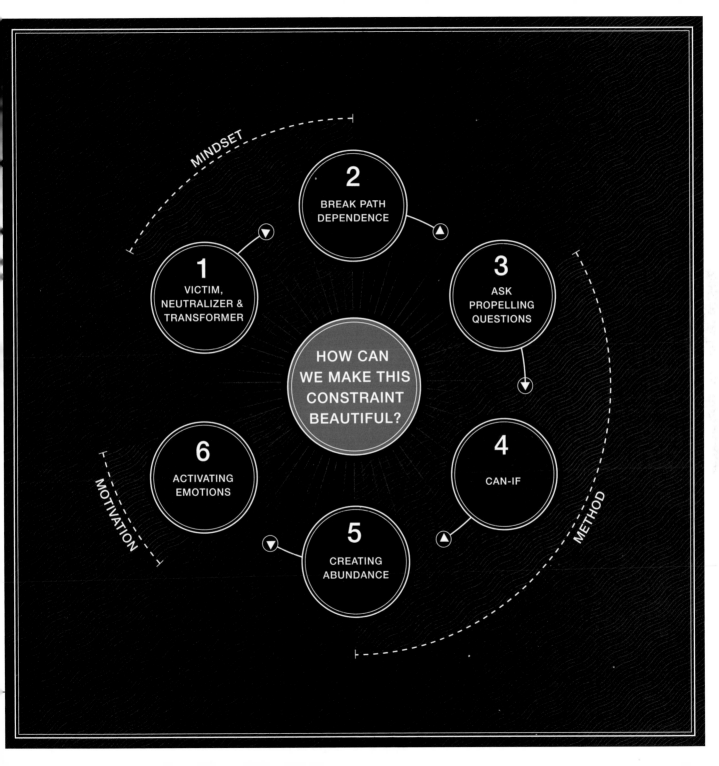

## PART TWO: The application of the concept, and why it matters now

We then pressure test our emerging point of view with two challenges. **Chapter Seven: The Fertile Zero** looks at brands and businesses that have been constrained to the point of having next to nothing of a key resource: is it possible for even this extreme nature of constraint to be fertile and, if so, how? And the second, **Chapter Eight: Constraint-Driven Cultures**, asks whether we are simply telling a story of one-offs from remarkable people. What's the evidence that this kind of mindset can take root in a large organization and become a repeatable method?

**Chapter Nine: Scarcity and Abundance** explores in more detail the critical context we have only touched on in this introduction: why the ability to embrace constraints will be more important than ever as we live in the tension between scarcity and abundance.

**Chapter Ten: Making Constraints Beautiful** draws together a summary of the learnings of the book and proposes a range of ways that we can use it ourselves. And **Chapter Eleven: Leadership and the Future of Constraints** concludes the book with a perspective on what transforming constraints in this way demands of a leader.

While there is a narrative across the book, it is not necessary to read it in order, although we would recommend that Chapters Three, Four, and Five be read in sequence. For those who find themselves constrained in attention, the beginning of each chapter lists the key questions that will be addressed in the pages that follow; you can browse and see if you are curious about the answers to those questions before reading the rest. For those constrained in time, there is a brief summary of the key points at the end of each chapter; these are boxed in red, to make them easy to find and reference. Collectively they can be read in 21 minutes and 20 seconds.

Let's go.

## INTRODUCTION: CHAPTER SUMMARY

- Most of us tend to see constraints as restrictive and adversely limiting. This book shows how and why the opposite is true: they are actually fertile forces of enhancement, stimulating new possibilities.

- We can, in fact, see the beneficial effects of constraints all around us in popular and business culture, from the video-game character Mario to the principles of good parenting.

- We define a constraint as a limitation that materially affects our ability to do something. In the chapters that follow, we will see constraints falling into one of four groups: constraints of foundation, resource, time, and method.

- In some cases, the people we discuss were responding to constraints imposed on them; in others, they have deliberately imposed a constraint on themselves to spur a new breakthrough.

- The capability to make constraints beautiful is increasingly important to all of us. We all live at the nexus of scarcity and abundance, and the capability to turn constraints into sources of opportunity will increasingly be a key definer of progress in our personal as well as our business lives.

# 1 VICTIM, NEUTRALIZER, & TRANSFORMER

Our starting relationship with constraints

1. How can we best assess our own starting relationship with constraints?

2. What are the keys to moving to a very different kind of relationship with constraints, one that would make us more able to take advantage of them?

3. What can a broader group of us learn from people who see constraints as inherently beneficial?

## Constraint and ambition

**Imagine you could** develop a new system that enabled your business to use 50 percent less of your most precious resource, while at the same time driving 20 percent growth. Not a promise of future growth, but immediate growth. What would that be worth to you?

To increase output by double digits while halving inputs in one year—even in today's efficiency-obsessed economy—this, surely, is almost impossible. If a team had found a way to achieve it, we would know about it; they would be on the cover of every business magazine.

And yet, somehow, they are not.

But while modern drip irrigation may so far have failed to set the dinner tables of the Twitterati alight (you are welcome to try it this evening), it remains a remarkable and ongoing story of growth in the face of constraints.

Until the mid-1960s, the Kibbutz Hatzerim eked out a living farming in the Negev desert of Southern Israel (Negev is the Hebrew word for dry). Though committed to farming, they realized that to thrive they would need to bolster their fragile existence with a business alongside their agriculture. Determined to find an industry that leveraged their expertise as farmers, they partnered with an engineer, Simcha Blass, to build and sell a new kind of irrigation system. Years earlier, Blass had noticed a line of trees, all planted at the same time, in which one tree stood considerably taller and fuller than the rest. Investigating, he discovered a small leak in a pipe that dripped constantly near the roots of the tree. Experiments led him to realize that drip irrigation, giving as it could just enough water at regular intervals, was both superior in growth effects to flood and even sprinkler irrigation, and vastly more efficient in water consumption. But it wasn't till plastic tubing became commercially available that he and the farmers of Hatzerim were able to commercialize his insight.

During initial trials of the dripperlines, their new plastic piping system, on Hatzerim's own crops, water use fell by 50 percent, while yields of peaches, pears, and apricots improved so dramatically that some of the kibbutz argued excitedly that they should keep the technology a secret, and just use it for themselves; many of them still, after all, simply thought of themselves as farmers. But there was a greater ambition at play—it was clear that this was an opportunity to launch a new industry, with much bigger benefits for the kibbutz than simply boosting their own crop. The joint venture between Blass and the kibbutz was called Netafim.

Netafim is now an $800 million company. Its success has been driven by the tension between ambition and constraint, above and beyond the initial need to grow crops in a desert. The company's growth put a strain on the resources of the kibbutz, who refused to compromise on one of their founding principles: that they wouldn't use hired help. So with only fourteen full time people assigned to work in the factory where they manufactured their drip systems, the only way to handle Netafim's growth and simultaneously maintain their principles was for everyone in the kibbutz to put in one shift a week on the production line, in addition to their other jobs. This in turn meant that everyone in the kibbutz became more connected to, and knowledgeable about, this new initiative that would be so critical to their future.

The new drip irrigation system boosted the kibbutz's (and the country's) fruit and vegetable production so much that they could begin exporting. But political tensions in the region meant that their neighboring countries wouldn't buy from them—a constraint requiring them to develop and grow fruits and vegetables with longer shelf lives, for export to Europe. And, finally, the challenges of clogging within the drippers forced a continuous quest for superior pressure-compensation and self-cleaning technology within the dripperlines themselves; what may look like a hosepipe with holes is a deceptively brilliant piece of engineering.

Netafim is now ambitious to have greater global impact. Their systems can contribute to food security in countries that must use less water but feed growing populations on finite arable land. They can help lift subsistence farmers out of poverty, and help solve gender issues: with drip irrigation, women in rural communities spend less time each day walking to collect water, and can spend that time instead developing new skills as well as being with their families.

Yet today only 5 percent of the world's irrigated fields use drip irrigation, in part because the system's initial cost is a barrier for the world's 500 million smallholder farmers. This tension between global ambitions and the constraint of price has driven the next stage of innovation for Netafim. Now they are aiming to produce cheaper systems, while developing programs with the Indian government to subsidize them with grants. Once they are able to demonstrate the impact of their systems, not just on yields and water use, but on the wider community, they believe they will be able to open up many more new markets.

Keeping the ambition high in the face of a succession of constraints, it seems, has been at the heart of much of Netafim's fertility.[1]

## Stages or personalities?

Michael Bierut routinely deals with constraints, although lack of water has yet to be one of them. A partner at the design firm Pentagram, he is one of the world's most successful graphic designers, creating elegant, inventive solutions to challenging briefs for the *New York Times*, Saks Fifth Avenue, Disney, and The Clinton Foundation.

When we met with him, the importance of the relationship between ambition and constraint had already become clear. Those who refused to scale back ambition in the face of constraint, like Netafim, seemed to be the ones most likely to find a way to make the constraint beautiful, whereas those who reduced their ambition were more likely to find the constraint constricting.

For the first group, the ambition was the vital, even dominant, part of their mindset. While they might not always know how to make the constraint work to their advantage, they used the tension between the scale of the ambition and the nature of the constraint to fuel the search. They had to make it work.

For the less ambitious, the opposite was the case; the constraint was the dominant dynamic. They looked to reduce the tension between the ambition and the constraint by trimming their ambition in line with the severity of the constraint. The constraint was allowed to limit them.

Our hypothesis at the time was that there were three kinds of people:

1. **Victim:** Someone who lowers their ambition when faced with a constraint.
2. **Neutralizer**: Someone who refuses to lower the ambition, but finds a different way to deliver the ambition instead.
3. **Transformer:** Someone who finds a way to use a constraint as an opportunity, possibly even increasing their ambition along the way.

But listening to us describe these different types, Bierut offered an alternative interpretation based on his own experience. He recognized, he said, all three types in himself; even today, despite his track record, he still finds himself passing through each of those stages when facing a brief with tough constraints.

His reaction each time was initially as a victim, bridling at the constraint and at the person who had put it there; he noted the spark one could get from kicking against that a little. Then as he spent more time with the brief, he passed into the neutralizer stage ("Wait a minute—maybe there's a way through this"); and finally, while exploring the possibilities, he moved into the transformative stage, where the ultimate solution lay. Indeed, making this journey was part of the energy of the problem-solving process for him.

These were not three kinds of people, then, but three stages that problem-solvers went through—even the most talented and experienced of them. And this was an important shift in our thinking: if we have a tendency to initially react one way to the imposition of a constraint, we need not see this as fixed and final. We all have the potential to move from victim to neutralizer to transformer. Bierut's suggestion, which our experience in working with the model seems to confirm, is that most of us are already proficient neutralizers, even transformers in other parts of our lives (perhaps in a hobby, or sports, or making music); we just haven't recognized that we can move through these stages in other areas of our lives, too.

Michael Bierut's insight changed the question that drives the rest of this project. It takes the more optimistic view that some people are not inherently victims, for example, but are instead temporarily stuck in one stage, needing to find a way to progress to the next.

So the key questions then become "Why are we stuck in the stage where we are? And how do we progress beyond it?"

## Progressing through the stages

One might argue that it is relatively easy for a creative professional such as Michael Bierut to proceed through the stages, armed as he is with experience, skills, methods, and a strong motivation to succeed. Once the victim mindset has released its temporary grip on him, he can address the situation more constructively.

But those of us not so used to finding the opportunity in constraints will need to be a little more rigorous in assessing our mindset, methods and motivations, all of which are important determinants of how well we will do in progressing through the stages.

Greater self-awareness yields valuable insights into where we might need the most help to progress from one stage to the next, and how best to use this book to get it.

So, think of a constraint-driven challenge of which you could be on the receiving end. Take an important and specific goal in your professional life: a revenue or share target, for instance; or the number of clients you need to add, throughput rates at the factory, and so on. Now impose a new constraint on that. Say you have to hit your target within six, not twelve months, or with half the budget, or a smaller team. The more real you can make this, the better.

A handful of questions can now help assess our mindset, method, and motivation with regard to that challenge.

### Do we believe it is possible? (Mindset)

We will only be open to exploring ways to make a constraint transformative if we believe it is possible. Some of us will see this naturally, through experience or an optimistic outlook; others will be more cautious, and some even cynical about the possibility. Questions that will help us better understand where we are and how to progress include:

- Have I done something like this in the past?
- Is that a key part of the way I think about myself?
- Has my organization done something like this in the past? Is it a story we tell about ourselves?
- Do we celebrate people who do this? Do we value it?
- Am I aware of others making these kinds of breakthroughs in areas that I can identify with—inside or outside my own organization?

At the outset, there needs to be an honest assessment of what the dominant narrative is—either your own, or that of your organization. It may be that some surfacing or reframing of hidden stories is needed to raise the initial level of self-belief; believing we tend toward a victim mindset can easily become a self-fulfilling prophecy.

Yet it is rare to find a situation without any evidence for transformation. When pressed, most people can find a time in their lives when they have responded as a transformer, and the history of any successful company will have moments of inventiveness that can be harnessed for ongoing inspiration and belief.

And the world is full of people like us transforming constraints. We need to look up and look around. They are not hard to find.

## Do we know how to start to do it? (Method)

We can be open to the possibility of success, but not know how to get started, because this situation, this kind of challenge, may not yield to the methods we use for more conventional problem-solving. The emphasis is on "start" rather than "complete," because we will not know how to answer the brief yet and will have to iterate our way to solutions. Questions to answer include:

- Do I understand how and why the usual ways of problem-solving may not work here, and may hold us back? (Chapter Two: Break Path Dependence, addresses this question.)
- Do I understand the best way to frame the challenge to be most productive? (Chapter Three: Ask Propelling Questions, answers this.)
- Do I understand how to best structure the search for solutions so we can maintain momentum in the face of such a difficult challenge? (We look at this in Chapter Four: Can-If.)

People and teams not accustomed to working with constraints will benefit from a shared sense of how to approach them, especially at the start. Chapters Three, Four, and Five introduce some of the tools that will make it easier to do this.

## How much do I want to do it? (Motivation)

We can believe that it might be possible, and know how to start doing it, but if we aren't driven to do it, then progress is unlikely. To get to the transformer stage, we will need to put our hands up to answer questions we don't know how to answer, and persist on a journey that will be frustrating. We'll need to be highly motivated to do so. Questions to answer include:

- How do I feel about this challenge? Is it emotionally charged for me?
- Is it important enough to me that I am prepared to push through the challenges that will come? Or does the organization see it as more important than I do?

- How can I (or we) understand this challenge differently so we will want to push through all the barriers and obstacles that come our way?

These kinds of questions will inevitably engage us with the larger issues of the organization, if we work in one, and the issues of scarcity and abundance in the wide world in which we operate. What's our purpose and how connected to it are we? How connected is this project to our purpose? Is our organization succeeding or in crisis, and does that lend extra motivation to this assignment? Am I excited about the opportunity we are going after? And so on. Personal motivation is crucial to the transformation process, and that can be sourced from the larger narrative of the organization, as well as our own makeup.

Reflecting on the questions in each area, we can arrive at an assessment of where we are in terms of mindset, method, and motivation. Figure 1 helps us to map our answers from low to high (illustrated as red crosses in the example below).

If we have a strong belief that the constraint can be made beautiful—say we have a strong team, with agile minds, that doesn't quit easily in the face of tough challenges—we would mark ourselves as high in that column. But if we then aren't sure how to get started, as we've never worked on something quite like this before, we'd mark ourselves as low in the second column. And if we have a reasonable degree of motivation to do this—we get why this is important, but are cautious about taking on something this hard, perhaps—we mark ourselves medium on the third question. So we are High/Low/Medium. HLM.

Get the members of the team to do it for themselves as individuals, and then for the group or organization as a whole. This will be a useful foundational understanding, both for beginning the

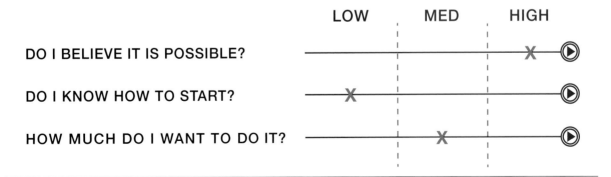

*Figure 1: What is our starting point in terms of mindset, method, and motivation around transforming this constraint?*

ABC approach—we'll be working as a team, after all—and also potentially outside the process (one client of ours has begun exploring it as a tool for professional development within their organization, for instance).

Simply scoring high on any one of these questions does not make us a transformer; we are only as strong as our weakest answer. If I am HLH, I am still at the victim stage; no matter how great my sense of possibility and my desire to make it happen. If I don't know how to start doing it, then I will not be able to find possibility and opportunity in the constraint. Moving from a victim to a transformer stage will only occur when we are HHH: with a high degree of belief, high degree of confidence in our own ability to lead the initial stages of a process, and high personal motivation to do so.

But is it possible, or even desirable, to create an environment that is high across mindset, method, and motivation all the time? Is that how cultures that repeatedly make constraints beautiful need to operate? And, if so, what can we learn from those who work this way about how they stay at that level?

We flew to Oregon to ask a man who would know.

## A gift in Portland

Dan Wieden, the legendary and charismatic co-founder of the global communications company Wieden+Kennedy, describes a gift that his fledgling agency was given as it started out—a gift that precipitated the beginning of a thirty-year sequence of famous, even iconic creative ideas on Nike, their founding client, and made both of them famous.

The gift was a constraint: the complete denial of everything they already knew about how to produce great advertising.

In giving them the Nike advertising account in the early 1980s, Phil Knight, Nike's CEO, briefed them personally, and was very clear on what he didn't want: he didn't want anything that looked or felt or smelled like "advertising." Knight didn't like or believe in advertising: a competitive college middle-distance runner himself, he had built his business selling footwear out of the back of his Plymouth Valiant at athletics meetings in the early days, and he wanted communications that spoke to the athletes with whom he had enjoyed that early relationship. They were not to run the same ad twice—you wouldn't write the same letter to a friend two weeks in a row, so why would you show them the same ad? And no models—definitely no models.

Wieden, a copywriter as well as the co-founder of the agency, was initially thrown: with this brief, there was no path he could follow. Nothing in his experience could help him. And the pressure to find a good solution did not simply come from a desire to meet Knight's brief; Wieden had started his new agency in Portland, Oregon, a long way from the business hubs of New York, Chicago, or San Francisco. Nike was a big opportunity, and it was the only big opportunity. Wieden needed this to work for himself and his agency, as well as for Knight.

Wieden+Kennedy's location presented another constraint. Few advertising stars would leave Madison Avenue for Oregon, and Wieden couldn't afford them anyway, so his initial team was made up of "kids right out of school and people who'd been fired everywhere else—a ship of fools" who didn't know how to do conventional advertising very well. The opportunity in that constraint would soon become apparent.

Prompted by Knight's challenge to connect with the athletes, Wieden tore out a picture of the Finnish Olympic runner Lasse Viren, taped it to the wall above his desk and sat down at his typewriter to answer a new kind of question: What could he say to the Finn that wouldn't make him laugh?

The first advertising created wasn't the mold-breaking work Nike became famous for. That took

## The gift was a constraint: the complete denial of everything they already knew about how to produce great advertising.

time. But it didn't feel like conventional advertising, and it connected with athletes. The client liked it enough to want more.

Wieden's band of misfits seized the opportunity to blend Nike's authentic connection to athletes with Knight's own irreverence and a sense that sport deserved to be center stage in culture. They were soon stirring up controversy using the Beatles' "Revolution" as the soundtrack to the new fitness boom, pairing up-and-coming filmmaker Spike Lee with emerging megastar Michael Jordan, and showing a bare-chested, toothless octogenarian running seventeen miles every morning. The world had never seen advertising like this before.

So, from this "gift" of denying the agency everything they thought they knew about how to do successful advertising, harnessed to Wieden's own constraint of not having talent to do that kind of advertising anyway, the most widely admired and consistently successful communications campaign in the world was born.

And with it a culture that came to believe that it could answer any impossible brief.[2]

## Transformers and their cultures

Over the last fifteen years, Wieden+Kennedy has defined its culture to ensure that the mindset of its early days is nurtured and developed as it grows. Some of that definition describes a method. They encourage each other to "Walk In Stupid Every Day," acknowledging that each problem is best solved from a place of humility, even ignorance of what is supposed to work. And a mantra to "Fail Harder" acknowledges that, while no one wants to fail, it is an expected part of the process when aiming for a breakthrough, and is not to be stigmatized or used as an excuse to quit. This method, enshrined in a culture code, and reinforced by success, instills belief. And Wieden credits culture as the main source of strength for his business.

Wieden understands how to motivate. One of the key factors in his own success has been a sense of crisis and urgency, with the best ideas coming right before deadlines, when the logical mind stops screening out novelty for want of something to put on the page. The line "Just Do It," for instance, was written during a long night right before the presentation of the first big TV campaign for Nike; the line itself taken from the final words of condemned murderer Gary Gilmore to his firing squad: "Let's do it."

One of his roles as leader, Wieden says, is to use the same dynamic to dial up motivation in his people. You need to keep telling them what a tough brief this is, he says, and what an incredible opportunity it is, "to create that sense of importance and urgency." While the internal contest for doing the best work is motive enough for many of his people, breakthrough comes from dialing up the intensity on a particular assignment.

A solver of different kinds of problems, Yves Behar is celebrated by *Fast Company* magazine as a superstar of the design world for his game-changing work with Jawbone, Sodastream, and the Ouya gaming console.[3] The One Laptop Per Child initiative sought out Behar's fuseproject in 2005, when seeking to bring the price of a laptop down to $100 from $1,000, in order to make it affordable enough to provide to children in developing countries. When pushing hard on so many complex and overlapping constraints of hardware and software necessary to make a tenfold impact on cost structure, he and his team were constantly confronted with "No."

*The reality, on a project like this, is that you hit a million snags and a million people tell you "it can't be done like this" or "it doesn't make sense," or "you shouldn't try this," or "the cost of this or the engineering of that is something that we can't do."*

*And every time you are presented with one of these challenges that potentially are crippling for the project, you say no. You go back to the big idea. You go back to the belief. You go back to what got you to work on this in the first place.*[4]

There were times, Behar confesses, "I myself thought it couldn't be done." When faced with that doubt, he goes back to the importance of a project. "The more noble the endeavor," he reflects, "the more, in a way, the constraint goes away." He dials up the motivation of his team time and again, using the power of the purpose.

One by one, in the case of One Laptop per Child (OLPC), solutions were found: The guts of the machine were all placed behind a small, one-color screen, in order to allow for a simple, durable, low-cost keyboard to be used. This necessitated a stand, which became where the battery was housed, and also a handle, which proved to be one of its most popular features. Flash memory was used instead of a hard drive, and a Linux Operating System developed. While there has been debate over the ultimate success of this program,[5] there's no doubting the inventiveness of the team that developed the XO-1 model. Behar's belief that he and his team can solve any problem is summed up by his tongue-in-cheek remark at the end of our interview: "We can bend the laws of gravity," he said. "We can do that."

Marissa Mayer, now CEO of Yahoo!, was at one time responsible for Google's search product and user experience. She understood well the positive impact of constraints on innovation and spoke about it often: "We need constraints in order to fuel passion and insight," she said, believing that the difficulty inherent in constraint enlivens her best engineers.[6] The Google Toolbar her team developed presented a number of challenges: it had to be restricted in size to just 625kb (back in 2005) to ensure it could work for any screen resolution, be downloadable fast, yet had to allow for user customization. She would add further constraint to this brief, deliberately limiting the size of the development team to three people and giving them a day to create the first prototype. She understood the need to create urgency and action in the face of potentially debilitating constraints that might lead to procrastination.

While Mayer understands that the interaction between constraints and a disregard for the impossible is where unexpected insights and inventiveness are born, she also understands how difficult this might be for a mere mortal. "Constraints alone can stifle and kill creativity," she observes. "They can lead to pessimism and despair, so … we also need a sense of hopefulness that keeps us engaged and unwaveringly in search of the right idea."

It seems that the victim made an occasional appearance even at Google.

## Knowing when and how to peak

Not even the superstar athletes featured in W+K's Nike campaigns operate at peak performance all the time. That leads to injury and burnout. In fact, many athletes carefully calibrate their training regimens to peak at the right time for the big events, and there's an art and science to that. The same is true of the transformer cultures we're highlighting here. They aren't operating at the highest level of belief, capability and motivation all the time. There are plenty of projects at Google, fuseproject and W+K that don't come with an onerous set of constraints. Few, if any cultures could live permanently in a transformer state.

But these individuals and cultures have developed the capability through conscious efforts over time, and have a base-level "fitness" that allows them to step up when needed. They have put in the work and they know they have methods to take it up a level. They understand how to dial up the emotional intensity, too. And they believe they will succeed when they have to, despite the "impossibility" of the assignment. They live at a threshold level, at the border of "medium" and "high" across mindset, method, and motivation, able to push to the critical stage when the right challenge is presented.

## A mindset that sees opportunity in constraint

A fundamental difference between these inventive people and teams and the rest of us is their core relationship with constraints. While we may see constraints as punitive, restrictive, and to be avoided, they see constraints as necessary, beneficial, and to be embraced.

Michael Bierut says he is incapable of working without constraints or limitations. The result of a completely open brief for him is simply paralysis. Now it might be tempting to think that an open brief would be liberating—imagine how exciting it would be to do anything one liked for a client like Nike. And yet Dan Wieden is candid about the one time they tried this, for the launch of the Nike 180 shoe in 1991, when they were given the shoe specs and full creative freedom:[7]

> *It was a disaster. There was no theme to anything; there was a bunch of weird film-makers that came in and did their own little things and it added up to nothing. It was a failure for us as an agency, and we didn't live up to the relationship we had with our client, Nike.*

Todd Batty, the Canadian Creative Director for video game giant Electronic Arts, offers an interestingly counterintuitive perspective on the result of complete freedom in his field. The absence of any constraints on video game designers, in his view, somehow leads not to an infinite range of possibilities, but the opposite: a predictable sameness, where everyone comes up with something like a massive, online multiplayer game where the city of New York has been turned into a Mafia playground.[8]

How do constraints help, then, for this group? What are they seeing in them that we are not? Trevor Davis, one of IBM's Distinguished Engineers, notes the fundamental importance of constraints in problem definition.[9] The reason a completely unconstrained project is the most challenging is because it is so difficult to grasp what it is that you're really trying to solve. To be very good at problem-solving, you need to be able to very clearly articulate the problem you are trying to solve, and constraints are key parameters of that definition (David Ogilvy's "tight brief"). Marissa Mayer shares this view. She needs the shape and focus of constraints to provide clear challenges to overcome, she says. This makes it easier for the problem-solvers to know where to direct their energy.[10]

What we are seeing in the experience of leaders in design, gaming, software engineering, and communications is confirmed in *The Blank Page*, a study of the effects of constraints on creativity. Dr. Caneel Joyce conducted a number of studies, both in the lab and with 43 new product development teams, to test the effect of choice on the creative process. Previous studies showed that giving people too much choice limits creativity, just as giving them no choice at all does. Her study explored the continuum between these two poles and found the sweet spot: just enough constraint incites us to explore solutions in new places and in new ways.[11]

Joyce uses the analogy of a playground.[12] Researchers found that when you put up a fence around a playground, children will use the entire space—they'll feel safe to play all the way to the edges. But if those walls are removed, creating a wide-open playground, the space the children choose to play in contracts: they stay toward the middle and they stick to each other, because that's what feels safe. This, Joyce suggests, is what happens in the creative process. When there are no clear limits in the brief itself, we aren't sure what boundaries to explore and push against. We end up without the necessary focus and passion of which Marissa Mayer speaks. In fact, one of Joyce's surprise findings was that in the absence of explicit constraints, the unconstrained teams created more conflict, stemming from all the different unarticulated assumptions and implicit constraints that team members created in their own heads, as if to fill the void.

There is, it could be said, one other key difference between most of these creative professionals and the rest of us, and that is their relationship with solving problems. Many of this group are, by their own admission, problem-solving junkies; they love the difficulty of the problems they solve. They like constraints because they like solving problems, and constraints make problems easier to solve.

But even if we don't enjoy solving difficult problems, we need to become more confident in how to approach them. Which means we need to get comfortable and confident in dealing with constraints.

## Deliberately imposing constraints upon ourselves

The power of constraints to force us beyond the familiar is a core part of comedian Jerry Seinfeld's approach. If Seinfeld is in the business of comedy, it is a very successful business, with syndication rights for *Seinfeld* alone bringing him over $30 million a year. Part of what makes his comedy different, Seinfeld has observed, is that he deliberately denies himself sources of the easiest laughs, such as sex or swearing—or for that matter, any topic people are interested in talking about. Seinfeld's comedy is deliberately about the humdrum minutiae of life:

> *I do a lot of material about the chair. I find the chair very funny. That excites me. No one's really interested in that—but I'm going to get you interested .... It's the entire basis of my career.*[13]

*Jerry Seinfeld in NBC's* **Seinfeld**

new possibilities and opportunities; he is a proactive, rather than reactive, transformer. We will look later at cases of organizations that have moved through each of the stages we have discussed in this chapter as they became more confident in their ability to turn constraint into opportunity.

Nike, for example, responded initially as a victim when singled out by labor activists for alleged sweatshop practices. But they developed a growing sense of confidence in their ability to turn these lemons into lemonade when a series of product improvements resulted from changes they were forced to make. Nike now sees its ability to define and transform constraints as a competitive advantage, and has moved into this proactive transformer stage. Michael Bierut was right, it seems: we are not by nature one or the other of these types. Even very large organizations can learn to move between them.

Up to now, we have been discussing constraints as those imposed on us by circumstance or by someone else. But Seinfeld is an example of a creative professional so confident in his ability to transform constraints into something positive that he proactively imposes them on himself, to make his content more original and fresh. Seinfeld is this good because he has performed live a couple of times a week every week since 2000, trying out new material each time. He sees his disciplined approach to practicing transforming his chosen constraints as having more in common with an exacting athlete than a creative artist.

Seinfeld's story highlights a crucial distinction between situations where we respond to a constraint that was not of our making, and situations where we impose constraints on ourselves to stimulate us to see

# We are not by nature victim or transformer; even very large organizations can learn to move between them.

## The stages and strategies in response to constraints

Table 1 below summarizes the different attitudinal stages we need to move through in order to evolve our mindset and approach towards constraints.

| | Foundational Premise | Types of Strategies |
|---|---|---|
| **Victim Stage** | This constraint will necessarily inhibit our ability to realize our ambition. | Avoidance strategies: denial of the constraint<br>or<br>Reduction strategies: reduce level of ambition to fit perceived impact of constraint. |
| **Neutralizing Stage** | Our ambition is too important to allow this constraint to inhibit it. | Workaround strategies: neutralize the effect of the constraint by finding another way around it. |
| **Responsive Transformer Stage** | This constraint that we need to respond to could catalyze arrival at a better solution. | Transformative strategies: use the constraint to prompt different, potentially breakthrough new approaches and solutions. |
| **Proactive Transformer Stage** | What constraints should we impose on ourselves to stimulate better thinking or new possibilities? | |

*Table 1: Stages in response to constraints*

Having defined the different stages, we'll now explore the first part of catalyzing that movement, and why we need to frame the challenge to ourselves not purely in terms of the constraint itself. We'll see what happens to our cognitive response when we link the constraint to a bold ambition.

## VICTIM, NEUTRALIZER & TRANSFORMER: CHAPTER SUMMARY

- To unlock the potential of a constraint, we need first to increase our level of ambition with regard to the constraint, not decrease it. The tension this creates is invaluable.

- We need not be defined by our initial attitude towards constraints. It is natural to adopt a victim mindset at the beginning; even the most experienced and skilled transformers of constraints can find themselves with this mindset at first.

- Moving from victim to transformer will require strength in mindset (Do we believe this is possible?), method (Do we know how to start doing this?), and motivation (How much does this matter to us?).

- To find the potential in a constraint, we need to reach a transformative threshold on each of these dimensions. It is only when we are at a high level in each of these that transformation is likely. And we are only as strong in this as our weakest dimension.

- Professional problem-solvers have a different relationship with constraints from the rest of us: they see them as inherently beneficial, because they provide clear problem definition and focus the problem-solver's energies; they set the boundaries to explore and push against.

- The most confident of these kinds of problem-solvers, in fact, will impose constraints on themselves to force them to unearth different, possibly transformative strategies and solutions.

# 2 BREAK PATH DEPENDENCE

The behaviors and practices that prevent us seeing opportunity in constraint

1. How does success today blind us to what could create success tomorrow?

2. How does the language we use lock us into ways of thinking and behaving that will limit our ability to see new possibilities?

3. What can we do to surface and move away from unhelpful paths on which we have become dependent, in order to reveal newer, more productive paths?

**Writer William Gibson once famously said that the 'The future is already here—it's just not very evenly distributed.' I worry more that the past is here—it's just so evenly distributed that we can't get to the future.**

—Paul Kedrosky[1]

**A few years ago,** we facilitated an event with a group of luxury car dealers in a Four Seasons hotel. They were all the owners or General Managers of the dealerships: wealthy, shrewd businesspeople with a track record of success going back a decade or more.

They had come to the event to learn from other luxury and service businesses. They were exposed to world-class stimuli over the two days: leading-edge technology retailing, high-end customer service, the latest and greatest in travel and hospitality. And yet one of the most illuminating conversations came after a visit to the laundry.

The trip was a part of a tour through the departments of the hotel: Room Service, Front Desk, Gardening, and so on. We met and spoke with Four Seasons' staff in each area.

And then we came to the laundry.

If you have ever spent any time in a hotel laundry, you will know it is not an exciting environment, in the conventional sense of the word. Typically hot, short of natural light, and full of damp, drying linen, it is a place that owes more to perspiration than inspiration. And yet the young man who stood on a chair to talk to the dealers about working in that Four Seasons laundry radiated enthusiasm and commitment; for twenty minutes he made it sound like the most important and fulfilling job in the world. We were rapt.

The visit over, we went upstairs to discuss the tour, and what we had learned. And the first question from one of the dealers was about the laundry. He had been very taken by the young man we'd met there, the dealer said. In his business, the stars (or quarterbacks as he called them) were the salespeople on the showroom floor. They got the big bucks, wore the good suits, "because they are the people who make sure we hit our numbers with the quality of customer engagement that we have become famous for." And yet he also had a group of people at the back end of the business servicing the cars, valeting, and washing them, who did not seem to be nearly as evangelical as that young man. How, the dealer asked, could he get his back end to be as motivated and engaged as that?

The relevant department head from the Four Seasons, a well-built man called Bob, stepped forward. "I'll tell you what a back end is," said Bob, and he pointed to his own behind: "That's a back end. Here we call those people our Heart of House." And that means you think of them very differently, he went on: if you think of them as Heart of House, then they are really important to you. You know their names and their children's names. You know what's going on in their lives. You know their birthdays. You go and talk to them twice a day. "How often," he asked the dealer, "do you walk over to your service area and talk to your people there?"

Once or twice a week, the dealer said.

"There you go," said Bob. "If you called them Heart of House you'd literally change the way you walked, as well as the way you thought. You'd be over there twice a day, asking them how you could all make the service experience better. They'd have a completely different relationship with what they did."

They'd become, in other words, our young evangelist in the laundry.

## Why we become "locked-in"

We are all familiar with aspects of modern life that are legacies of history, and have simply become such an integrated part of the way we all work now that they are too difficult or too expensive to change, even though better solutions might be available. When the two solid fuel engines that power the Space Shuttle into space were designed, for example, they could not be much more than 4 feet 8.5 inches wide—the width of the rail line that was to transport them from Utah to Florida. This was the width of the line because the laborers who built it last century came from England, and their forefathers had built the tramlines in England along the paths made by the horses and carts that preceded them. These paths were 4 feet 8.5 inches wide because that was the width of the roads, built by the Romans, on which they were based. Which is why a design feature of one of the most advanced pieces of technology ever produced was determined by a Roman road engineer over 2000 years ago.[2]

Path dependence is the term, borrowed from mathematics, that is used to describe the persistence of features like the width of railway tracks. We can see it in the QWERTY keyboard, the internal combustion engine, and even in formulations like the famous Moore's Law (see sidebar on page 41). And we can also see it in how organizations lock-in self-reinforcing processes and the cognitive rigidities that can come with them.

In our case, the way our dealer had been motivating and rewarding his people, the priorities and systems he had put in place, the way he divided his time, even the way he physically walked the dealership day in day out, all of these had been key to driving the success he had enjoyed to date.

But the stimuli from the Four Seasons were not about codifying what had made him successful in the past, but what would make him successful in the future. And what Bob had highlighted for the dealer was that what had created success in the past was preventing him from seeing and driving the initiatives that would create success in the future. In fact, data shows that the ownership experience has twice the impact of the buying experience in determining whether a customer will buy again from a dealer. And yet the business model was biased to quality acquisition, rather than a quality experience all the way through. The dealer was not set up to maximize the lifetime value of each customer.

## Today's path is really yesterday's path

Sydow, Schreyögg, and Koch[3] have suggested that organizations go through three phases in developing path dependence. In the first phase, there is a broad range of approaches used within the organization, and a high degree of managerial discretion on which to use and when.

During this phase, an event occurs (an important success of some kind, for instance) that leads to a dominant approach developing in phase two ("That worked well—let's do more of that"); in this phase there is still some flexibility, but the dominant example is visible and celebrated. Phase three is the lock-in phase in which a greater degree of self-reinforcing processes and behavior patterns predominate, and there is much less room for variations in approach.

Path dependence manifests in different ways. It can be formal and easily visible—the large manual on our desk, titled "The ACME Way." Or it can exist in a more informal, pervasive sense of "the way we do things around here"—the learned best practices, processes, values, data sources, and partners that people pay attention to (and, as importantly, the processes, values, data sources, and partners that people ignore). In a workplace culture that prizes efficiency and repeatability, these are the ones that endure, because they have worked before.[4] They have become part of the identity of the company. And they can be almost invisible to the people working there, glimpsed only in the telltale indicators of language and KPIs that persist—our dealers' "back end," for example.

In other words, today's approaches are in effect yesterday's approaches, based on what was appropriate then, not necessarily now. They are not simply processes, but paths made up of self-reinforcing bundles of beliefs, assumptions, and behaviors, whose nature—and underlying rationale—may no longer be visible, and rarely questioned.

## The profits and pitfalls of our habits

Because path dependence is about beliefs and behaviors, it is a personal phenomenon as much as an organizational one. It's about our own habits of mind. Consider the last five problems you have been asked to solve in your work, especially if you have some tenure in the role. Chances are you will have:

- Defined the problem in the same kinds of terms.
- Used the sources of data you have at hand, because they have been valuable on past questions.
- Asked similar kinds of questions of that data.
- Analyzed the answers in the same way.
- Involved the same kinds of partners to help.
- Asked the same colleagues for advice at key stages.

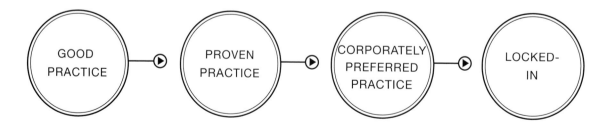

*Figure 2: A simple model of how path dependence develops (based on the work of Sydow, Schreyögg, and Koch).*

- Used a similar kind of overall process.
- Looked for solutions in the places that have worked for you and the category in the past.
- Evaluated options in the usual ways before making the final decision.
- Put in place similar measures of success.

It makes sense to do all these things. These paths, after all, have good résumés: they are the paths we took to success, and they got us promoted. And habits can be efficient, saving us from all kinds of unnecessary mental processing. President Obama wears only two types of suit, a gray one and a blue one, so he can save his cognitive load for more important things. Repetition and habit are important features of a productive life.[5]

Moreover, the faster and harder we are asked to work, the more we will want to lean on these protocols. You don't want your team to use their finite resources questioning every good decision you made yesterday, when the pace of work is only increasing. Indeed, research suggests that we're more likely to stick to habits when stressed, because change requires more cognitive energy than we have in those moments.[6] When a track record of proven success meets an increased demand to do more, the tendency to become locked-in is greater than ever.

The language we use both represents and reinforces this lock-in. You can see path dependence in language everywhere. The car dealer's use of "back end" framed and reinforced relationships and behaviors. The U.S. government continues to report employment in terms of "non-farm payroll" long after this was a useful way to segment employment, simply because it always has. When pitching an innovation to a mobile phone company a couple of years ago, we had the idea that the phone could produce a funny noise or line of comedy just before you took a picture of your children—so you could take a more candid photo of them smiling or laughing, rather than the usual fake grin. Our client loved the idea. Now, they said, you need to go and talk to Optics about it. Needless to say, Optics weren't interested in hearing about sound. The underlying premise of having innovation handled by a department called Optics was that all good innovation was going to be, well, optical. Because up to then, it always had been.

All of these are obvious and explicit. But words can come with a particular cultural interpretation, and act as limiters in a similar but subtler way. So, for instance, in most confectionery companies, the word "innovation" means, in practice, product innovation. There are many other kinds of innovations they could use to build their brands—new dispense methods, packaging structures, distribution means, and strategic relationships, for example. But because they understand the word in that way, they hire product innovation experts who focus on optimizing product innovation processes, and feed product innovation ideas through them, whether that is the most valuable form of innovation for the future or not. What innovation is and isn't understood to mean in an organization is often a reflection of path dependence.

## So why do path dependence and lock-in matter, if it has driven past success?

There is a great deal to be said for the consistency and clarity of purpose of habitual ways of doing things. But when confronted with a constraint that we are not used to dealing with, path dependence can limit us in several ways.

Path dependence can:
- Create lock-in to foundational assumptions that are no longer best for the future.
- Create lock-in to criteria for success that are no longer relevant or the most important.
- Create lock-in to organizational biases and priorities that are no longer appropriate.
- Make us closed to what might be possible, when we need to be open; we confuse what is possible with "what is possible within the way we do things at the moment."
- Make us blind to new kinds of information that don't serve the efficiency of today's path.
- Lead us to follow approaches that are not going to be the best to solve this problem.

The forms of lock-ins here are cognitive (personal), cultural (collective), and procedural. Perhaps one of the most striking examples of blindness that path dependence can create is that of Intel. Moore's Law—the processes and practices that underpin semiconductor development—drove years of immensely profitable growth for Intel, but then somehow they missed one of the largest (and arguably very obvious) shifts in the industry ever: the move to mobile. Intel's CEO himself, struggling to explain why, noted their inability to see what their well-grooved machine had made them blind to: "it took a while for us to acknowledge and accept the data."[7]

One of the reasons why people find themselves shrinking back to the victim mindset in the face of constraints is that their paths have become so well-grooved as to become ruts, and they can't answer the challenge of the constraints by staying within them. The most significant and disabling constraints we face may not be the external ones, but the internal ones that determine how open-minded and flexible we are in our problem-solving ability. Some constraints are inherent to the challenge itself, and some inherent in our approach.

**Let's go back to mindset, method, and motivation.** In our interviews, people with good track records as transformers advanced the view that most, if not all, constraints could potentially be enabling. The most disabling were the ones in our heads (cynicism, or limiting beliefs) or in our culture (the blindness of path dependence). IDEO, for example, is one of the most celebrated innovation companies in the world, responsible for breakthrough solutions in healthcare, finance, education, and toy design. Tim Brown, their CEO, notes how frequently the most significant constraints imposed on them are largely in the minds of the commissioning client: how large healthcare clients, for example, tend to over-interpret the necessary impact of the legal and regulatory issues involved. Brown divides the relevant constraints IDEO has to overcome in these situations as constraints of

## Moore's Law versus Reverse Innovation

Some commentators suggest that the much-lauded Moore's Law—the presumed doubling of the number of transistors on an integrated circuit every eighteen months—is less a story of the physics of silicon, and more a set of beliefs and attitudes baked into the planning cycles of Intel and others. It takes one to two years to conceive, design, prototype, test, manufacture, and market an improvement; and, it is suggested, a good engineer can double performance in that period. A more complete explanation of Moore's Law "has to do with the confluence and aggregation of individuals' expectations, manifested in organizational and social systems which serve to self-reinforce the fulfillment of Moore's prediction." In other words, Moore's Law is a form of path dependence—a self-fulfilling prophecy.[8]

Contrast this with the approach of Reverse Innovation, where an innovation conceived in a developing market, and driven by a very different set of constraints to those of a developed market, succeeds in creating something new, which is ultimately imported into the developed market. This is a way of vaulting over path dependence in more developed markets, and why so many leaders in major corporations are looking to developing economies to help pioneer mobile phone features, medical devices, and personal care products.[9]

# We need to be deliberate in the way we make visible and overcome the rigidity of our mindset and method.

the world (factually-based constraints of budget or space, for example) and constraints of the mind (perceptual barriers erected by the culture around the problem).

Having a positive attitude toward problem-solving is not enough. To be open, we need to see what is making us closed, and why. And we need language that allows us to talk about it with others. We need to be deliberate in the way we make visible and overcome the rigidity of our mindset and method. Let's look at how this worked in practice in transforming education in four schools in Northern California.

## Breaking path dependence in California charter schools

Dr. Louise Waters is the Superintendent and CEO of Leadership Public Schools (LPS) in the East Bay of San Francisco. Here's how she describes her challenge:[10]

> A lot of our families don't have steady employment, so our kids may be major contributors to the household income, or provide childcare while their parents work night shifts. Some might be homeless, undocumented, in gangs, or foster care. Since the Great Recession of 2008, the social safety net has come unraveled and we've seen hunger and medical issues. Kids fall so far behind that by the time they get to high school they are four or five years below grade level, and no longer believe that they can succeed. Talk about constraints....

Dr. Waters and her team did not allow the constraint to limit the ambition. On the contrary, they set an enormously ambitious goal: in time, they wanted all LPS students to leave school ready for college without remediation (i.e., with no need to take catch-up classes), representing a 1,000-percent increase in the level she found when she arrived. To make this possible, students would need to progress two to three grade levels each year through high school. But there was no extra money to feed the realization of this elevated ambition: Dr. Waters and her team would need to achieve it in the face of budget cuts for her schools, along with everybody else's. There was, they realized, no conventional prescription for achieving anything like this. LPS would need to find an entirely new way to do it.[11]

So they brainstormed as a team using whiteboards to capture, pull apart, and interrogate all the elements of the situation. They knew what their goals were, how they might typically be expected to achieve them, and what wouldn't work in their circumstances. Two things they knew would be important were the Holy Grails for accelerating student achievement—differentiation and intervention:

- **Differentiation:** Each student requires a differentiated approach, because each has a different learning style, language proficiency, and area of "stuckness."
- **Intervention:** Having the ability to spot an issue of poor understanding around a topic as it emerges, address it immediately, and keep the learning process going. Circling back days later has far less impact—the student will have already moved on.

The traditional paths for addressing differentiation and intervention lie in hundreds of hours of one-on-one tutoring, many of those after school. But this was not a path they could take: even if LPS had the resources to deliver this, they didn't have kids who could always stay after hours, and they certainly didn't have the quality of pupil feedback they needed—giving instant feedback on their grasp of a topic is not something many teens excel at, especially those insecure in their abilities. If you're already three grade levels behind, you feel raising a hand only confirms how dumb you are.

But from her prior role as an academic, Dr. Waters had a strong sense that getting this kind of data held the key, and her team felt that a smart application of technology in the classroom could help address the feedback constraint and create a new path to accelerated learning. By chance, a foundation had donated some "clickers" to the school—simple remote-control devices used to poll audiences at conferences. Right-click to agree, left-click to disagree, and the feedback appears on the screen. Could this work to get an immediate student-by-student reading on how well they understood a lesson?

They tried it out with one teacher and one class at one school; though the technology was clunky, the results were compelling. The teacher was able to clearly assess how every member of the class was doing, and intervene immediately with the ones who were struggling, on their own terms. So the question became how to scale this: how to design the ultimate clicker?

Dr. Waters now gambled, committing her limited resource slack to hire a Chief Innovation Officer, and immersing him in classroom-based R&D. If she could show promising, scalable results, she'd be able to attract grant support to build their dream. And if they could prove its value, they might be able sell this new technology-based approach to other schools, recoup their investment, and fund further R&D. This was not just a teaching innovation now, but business-model innovation.

*The ExitTicket app on tablet: offering real time data to teachers on performance for each individual student and the class as a whole.*

The introduction of the ExitTicket app (as they named the evolution of this tech-based instant feedback) was immediately popular with kids. It was new, different, and offered the kind of text-based interactivity they knew. At first, teachers shared aggregate data with the class on how they were improving collectively, so as not to embarrass individual pupils. But the class wanted to see their individual scores improve, as one would with any game. So they sat up straight, paid more attention, and tried to beat their scores, while the teacher made quick interventions to help. Scores continued to rise and a sense of agency developed amongst the kids, who were soon participating in further design iterations. The cycle of hope and energy and excitement, as Dr. Waters described it, started turning in a positive direction.

In 2013, 97 percent of LPS students were accepted to college with over 33 percent ready to start without remediation. They're a long way still from the 100-percent goal, but have traveled far from their 10-percent start. It is remarkable that so many students have been able to make up two to three years' worth of improvement in a single year and, by that metric, the program has paid for itself. LPS launched ExitTicket for other schools in August,

2013, and already 100,000 students use it in 4,800 schools in 108 countries. Though money is very tight in education, the program should be financially self-sustaining within a couple of years and able to provide the funds for further classroom innovation.

The LPS team refused to accept that resource constraints would necessitate reducing ambitions. The future of their kids was just too important to them. And they refused to accept that the conventional path to deliver differentiation and intervention was the only path. They were both opportunistic and resourceful in breaking path dependence—open-minded enough to seize an opportunity when it presented itself (donated clickers) and willing to step outside of accepted methods to take full advantage of it (hiring a CIO to embed in the classroom). And while they are keen to point out that Ed Tech, as these tech-enabled classroom initiatives are known, is no panacea, and not the only thing they did in order to achieve their results, they are thrilled with how much they have been able to achieve with so little.

Let's summarize exactly what LPS did to succeed:

- They had a very clear-eyed view of all the constraints they faced, yet still set themselves an even bigger goal—100 percent college readiness without remediation.
- They knew that if they simply continued to do what they had done before they would fail to meet their bold ambition—they would need a different approach.
- So they went to the whiteboards, mapped out what they knew, unbundling and interrogating component parts, deciding what to keep, what to change, and where to focus.
- They knew what really mattered—differentiation and intervention—but they couldn't achieve that in the conventional way given their constraints of time and money.
- And they valued a different kind of intervention anyway—immediate feedback—which would be a better fit with their students.
- So when the clickers were donated they sensed the opportunity to use them for immediate feedback—this became a potential new path to deliver differentiation and intervention.
- To realize the opportunity they had to commit to it, hiring a part time CIO

to build the tool alongside the teachers—the new path required a new kind of resource.

- They iterated in one classroom, in one subject, creating many prototypes until they had confidence that it worked for the students and could scale.
- Then they rolled it out across all four schools and in different subjects.
- And in selling ExitTicket to other schools, they broke their own business model path dependency, creating new revenues that should continue to fund further R&D.

This wasn't the punky, slash-and-burn of a maverick young start-up—the LPS team deals in children's futures. But by diligently identifying and naming what they knew to be true about accelerated learning, generating the insight that immediacy of feedback was the key, they were ready to seize the initiative when the moment came. And that's why we must take the time and effort to analyze and label the biases inherent in current paths. By making them visible we make it easier to discuss how and when they might hinder our progress.

### What's in a name?

This power of labeling has been noted by Daniel Kahneman, the Nobel Prize-winning psychologist. With his work on decision making, he wanted to enrich our vocabulary by labeling the unhelpful biases of judgment he uncovered over decades of research: the negativity bias (our tendency to over-interpret bad news) and the confirmation bias (our tendency to select data that supports our existing opinion). He feels we need more intelligent gossip on how to make better decisions. In the same way, it will be helpful for us to identify our own path dependence and name the paths that are most and least useful going forward.[12] Names make the invisible visible, and easier to discuss. Names make us aware, and help us remember. Names can start to change the way we see and behave. New names can stimulate new beginnings.

Southcentral Foundation, for example, is a healthcare provider to native peoples in Alaska. It credits a huge turnaround in its fortunes, in part, to a change of language. As a nonprofit organization owned through a foundation by the native peoples themselves, their young CEO questioned why they referred to people as patients. She suggested they start using the term customer-owner instead, and begin to shift responsibility for health outcomes onto the community as a whole to reflect the meaning of this new idea. People would not be thought of as a set of symptoms walking in the door, but as people whose health is influenced by a complex blend of cultural and lifestyle factors. This simple yet profound change precipitated a series of subsequent changes throughout the system for over two decades, the extraordinary results of which we will see more of in Chapter Six.

## How does one overcome path dependence?

Changing path dependence can sound intimidating. We may recognize it, but feel it sounds as if we need to re-engineer the whole organization if we want to really enable ourselves to move from victim to transformer in this regard. But we can overcome path dependence in small as well as big ways, tackling one or two dated assumptions first, making an impact with that, and growing in confidence to take on the larger issues. When Nike launched the Flyknit shoe in 2012, they spoke about the need to "forget everything we knew about how uppers were made," but only arrived at that mindset after many years of smaller victories, born of questioning how and why they do individual things.[13] Breaking path dependence for Nike happened one step at a time.

Later in the book, we will explore how Unilever are delivering their Unilever Sustainable Living Plan, a key part of their commitment to double their size while halving their environmental footprint by 2020. The challenge of this ambition means that in the supply chain, for instance, they have set themselves a target of reducing wastage in a crop like tomatoes by 50 percent. In geographies where tomatoes are harvested mechanically, an optical scanner looks for red and rejects the green; as part of their interrogation of their existing approach, the Unilever team discovered that their own sourcing specification allowed for just 5 percent of green tomatoes to be allowed past this optical scanner. So what, they asked, would be the difference in taste performance if they doubled that permitted specification to 10 percent? None, said R&D; it was a criterion that had been set for different reasons a number of years ago. That one change in specification across the entire system has made a significant contribution to their wastage goal against that crop, as well as increasing yield and profit for the farmers, and indeed Unilever's own margins as well. As their Chief Supply Chain Officer says: "It's simply a matter of challenging assumptions."[14]

So first we need to see the paths for what they are—surface them, name them and the assumptions they contain, and unbundle complex wholes into constituent parts so we can choose those we want to pursue. Here, then, are two simple techniques to create an awareness of how we might be path-dependent and where we could start to break that dependence. These could easily be a formal or informal part of any strategic planning process.

## Naming our tendencies and biases

Surface and make visible path dependences by naming practices, beliefs, and assumptions that may have served us well in the past, but are potentially limiting for the future.

An easy way to start is to take the six words that are most important to the organization, and articulate what you mean by them: What do we really mean when we say innovation, or marketing, or customer satisfaction, or growth, or consumer insight, or production efficiency, or strategic partnerships, or operating discipline, or healthy, for example?

This will make it easier to articulate the biases in our path dependence, and discuss alternatives for the future. If we decide what we really mean by marketing is sell this month's allocation of product, we clearly have a short-term, sales-led bias, at the expense of building a truly differentiated brand equity or experience. Let's give it a name that reflects that bias. If what we mean by consumer insight is paying other people to study our consumers, recognizing and naming that bias might encourage us to find ways to create a more visceral, personal understanding of the people with whom we do business. The aim is not to be critical, but to clarify which paths to keep and which to break as we transform our constraint.

## Surfacing and interrogating the constituent parts of our path dependence

Sometimes larger systems turn on smaller, underlying assumptions, and we'll need to break down the larger dependences into constituent parts. Once we have an overall sense of our biases, we can start to unbundle and name the components on which we are most dependent—those impacted most by the constraint—and explore alternatives. For instance:

### Beginning assumptions

The Question: What are the foundational assumptions underpinning our current approach? Which might be no longer valid as we look to make our constraint beautiful? What should they be changed to?

Example: Hannah Jones, VP of Corporate Responsibility at Nike at the time, visited a factory and was confounded by the impossibility of policing the use of protective facemasks to prevent the inhalation of glue fumes.[15] Ensuring compliance across such a huge network of factories was simply too difficult so rather than implement new safety processes she challenged the initial assumption that glue fumes have to be toxic in the first place, and pushed Nike designers to make a nontoxic glue. The new glue that they developed was not only safer, but also performed better. This moment was an epiphany for Jones, and was one of a number of initiatives that led Nike to review all design and manufacturing processes and the historical assumptions that had become locked-in.

### Routines and processes

The Question: What are the processes and routines we habitually use? Which parts of them are integral and necessary, and which could we relax and explore alternatives to, if they would help us move from victim to neutralizer or transformer?

Example: We tend to think of processes as big. But changing processes in even small ways can open up new senses of opportunity and possibility.

When we began working to reposition the global detergent brand Surf, it needed to grow and become more profitable. But as Unilever's value detergent (below the top-performance brand Omo) it faced constraints: for cost reasons it didn't have access to the best cleaning ingredients, was unable to innovate in structural packaging, and had a limited communications budget—some of the usual things a laundry brand relies on for success. We asked the Consumer Insight Director to present to the team. He sighed:

everyone in the room had heard his presentation on "The Savvy Shopper" before. How could he find something fresh in it? We suggested that he talk us through her entire day (she's typically female) through the lens of the children's game of Snakes and Ladders. Where were the unexpected ladders to boost her? Where were the predictable snakes to bring her down? This created more energy around familiar data, but also highlighted where an opportunity might lie: the final, long snake down was the moment when our customer found herself still folding socks in a badly-lit basement at midnight, with yet another load to do, while her partner snored contently in front of the television.

The team saw her in a new light, past the dominant "Savvy Shopper" narrative of bargain-conscious mom to the more fundamental insight about the lonely joylessness of doing laundry. That was the beginning of a new way forward, with the chance for Surf to put new emotion—which they called delight—into the laundry experience. We'll return to Surf later to see how they used this insight to break through, and how it came because of, rather than despite, the constraints.

### Expected sources of solutions

The Question: There are habitual places we go to for solutions. What would happen if we took some of these away? How would that make us think differently about where future solutions might lie? Where should we be looking more actively in future?

Example: The prevalent way for image-conscious alcohol brands to boost sales is to advertise. In so-called dark markets, advertising is significantly restricted or banned— that is, the primary solution for growth has been taken away. Alcohol brands in those dark markets consequently have to think harder about how they use their other assets, such as packaging, and often end up being more inventive and engaging through these new sources of solutions as a consequence. (Perversely, those same brands in markets that are not dark seem to learn little from them. They rely on that default, habitual path of advertising.)

Challengers are particularly interesting in this regard, because their lack of advertising budget relative to the Big Fish renders them effectively dark in advertising terms anyway, and needing to find sources of engaging communication in other areas. Air New Zealand and Virgin America, for example, take what most airlines don't even consider media—the flight safety video—and use it as one of the primary tools for creating awareness and personality. Air New Zealand's Bare Essentials safety video has seven million views worldwide on YouTube, and their safety video partnership with *Sports Illustrated* has six million.

### Associations and relationships

The Question: What internal and external relationships do we normally rely on? Why are these no longer sufficient? What new kinds of relationships would make us more flexible, agile, open to new possibilities?

Example: Netafim, the Israeli irrigation company, grew by selling commercial systems to "Big Ag." But the majority of the world's 500 million farmers are smallholders in developing economies, unable to invest in their systems while arguably the most in need of them. The price constraint forced Netafim to develop a new path for small holders via government-subsidized programs. In India, for example, they lowered the initial cost to palm oil farmers by 50 percent through partnering with the government, subsequently reducing water use by one-third and increasing productivity by 25 percent.

### KPIs and measures of success

The Question: How do we currently measure success? Do any of these measures restrict possibilities for the future? Could new measures open up new possibilities and ways of thinking for us?

Example: LPS. Much of the differentiation and intervention in a typical educational environment happens several days after a test or homework assignment. Dr. Waters and her team felt and proved that there's no time like the present when accelerated learning is the goal. There was simply no time to go back and course-correct later. Using ExitTicket, their feedback metric went from in several days to immediate.

Several years ago, we worked with the Visa marketing team. At the time, they benchmarked mostly against their immediate competitors, Mastercard and AmEx. And yet people who carry Visa cards benchmark the brand against everyone else they engage with—they don't think in terms of categories. The team wanted to address that. Consistent with their overarching goal to drive more transactions, they also set a new bar: to be considered one of the world's most powerful brands and a leading innovator, on a par with Nike and Apple; they mocked up the cover of a leading business magazine with the headline "Visa: Most Innovative Brand in the World," to signal their

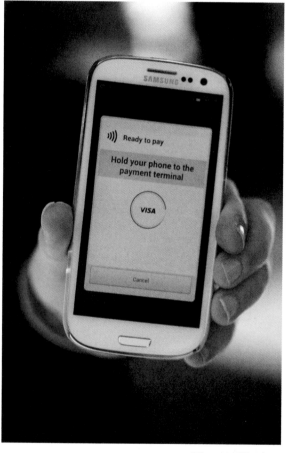

**Visa payWave**

intent. Since then, product innovations like Visa Checkout and Visa payWave have been matched by innovative social-media driven marketing ideas such as "The Samba of the World" and "United in Rivalry" at the World Cup in Brazil. Based on recent tracking studies Visa is moving closer and closer to its goal.[16]

## Repeatability and renewal

All organizations, big and small, need to design repeatability into their methods, based on historic drivers of success: they achieve efficiencies to make them more competitive, provide confidence around a path to growth, set clear expectations of behavior, and create a sense of identity around shared practices.

But we need to be vigilant in assessing the degree to which these habitual ways become dogmas that blind us to opportunity, and create ruts that can be hard to escape—particularly ruts that keep us from the openness and flexibility that will allow us to move from the victim to transformative stages. As we saw above, there may well be a natural tendency for someone to tell us that something is impossible, but, by and large, they don't really mean that. What they mean is that it is impossible within the current paths on which they and the organization are dependent. If we want to open up a greater sense of what is possible, to misquote Robin Wight, we need to interrogate the paths until they confess their weaknesses.[17]

But this chapter does not argue for relentless disruption as much as an acknowledgement that, as Nike would put it, there is no finish line. When the

## Path Dependence and the Invention of the Aircraft Carrier

Captain James Housinger, U.S. Navy, and Professor at University of Utah, cites the introduction of the first aircraft into the Navy in the early part of the 20th century as a good illustration of one form of path dependence in an organization. At first, it was hard for the Navy to see the potential role in warfare of these fragile flying machines, and they used them for reconnaissance, to get better intelligence on where to point the ships' guns; the aircraft, with all its potential, was initially integrated into the way the Navy already thought about fighting (using a new technology in service of the existing path).

With evidence mounting from World War I of the growing potential role of aircraft in warfare, it was apparent that the Navy would need to embrace aircraft, and not just on shore. The outlandish idea of sea-borne runways started to take hold, but the issues that engineers had to deal with were considerable, and their inventive solutions required them to abandon the previous path of warship design entirely.

For example:

- The deck of a ship is cluttered with equipment, so how could they make room for a flat surface to land on? They could if they moved the superstructure off to the side and put the rest of the equipment underneath to act as ballast against all that weight on one side.

- How could they take off and land when the ship isn't long enough for a runway? They could if they used a catapult to propel planes faster and a wire to catch them when they land.

- How could they fit enough planes on ships to create a true fighting force? They could if they built planes with folding wings, stored them below decks, and moved them with elevators.

Even after it became apparent just how important a role the new aircraft carriers would play in modern warfare, according to some commentators, the U.S. Navy remained locked-in to building too many destroyers at the expense of carriers and planes. The debates were intense. The colorful Brigadier General Billy Mitchell was ultimately court-martialed for insubordination after accusing Army and Navy leaders of "an almost treasonable administration of the nation's defense" by staying on the old path and building the wrong kind of fleet.[18]

only constant is change, and the realities of a world of scarcity start to bear down on business models built for abundance, continued success means continued renewal—renewal driven and directed by the transformative power of constraints. This is no time for blue-sky fantasies.

Becoming locked-in to path dependence is inevitable unless we deliberately create methods to break it.

The first of these is to ask propelling questions.

## BREAK PATH DEPENDENCE: CHAPTER SUMMARY

- The past is a powerful influencer of the future. If we let them, the decisions we made yesterday will determine what is possible tomorrow.

- Path Dependence describes the bundle of premises, processes, assumptions, relationships, and ways of thinking about solutions that define "the way we do things around here."

- The dominant path defines our, or our organization's, way of approaching challenges for good reason: that path has worked before.

- Having a locked-in path is particularly valuable, and therefore prevalent, in large, efficiency-driven organizations, where the ability to repeat at scale and speed is an essential driver of success.

- The language we use tends to reinforce that path and its inherent beliefs and assumptions.

- A precondition for success in the journey to transforming constraints, however, is the willingness and ability to examine all the ingrained habits that may stand in the way of our being able to see and realize the possibilities in it.

- The most disabling constraints we face, in this respect, may be those inside our heads (preconceptions, the stories we tell about ourselves) and our culture (the path we have become locked into). This form of lock-in can prevent us moving from the victim mindset to a more productive one.

- The chapter explores two key parts to breaking path dependence. The first is surfacing and naming the tendencies and biases we have as a group, reflected in the language we use and what we mean by it. The second is surfacing and interrogating the constituent parts of our path dependence.

# 3 ASK PROPELLING QUESTIONS

How to frame the constraint to force breakthrough

**THIS CHAPTER FOCUSES ON:**

1. Why is it key to frame questions in the right way to find new paths and transform our constraint?

2. How does framing these questions differ if you are responding to a constraint or imposing one on yourself?

3. Why must we be proactive in generating these kinds of questions?

# PART ONE: Uncomfortable Questions

**Larry Page, Google's co-founder and CEO,** has little patience for the kind of incremental thinking he sees from most large corporations; it is, he believes, guaranteed to become obsolete over time. And he feels that the obsession with competition as the sole driver of innovation—with media coverage he compares to that of a sporting event—is also off the mark: "It's hard," he says, "to find actual examples of really amazing things that happened solely due to competition."[1]

Page has a different measure of success. He's not interested in simply being "better than," but in being "really amazing." And with that as the goal, he sees his role as to look up from the daily contest and ask bigger questions, what he calls 10x questions: those requiring answers that have ten times the impact of previous solutions.

Now Google is the second largest company in the world, with a market cap approaching $400 billion and annual revenues in excess of $50 billion,[2] so one might ask what they are doing in a book about constraints at all. But despite their obvious lack of financial restrictions, what's helpful for us to understand is the effect the scale of Page's ambition is having on the way his project teams behave.

In a semi-secret facility a half a mile away from the Googleplex in Mountain View, California, Page's partner, Sergey Brin, oversees the Google X projects, which look to answer these 10x questions, many of which must seem almost impossible at first. The first of these, for instance, is the famous driverless car, whose ambition is openly shared on Google's blog: "Our goal is to help prevent traffic accidents, free up people's time and reduce carbon emissions by fundamentally changing car use." The more curious can find the key rationale for this ambition in Larry Page's own Google+ post: of the accidents that killed 370,000 people on America's roads in 2009, 93 percent were due to human error.[3]

Google's 10x question here is not the incremental question of "How can we reduce car accidents?" but, in effect: "How can we prevent all traffic accidents that result from human error?" The question clearly defines the size of the ambition while pointing to the constraint in which the answer lies: to remove the driver from the equation. And this question has both legitimacy and authority. It has authority, in the sense that the question is being asked by one of the founders and the solution being led by the other, and it has legitimacy, in that 344,100 people were killed on American roads due to driver error in 2009. This concept of legitimacy and authority will be important to us later in the chapter.[4]

Google's semi-autonomous vehicles are making progress so fast that commentators believe they will be ready before lawmakers have had a chance to fully understand and legislate around the consequences. How Page will deal with that constraint will be interesting to see.

## The effect of being asked to do the impossible

Questions that are apparently impossible to answer are not always reserved for world-changing technology; they are powerfully framed and used by any company with a strong sense of purpose and a desire to create significant breakthrough. IKEA, for example, is on the side of what it calls "the many"—the vast majority of the people in the world who love their homes, but don't have a lot of money to spend on them. So reducing the price of good design is a key part of how they progress. And to make this kind of progress with the speed and impact they need, they will ask a team to find an answer to a question that, at first, appears impossible to answer.

Michael Hay, whose fifteen years at IKEA included roles as Creative Director and Strategic Planner for global communication, as well as range development, describes what it is like to be on the receiving end of a question like this: for example, the brief to produce a well-designed, durable table that could be made and sold profitably for five euros.

Just think about it for a moment. How would you begin to design a table that could be made and sold, at a profit, for five euros? A solid, durable table that is going to cost just twice the price of the latte that might at some point adorn it? Where on earth would one even begin?

The nature of this kind of question, Hay observes, means that it is impossible to answer by using an approach you have used before; it forces you off the path you have become dependent on. You can't answer it by looking at competitors, simply because there are no competitors who are making tables for five euros and might never be any. You recognize that you can't answer this on your own, or even within your specialist team—you're going to have to work in a much more multidisciplinary way, talking to other people in the organization who will help you look hard at potential opportunities within supply chain and materials, for example. And as you explore entirely new kinds of materials, there may not even be the expertise and knowledge within the company itself. The question may push you further outward, to talk to universities about new research that might help contribute part of the answer.

It is the constraint at the heart of the question—the unreasonably low price point that has never even been approached before—that ensures the IKEA team will need to abandon all of its habitual thinking about design and manufacture. The degree of invention required to meet this brief will be significant, rather than incremental. In this particular case, their journey led them to door manufacturers. Their solution to the impossible question was to cut a door in two and make it into a five-euro table; a type of solution and business partner that they would never have considered if the question had asked for mere incremental improvement. And the result was a table that opened up a dramatically new price point for them, while better meeting the needs of the consumers that they champion.

## The nature of a propelling question

In Chapter Two, we saw that a key difference between being victim to a constraint and transforming it is the relationship between the constraint and the ambition attached to it—they are intrinsically linked. We saw that people in the victim stage tended to reduce the ambition to fit the constraint, while those in the transformer stage tended to leave the ambition

## A propelling question is one that has both a bold ambition and a significant constraint linked together.

high, and use the tension between the ambition and the constraint to drive the search for solutions. We can see this relationship between high ambition and significant constraint in many of the cases we are exploring here, and making their relationship an integral part of the framing question is a key part of driving the successful solution development that follows.

How we frame the question is critical to making a constraint beautiful, because it forces us to think and behave in a different way. We call these kinds of questions *propelling questions*. A propelling question is one that has both a bold ambition and a significant constraint linked together. It is called a propelling question because the presence of those two different elements together in the same question does not allow it to be answered in the way we have answered previous questions; it propels us off the path on which we have become dependent.

Scott Keogh, the CEO of Audi of America, tells the story of how Audi developed the R10 TDI car for the famous 24-hour Le Mans race in 2006. The obvious question for a team working to develop a new race car would have been "How can we build a faster car?" But Audi is a company that has at its heart being progressive, and so instead of asking his team the obvious question, the Chief Engineer asked

*The Audi R10 TDI*

a more progressive one: "How could we win Le Mans if our car could go no faster than anyone else's?" A bold ambition with a significant constraint, plus a propelling question, took them to put diesel technology into their race cars for the first time. For the answer was fuel efficiency: they could win Le Mans with a car that wasn't faster than any of the other cars, if it took fewer pit stops. And they were right: the R10 TDI placed first at Le Mans for the next three years.[5]

We can see propelling questions of this kind, coupling bold ambitions with significant constraints, used at different levels in companies and enterprises. When it is the frame for the overarching corporate mission, for example, such as Unilever's promise to double its growth while reducing its environmental footprint, it forces the entire organization to rethink every path and assumption—from how to source tomatoes, to the role of packaging, to how to engage consumers in behaving more sustainably. But it can also be used more specifically and tactically, as in the case of the fast-growing designer furniture retailer Made.com, who asked, "How can we exhibit at the world's most prestigious furniture exhibition in Milan without paying for an exhibition hall?" (We will see how they answered this on page 106). And at some level, it is the defining question for every CMO of every challenger brand: How do we build a stronger relationship with our target market than the market leader, without a communications budget? It is the tension in that question that forces a challenger brand team to rethink the role and potential nature of packaging (cleaning brand method's breakthrough use of structural design), or how to introduce more character and distinctiveness into their offer (rideshare brand Lyft's cars sport pink mustaches), or leverage its community (Airbnb's photographers), or create entirely new kinds of user value (Warby Parker sending you five different frames so you can ask your friends what they think).

Let's explore how a propelling question works at an individual level, and the changes it can drive in an individual's approach to answering a question that the organization as a whole must answer.

## Growing a better quality crop with less water

Frikkie Lubbe is an agriculturalist for South African Breweries (SAB) in the Northern Cape region of South Africa, part of a team given a considerable degree of autonomy in how they approach the company's key challenges and ambitions.

In 2010, he needed to respond to two different ambitions for SAB that, taken together, made up a propelling question. As a brewer, the company wanted to produce better beer—so he needed to find a way of getting a superior quality yield from his barley, the key ingredient in beer. And at the same time, as a responsible corporate citizen of South Africa, SAB wanted to find ways to significantly reduce water consumption in producing beer. Water was a precious resource for farmers, and barley for beer, a non-essential crop that demanded 155 liters of water for each liter of beer produced. So the propelling question Lubbe faced was "How can we increase barley yield and quality while reducing water consumption by ten percent?" He was, he admits, initially unsure this was possible—the constraint of even only a 10-percent reduction in this context seemed "very challenging."[6]

To start to answer that propelling question, Lubbe knew he'd need new insights from new sources. He did something he had never done before: visiting a meeting of his local barley farmers, he asked if any of them had been forced to irrigate less in recent years, but had still produced a strong barley crop. Some put their hands up: yes, they told him, in 2009 they'd had problems with getting spare parts for their irrigation equipment and hadn't been able to irrigate properly, yet had still produced a crop with good heads and yields, although it hadn't grown as high. Putting a new kind of question to an existing data source had given Lubbe an initial clue.

He took this emerging idea to a new source of information outside the company— recent academic research into barley growth, which found that there were three stages to it: an initial stage when the head developed, a second stage when the stalk grew but the head was dormant, and a third stage when the head grew again. Putting these two together gave him the breakthrough insight: if they stressed the barley at the second stage of growth by significantly reducing the amount of water they gave it, Lubbe reasoned, the barley wouldn't grow as high, but the quality of the heads would be just as good. And because the stalks didn't grow as high, there would be less incidence of a barley problem called lodging, where the stalks become too tall and fall over, spoiling the heads. If this new irrigation approach worked, they would be able to reduce the amount of water used while increasing the quality and yield of the crop.

Lubbe's conversations with the farmers had also revealed why they weren't thinking in this way already: these were mainly wheat farmers applying the same irrigation practices for both crops, even though barley didn't require the same amount of water across all three stages of its life. They were blindly applying the approach for wheat to barley, a path dependence revealed only by the demands of the propelling question.

Lubbe now needed real evidence that his theory would work in practice; the final challenge was to find farmers prepared to try this new method. The difficulty here was that these were independent farmers, for whom farming was their only income, and SAB couldn't give them any kind of guarantee if the crop failed; the stakes seemed high. So Lubbe identified those for whom the lodging problem had been greatest as having the most emotional incentive to participate, and persuaded them to limit their risk by trying this new method on just 20 percent of their crop. Nine farmers signed up, and Lubbe and two colleagues committed to visiting them every week throughout the growing season.

The results over the following year surprised even the most optimistic. The new approach reduced water consumption by up to 48 percent, easily beating the initial target of 10 percent, while at the same time improving the yield and quality of the barley by reducing lodging. And there was an additional benefit to the farmer: a saving of $40 per hectare in electricity costs because of the reduced irrigation needs—a saving that went straight to his bottom line. SAB is now implementing the new approach across all of South Africa.

While this is a story about barley irrigation, it is also about a determined individual responding to a propelling question. First, he accepts the question as a legitimate and important one to work on, even though he finds it very challenging. Then, in beginning to work on it, he breaks his own path dependence: he works with an existing data source, but asks a different kind of question. He goes on to look outside his organization for new thinking that might offer further insight. Once he has his initial potential solution, he recognizes that to turn this theory into something more substantive, he will have to work with his regular partners in a new way. He creates a trial to give credibility to his answer, in a way that limits risks to the people it is most likely to impact. He overcommits his time and attention to that trial, running alongside his usual job. In doing so, he creates the hard data that convinces the rest of the organization—as well as the independent partners that they need—that they have found a significantly better solution for both sides.

And one that more than answers the propelling question he originally accepted.

## What makes propelling questions powerful?

If we want to make constraints beautiful, then it matters how we ask the questions that contain them. All of these questions harness the constraint to the ambition, ensuring that the constraint drives the solution:

- How do we win the race with a car that is no faster than anyone else's?
- How do we build a well-designed, durable table for five euros?
- How do we establish a stronger relationship with this buyer than the market

leader, without a communications budget?
- How do we grow more and better quality barley using less water?

Both sides of the propelling question are critical. The specificity and scale of the ambition needs to set a clear but high bar, a target we know represents our highest hope (100 percent college readiness without remediation for LPS) or something we haven't been able to achieve before (giving every child in the world the quality of education of the wealthiest child in Manhattan, in the case of One Laptop Per Child). The ambition defines the impact we wish to make.

And the constraint denies us something that would make the question easy to answer (budget,

---

## The Value of Paradoxical Frames

Researchers conducted four experiments to evaluate the role of paradox in prompting creativity. One experiment asked people to assess a toy after reading the supposed comments of judges in a toy design contest; some groups were shown comments describing the toy as low-cost, some as creative, and some as both. The latter case had supposedly surprised the judges, who thought low-cost and creativity to be at odds (i.e. somewhat paradoxical). Those primed with the idea of a paradox then proceeded to score the toy higher on a creativity test than the others. Another experiment first created a sense of internal conflict in some respondents (an internal paradox); these subsequently scored higher on a creativity test. A third experiment asked people to assess different, contradictory information and then try to integrate it all—they too became more creative in subsequent testing. And the fourth experiment integrated all of the above elements into one.

The researchers observed that paradoxical frames had a number of beneficial effects:

- They create a sense of conflict and discomfort, and this tension can be a valuable trigger to getting people to think in new ways, as well as engaging in deeper scrutiny.
- They reduce the likelihood that people will fall back into habitual lines of thought.
- They force participants to re-interrogate the relationships between key elements.
- They prompt "and" thinking rather than "either/or" thinking.
- They increase the level of integrative complexity—the ability to be open to ambiguity and contradictions. Previously this was thought to be stable (i.e. you either were high or low on this by nature); recent research, however, shows that this can in fact be influenced by circumstances.

*Source:* Miron-Spektor, Gino, and Argote[7]

distribution, know-how, a price point, user engagement), and that denial seems, ultimately, to make it more creatively fertile. Irritating, even confounding, in the beginning, but in the end, fertile.

Propelling questions are, then, not merely difficult questions to answer, like "How do we double volume in three years?" or "How do we reduce cost by twenty percent?" And propelling questions are not merely stimulating, like "Who is the customer of the future?" or "What new technologies are reshaping our industry today?" Propelling questions contain a directional tension—this constraint is what you must use as a key parameter to meet this stretching ambition.

This tension is more than a piece of inspiring rhetoric; research suggests it actually affects the way we cognitively process a question. The breakout box shows the results of a 2010 study into the effects of priming people with seemingly contradictory problem statements.[7] This kind of challenge, it found, made people productively uncomfortable, preventing them from falling back on habitual lines of thinking, forcing participants to re-interrogate relationships between constituent elements of the problem, and prompting "and" thinking, rather than "either/or" thinking.

The discomfort of propelling questions makes us think differently. While they might at first leave us perplexed, they change the starting point of the journey, make us re-examine what we thought we knew, set a new course, and ultimately open us up to new possibilities. And this, as Dan Wieden might put it, is their gift: they break path dependence and propel us toward new solutions.

> # The discomfort of propelling questions makes us think differently; they break path dependence and propel us toward new solutions.

While challenging, the tension they capture can also be compelling. One of the top ten highlighted books of all time on Kindle, for instance, is essentially a propelling question. Tim Ferriss' *The 4-Hour Workweek: Escape 9-5, Live Anywhere, and Join the New Rich* is in its very concept linking a bold ambition (joining the rich) paired with a specific and significant constraint (working four hours a week). And Ferriss' answers to that question—extensively outsourcing to virtual personal assistants, migrating to automated sources of revenue, for example—make us challenge some of the upstream assumptions about the foundations of our businesses and personal lives, assumptions that we no longer really see or question. Which is why we highlight them so assiduously on our Kindle.

## Starting to use propelling questions: the different families of constraint and ambition

In starting to work with this way of framing the challenge around our constraint, we will all need to define what our own propelling question is. While there might be some obvious ones that a number of us share—large companies needing to increase their innovation impact while also significantly reducing costs and time, for example[8]—for most of us they will be explicitly individual.

One element of this question might already be thrust on us; we may be responding to outside pressures as the constraint to our own ambition—we might have to achieve our ambition in a much more accelerated time frame, for instance. And one element might be the desired impact of our purpose or mission, if we have one.

But for those of us with more room to ask ourselves the most powerful question, it will be useful to break down both constraints and ambitions into different families. There are several different ways to explore which propelling question could work for us best. We saw in the introduction that we can broadly group constraints into those of foundation, resource, time, and method.

### Constraints of Foundation

A constraint around something typically regarded as an essential foundation for success in this area—lack of a physical restaurant for restaurateurs in the food-cart movement, for example, or lack of brick-and-mortar retail space for a product that supposedly needs trying or experiencing.

### Constraints of Resource

A limitation on an essential resource for creating success and driving growth off those foundations—typically the resources of budget, people, and knowledge or expertise. Think of Sailor Jerry rum, for example, launching successfully against Captain Morgan rum without an advertising budget.

### Constraints of Time

The composer and conductor Leonard Bernstein remarked that "to achieve great things, two things are needed: a plan, and not quite enough time." Constraints of time are ones that we experience throughout our day, every day—and also live large in some of the most ambitious projects in the world around us. Think of regulatory requirements to hit emission targets by a certain date, for example. Or Sky City in Changsha in China, which, at twice the height of the Empire State Building, will be the tallest skyscraper in the world, with 202 floors that the construction company has set itself the goal of erecting in just 90 days. (Their solution to this extremely tight time parameter is to pre-fabricate the floors elsewhere and then assemble them on-site.)

### Constraints of Method

A constraint which requires the solution to be delivered in a certain way, such as Audi's R10 having to win without being able to go faster, or IKEA having to deliver a table at a certain price point.

On the other side of our question, we can also see ambitions falling into different groups:

### Ambitions of Growth

These, of course, lie at the heart of any company, and can be framed in terms of revenue or profit, numbers of customers or subscribers, or different kinds of category growth. But they can be more imaginatively framed. Think of the famous ambition of Robert Woodruff as the 33-year-old President of Coca-Cola in 1923—that Coca-Cola should always be "within an arm's reach of desire," a growth ambition that then drove both dispense innovation in the United States and the company's first push into global expansion.

### Ambitions of Impact

These are usually ambitions coming out of the purpose or mission of the company: the impact on the world that it wants to have. Unilever's Domestos, for instance, has a Social Mission program with a target to help build a "clean, safe toilet for all."[9] But the desired impact can also be on the category (Warby Parker's desire to radically transform the eyewear industry), or people's relationship with it.

### Ambitions of Quality

These are ambitions defining a certain quality of the company or brand we want to be. Think of Chipotle's mission to be "food with integrity," a fast-food company of size, certainly, but one that sources meat from naturally raised, antibiotic-free animals.[10]

### Ambitions of Superiority

These are ambitions around superior service or innovation, or superior servicing of a customer's needs. Xbox in Europe, for example, has a stated ambition of being "the best gaming console for fans ... that plays the best games and has the best entertainment." In what it seems to regard as a zero-sum game against a resurgent PlayStation, it feels relative superiority will drive success.[11]

### Ambitions of Experience

Finally, the ambition can be about the consistent delivery of a certain kind of experience. This kind of ambition is much more customer-centric than some of the others here. Tony Hsieh, for example, describes the ambition of Zappos as "to deliver happiness in a box." This encapsulates not simply the contents of the box (important though those are), but the quality of customer service at the heart of what Zappos feels makes it different.[12]

While we are not proposing that these are the only families of constraints and ambitions, they can stimulate us to develop different types of propelling questions with greater precision. Sometimes our constraints might be fixed (SAB's water limits, for example), and we could experiment with different ambitions in relation to that fixed constraint to develop the most promising propelling question. This will typically be the situation if we are responding to a constraint.

If, on the other hand, we are interested in imposing a constraint on ourselves, to stimulate new ways of seeing and thinking about possibilities, then it is more likely that our starting point will be a fixed ambition (Audi's "win the race"), and we can experiment with different forms of constraints set alongside that ambition. It may be valuable for us to try a few, to help us find where the opportunity might lie.

## Specificity, Authority, Legitimacy

It is essential that the constraint be framed to be as specific as possible. A constraint without specificity, IBM's Trevor Davis noted, is very hard to work with—"we have a constraint around time," for example, offers no beneficial stimulus to creativity and possibility. "We have to be on sale within sixty days" or "We have to be able to free the

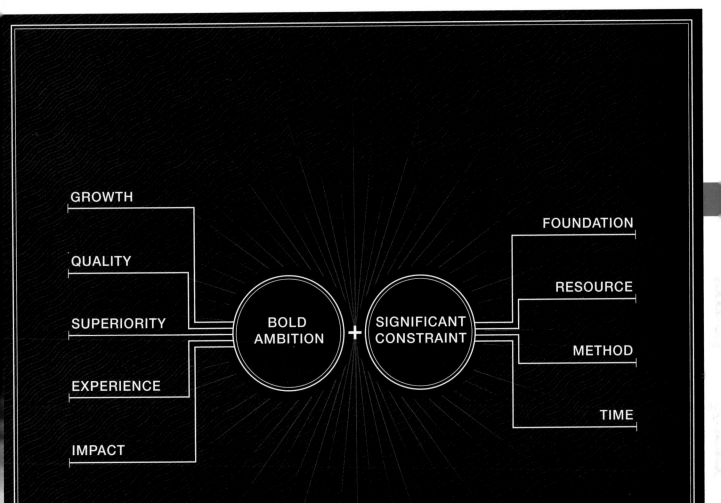

GROWTH

QUALITY

SUPERIORITY

EXPERIENCE

IMPACT

BOLD AMBITION + SIGNIFICANT CONSTRAINT

FOUNDATION

RESOURCE

METHOD

TIME

FAMILIES OF AMBITION

FAMILIES OF CONSTRAINT

captive within three minutes,"[13] on the other hand, have a focusing specificity that is an offer to unlock new ways to think about the solution.

And as we noted above, for the propelling question to work well, to be taken seriously enough to lead a team to find a way to answer it, and rethink existing approaches in doing so, it will need to have legitimacy and authority. It will need to be legitimate in the sense that people will recognize the rationale for the nature of the chosen ambition and constraint—that, far from being arbitrary, they accurately reflect the nature of the business and the context in which it operates or is about to operate.

And it will need to have authority: it will need to be asked by someone who has to be given an answer, whether outside (a key customer, for instance) or inside the organization.

The rest of this chapter will explore how, if we don't ask propelling questions of ourselves, we may find other people asking them of us, and what the consequences might be. For those who are already comfortable with an understanding of how to frame the question around a constraint, and wish to move on, the next chapter will explore how to begin to answer these kinds of difficult questions, and how to maintain momentum in answering those constraint-driven challenges if we lack experience in this kind of problem solving.

# Part 2: The Rise of Unreasonableness

## Who else might ask propelling questions of us, and what happens when they do?

Twenty-five years ago, Charles Handy wrote the highly influential *The Age of Unreason*, in which he described forces which were already shaping the world, but about to become much more important. First, discontinuous change—major shifts brought on by developments in IT, biotech, and economics. Second, smaller changes in the way we work that would affect the way we live—his "shamrock organization" foreshadowed subcontracting, flexible work hours, and telecommuting trends, as well as the idea of having customers do some of the work of the business (common now, but a radical prescience in 1989). And third, "upside-down thinking," in which he invited us to challenge many of our deeply held views about how the world worked and to look at everything in a new way. [14]

Quoting George Bernard Shaw's celebrated maxim ("The reasonable man adapts himself to the world, while the unreasonable man persists in adapting the world to himself … therefore all progress belongs to the unreasonable man"), Handy called for unreasonableness in the modern organization, in order to seize the opportunities presented by change. Yet just four years later, in The Age of Paradox, the same Handy was lamenting the chaos that all the unreasonableness seemed to have unleashed: "too many have been unsettled by the changes…. Life is a struggle for many and a puzzle for most," he said, "so many things seem to contain their own contradictions."[16]

And now here we are, a quarter of a century later, with greater change swirling around us than even Handy could have imagined, with new and different sources of unreasonableness spurring still more change almost every day. For the purposes of the rest of this chapter, we are going to focus on a very particular kind of unreasonableness as it relates to constraints: external forces imposing constraint-related demands on us, whether regulator, buyer, customer, or competitor.

The box on the next page sets out the different sources of unreasonable demands. At the heart of each of them, in some way, is the imposition of a specific limitation on how we have to grow—a constraint that we have to observe if we want to flourish.

## Uber's children and the death of the trade-off

We don't just expect Wi-Fi on planes now, we demand it. We demand high-speed Internet that never drops, as we hurtle through the sky at 400mph, 30,000 feet up. And the odds are we moan about having to pay for it.[18] After all, Wi-Fi at Starbucks is free. And email. So is Skype. Oh, and we'd like a better quality of Cabernet, please, flight attendant; this one tastes like Listerine.

As a new generation of companies teaches us that the old trade-offs we used to consider reasonable no longer apply, they simultaneously train us to want more. My own private driver for the cost of a taxi? Thank you, Uber. Use my credit card to buy carrots directly from the farmer? Bless you, Square. Eggs delivered directly to my house the day after they are laid via a web service? Yes please, Rakuten. A new generation of consumers sees no reason why two seemingly irreconcilable demands shouldn't be put together. These are Uber's children. And this is the death of the trade-off.

# The Four Sources of Unreasonableness

## The Unreasonable Regulator

In a world of increasingly scarce resources, rising commodity prices, and environmental degradation, regulators are imposing, or threatening to impose, "unreasonable" demands in many areas, such as water use and engine efficiency. U.S. Congress, for instance, imposed Corporate Average Fuel Economy (CAFE) standards following the Arab Oil Embargo of 1975: in 2012, an ambitious goal of 54.5 miles per gallon by 2025 was set, giving the industry twelve years to invent their way to meeting that goal. Ford and Toyota are now working together to develop hybrid powertrains for light-duty trucks and SUVs; many experts predict more of this kind of collaboration as industry competitors are forced to make new kinds of alliances in order to hit the regulatory targets.[17]

## The Unreasonable Consumer

Consumers no longer tolerate trade-offs they once accepted. Why can't I rent a car for an hour (City Car Share), or buy fast food that's healthy and ethical (Chipotle), or afford to enjoy high fashion on a basic wage (Zara, H&M, and Rent The Runway)? And they take these new, unreasonable expectations into every other category (see "Death of the Trade-Off").

## The Unreasonable Customer

Retailers pass on their own business pressures to suppliers—more impactful promotions, more successful innovation, keener price points, fewer SKUs—and they also pass on their business ambitions: when Walmart changed its approach to sustainability following Hurricane Katrina, for instance, it demanded that its suppliers deliver to the standard of that new ambition as well. These higher bars are matched with fiercer terms—an unreasonable combination, but the reality of the power the retailers hold.

## The Unreasonable Challenger

Three years ago, did the giant hotel brands imagine that they would be competing with me and you and our spare rooms for the custom of this new generation of travelers? And yet Airbnb, the fastest growing hospitality brand in the world today, rented more rooms last year than the Hilton brand.[18] That's a vastly different competitive offering to which the hotels must respond—and unreasonable to expect a legacy business to be able to respond so quickly to this new kind of challenger. But respond it must, and fast—just as Mercedes must respond to Tesla, Tesco to Aldi, and every cab company in the world to Uber.

In financial services, for instance, we might once have accepted an interest-bearing checking account, from a free online bank with online customer service 24/7, as a reasonable trade-off for having no actual retail branches. There was demand for a great online bank (ING, First Direct) and demand for a full-service bank with branches (Wells Fargo, NatWest), but with an understanding of the trade-offs on fees and rates. Not anymore. Today's banking customers want it free, accessible from anywhere in the world, anytime, with real people in case anything goes wrong, and a branch to drop in on when in town. But they don't want banks to get big. They don't like big.

The modern consumer is, in fact, the incarnation of Shaw and Handy's unreasonable man and woman, forcing businesses to get beyond "either/or" and work out how to give them the "and." The unreasonable consumer is, in effect, asking us propelling questions. And the answers they are getting are starting to change the face of the categories in which they appear. Just look at the United States alone:

- Fast food: I need a fast, cheap meal but I'd like it to be better quality and healthier. Chipotle's commitment to simple, hearty Mexican food with a side of sustainability has lead to double-digit growth three years in a row.
- Cleaning: I want cleaning products that clean, but I expect them to be green too. method makes gorgeous green products that "clean like a mother" and is now in its twelfth successful year.
- Mobile carriers: I want the best phones and the best network, but without being tied into a contract. T-Mobile now gives a smartphone without any contract, and it will pay off the early-termination fees charged by those who won't. Small wonder that it is currently acquiring customers faster than ATT.[19]
- Cars: I want a car that drives like a rocket and looks like a dream while being completely electric. Tesla's plug-in Model S is beautiful and fast, gets the equivalent of 89 mpg and was recently voted the safest car ever tested by the National Highway Traffic Safety Administration (NHTSA).

The point is that if we don't ask propelling questions of ourselves, someone is going to ask them of us, someone with authority and legitimacy. It may be our largest or most influential customer, or our noisiest challenger, but if we don't anticipate this, by the time we hear them we will already be behind the curve. This is the corollary of the new generation of inventiveness: if we are not leading in being that inventive, then we risk becoming an important part of the past, rather than a shaper of the future.

So this chapter has taken us on a journey. We started by exploring the value of how we framed the question around a constraint, to open up the beautiful possibilities it might contain. And now we are looking back and reviewing our competitive context, and the transformative power of propelling questions in our category as a whole— perhaps finding ourselves on the receiving end of a sharply competitive answer from an unreasonable challenger. One who asks a question that combines two different elements—a particular type of ambition with a certain kind of constraint—and is unreasonable, given everything we know about the category, to ask. And that, once answered, changes consumer expectations about the category, to our disadvantage.

But let's finish by flipping it: what are the benefits of offense as well as defense here? What if we impose that constraint on ourselves—ask and answer the propelling question first? Is there any hard data on the benefits of being the unreasonable challenger?

## The rewards for the unreasonable challenger

John Gerzema runs WPP's Brand Asset Valuator, a databank of an annual global survey of 50,000 brands in over 200 categories, amongst 800,000 people. Gerzema himself is a *New York Times* bestselling author whose work includes studies of the effects that lifestyle ambitions and budget constraints have on changing consumer habits. In the concept of Cinderellanomics, for example, he describes strategies of those who desire a luxury lifestyle but cannot afford to maintain it; their solution is to have it on a temporary basis, to rent luxury goods for a while and then give them back.[20] Unreasonable, perhaps, but smart if there's someone prepared to enable it for them (Rent The Runway, for instance).

The database Gerzema manages is the largest analysis of the changes in people's relationships with brands and categories over time; it can now identify and analyze key brand and consumer trends for over twenty years. BAV assesses brand energy as a combination of relevant differentiation and a sense of momentum. Working with professors Robert Jacobson at the University of Washington and Natalie Mizik at Columbia, they found a strong correlation between brand energy and market valuation, and believe consumers short brands in much the same way that investors short stocks—

**If we don't ask propelling questions of ourselves, someone is going to ask them of us, and by that time we will be behind the curve.**

brands that are losing energy get mentally sold to make way for brands with more energy. [21]

So where does unreasonableness fit into this? Categories tend to have poles of qualities which brands focus on delivering (high-performance, economical, rugged, and stylish in automotive, for instance). There is a range of these poles in any category, and the relationships between these different poles often contain trade-offs: people have historically accepted that they shouldn't expect a brand in that category to be able to offer them both high performance and be economical, for instance—it is reasonable to expect there to be a trade-off as a buyer that one makes between one and the other.

But we wanted to know if there was any evidence in the data that an unreasonable challenger—which we define here as a brand with an offer that unreasonably resolved what the category had previously seen as reasonable trade-offs, such as Chipotle and Tesla—would see an increase in brand energy, and hence their long-term value. And, indeed, what the effect on the rest of their category would be if they did.

To make things simple, we looked with BAV, using their data, at some of the more obvious poles in each category. In cars, we took the green versus performance poles and looked at Tesla versus other luxury auto brands. In fast food, we looked at value versus quality and healthy, and used Chipotle against Taco Bell. And in household cleaning, we looked at socially conscious versus efficient (a proxy for performance in cleaning) and looked at method against other leading cleaning brands.

The analysis is reproduced in the appendix. In short, what it found was that while there were inevitably variations in the magnitude of the effects by category, a consistent picture emerged:

- The poles we looked for are quite easy to see in the data, and have been stubborn over time; there has been until now a clear trade-off, with few brands seen as being able to deliver against both.
- Those who are now seen to be delivering against both of these two trade-off poles, resolving the trade-off, have a stronger brand energy score than those who don't.
- These unreasonable challengers who resolve trade-offs are gaining energy. Those in the same category that aren't are now losing energy, possibly depositioned by this new dynamic.

John Gerzema notes the significant shift this represents in the way buyers are thinking about categories, and their brand choices within them:

*According to our data, there have always been clear and discernible patterns in the ways consumers think about product categories. Historically, these patterns were driven by perceived trade-offs. In other words, brands would carve out a space around a few attributes that naturally clustered together into a territory, and that's how brands in categories thought about differentiation—as coming from "natural" clusters. However, the data now shows that brands able to unite attributes that have previously been perceived as disparate are showing considerably more momentum and energy than the ones that are stuck in their old one-dimensional territory. These brands are the ones that people want to do business with because they're offering something new, and reinventing what is considered reasonable—or even what is considered possible.*[22]

The future, it seems, belongs to the unreasonable challenger, who imposes on themselves the constraint of having to satisfy two apparently contradictory poles at the same time, and finds a way to do so. These are the brands that are gaining energy. And those brands that are slow to ask themselves this particular kind of propelling question are also the ones finding themselves starting to lose brand energy.[23]

So what do we do about this? Set up an unreasonable innovation stream within our innovation pipeline? Perhaps. But Yves Behar, the designer behind Jawbone and OLPC whom we met in Chapter One, goes further. Behar feels that this is the new normal—or at least, that we need to think of it as such:

*I think the consumer today wants it all, and it's our job to deliver it to them … to deliver the better experience that's green and less expensive, all at the same time. There's no reason why it can't be done, outside of the fact that somebody somewhere in a corporation is saying it can't be done. But the kind of era we're moving in is an era of much deeper and truer creativity, creativity that's all-encompassing in solving a problem, commercial or not, rather than compartmentalized solutions.*[24]

In other words, we must all be prepared to answer to Uber's children.

**ASK PROPELLING QUESTIONS: CHAPTER SUMMARY**

- There are many kinds of questioning techniques: the five whys, and "what if …" being perhaps two of the best known. This chapter argues that a new kind of powerful and relevant kind of question for the times we live in is a propelling question.

- Propelling questions bind a bold ambition to a significant constraint. The solution has to make use of the constraint, denying us what would make the answer easier, ensuring that we address real challenges and not indulge in blue-sky fantasies.

- Propelling questions force us off our well-worn paths, help us break path dependence, and spur us to entirely new kinds of solutions.

- A propelling question is most powerful when it has specificity, legitimacy, and authority.

- We can use different families of ambition and constraint to help define the most potent propelling question for our situation.

- Some of the most successful people and businesses achieve that success by routinely posing these kinds of impossible questions for themselves and their teams (IKEA, Google, Nike). It's a part of their make-up to propel themselves forward by setting ambitions that they don't know how they'll achieve.

- We all need to be more proactive in asking and answering propelling questions of ourselves, before someone else asks them of us—whether a regulator, a competitor or even our consumer.

# 4 CAN-IF

How to find solutions to constraint-driven problems

1. What's the best way to begin answering these challenging kinds of questions?

2. How do we maintain momentum in finding possible answers?

3. What might be the most fertile places to start to look for answers?

# PART 1: How we need to think about answers

## Optimism decays

Propelling questions—using a higher level of ambition to force us to find the opportunity in apparent constraints—require us to work towards solutions that lie outside our experience and comfort zone. Sir Jonathan Ive, Apple's design chief, has spoken about what it takes to confront these kinds of challenges. It takes, he notes, both a "remarkable focus" and "being inquisitive and optimistic"—qualities which, he says, one doesn't see in combination very often; optimism and persistent inquisitiveness are hard to sustain over testing periods of trial and error.[1]

Some scientists have suggested that there's an evolutionary advantage to optimism. Optimism underpins progress by allowing us to believe in a better future, and so make it more likely that we will plan for and begin creating it. This optimism bias[2] exists across race, region, class, and caste and explains why so many cultures have a version of the "every cloud has a silver lining" aphorism.

Academics also show that positivity correlates strongly with both resilience and openness, two characteristics we are going to need to draw on as we commit to exploring and testing inventive new approaches from unusual sources.[3]

But our optimism bias can't be fully relied upon. It tends to overestimate our chance of success, so that we underprepare for challenges, and it tends to be far more personal than collective: I am optimistic about *my* future, but pessimistic about *our* future. As we'll almost certainly be working in teams and involving new people, we'll need to find a way to build a greater collective sense of positivity, as we search for the beauty in our constraint, than our own inbuilt bias might be capable of delivering.

So the challenge is not simply "How do we answer this question?" It is "How do we create the conversational climate that gives us the best possible chance to answer this question?" One that's a little more helpful than a simple exhortation to be positive.

## Can-If

Colin Kelly is the Director of Research and Development at Warburton's, a Bolton-based British bakery that has grown from a regional challenger twenty years ago to the UK's brand leader in bread and baked goods; it is one of the most remarkable and unsung success stories in European business. Kelly and his team are quietly reinventing a 50-year-old baking process that the rest of the industry no longer questions.

Kelly emphasizes the importance of the flow in problem-solving, by which he means keeping the conversation focused on movement toward possible solutions, unchecked by the presentation of potential problems. His views about how to maintain this flow were strongly influenced by his experience leading a team in Russia in 2006. In the conservative culture of the time, the potentially strong solutions his team proposed were frequently blocked by others explaining that "we can't do this because…." The nature of the "can't because" varied. Sometimes it had to do with cost or capability, sometimes impact on other processes, sometimes simply the sheer degree of difficulty involved. But the effect was the same: every time someone introduced a "can't because," Kelly noted, the conversation reached a dead end. The flow had stopped.[4]

Kelly couldn't change the nature of the organization, but he could change the nature of the conversation, particularly the beginning of each sentence in the problem-solving process. He didn't let people start with "We can't because." He forced them to start with "We can if." So, for example, instead of saying "We can't use that type of new packaging because it will slow the line down," the person would be forced to say "We can use that kind of new packaging if we run it on someone else's line." The flow is maintained, and the group moves on to the next question in the chain (in this case, how to find the right line).

As Kelly notes, "can't because" is an understandable reaction to a difficult challenge. People are used to putting up their hands to solve a problem they know how to solve; what is much harder, and more unusual, is putting up their hands to solve a problem they don't know how to solve. And yet that is precisely what is required in constraint-driven problem solving. Without a positive construct to guide the team, the inability to have a ready answer to a difficult question kills the momentum and the flow of exploration.

Let's unpack why *can-if* is so powerful as a frame for our conversations in answering a propelling question, and finding the potential in an apparently challenging constraint:

**It keeps the conversation on the right question.** It keeps the conversation about how something could be possible, rather than whether it would be possible.

**It keeps the oxygen of optimism continually in the process.** It keeps optimism and inquisitiveness alive at the same time.

**It forces everyone involved in the conversation to take responsibility for finding answers, rather than identifying barriers.** It doesn't allow someone to identify obstacles, without looking for a solution to that obstacle in the same sentence.

**The story it tells us about ourselves is that we are people who look for solutions, rather than a group of people who find problems and obstacles.** It builds and reinforces our thinking about ourselves as a culture of potential transformers, rather than impotent victims of insuperable circumstance.

**It is a method that maintains a mindset.** The failure to generate an answer with one line of enquiry simply leads to another can-if, another how.

### Can-If sequences

IDEO's Tim Brown notes that constraints are rarely one-dimensional. There tend to be systems of interlocking constraints within a particular challenge that might encompass, for example, engineering, marketing, and legal. This kind of system requires vision from a leader to cut through to the key challenges, and the understanding that the process is unlikely to stop at a single first can-if, but instead become a sequence in which one solution leads to another challenge, which, in turn, needs a solution, and so on. It is the nature of this sequence of challenge-potential solution, challenge-potential solution, challenge-potential solution, that makes maintaining a culture of optimism and openness so vital.

The nature of a sequence of cascading can-ifs is illustrated well by a group that faced considerable constraints, but nevertheless wanted to be a serious competitor. In this case, the group was the government of a country: Taiwan.

Thomas Friedman once described Taiwan as "a barren rock in a typhoon-laden sea with no natural resources to live off"[5]—not an ideal choice, then, for the two million people who left mainland China at the end of the Civil War in 1949. Chiang Kai-shek's new government needed to build a strong economic foundation as a base from which to resist the sovereignty claims of their gigantic neighbor to the west, the People's

Republic of China. With few natural resources, the infrastructure destruction of World War II, and two million new citizens, Taiwan faced a number of very challenging constraints. But stasis was not an option. They needed to find a way forward.

So the Taiwanese central government asked themselves a propelling question: How do we boost our economy without natural resources?

Their first can-if was to change the definition of natural resources. If they thought of their people as natural resources, they reasoned, they could grow them to progress beyond their current agrarian base. Taiwan had already begun to transition from agriculture to light industry under Japanese rule prior to World War II, and the land reforms of the new government continued this by encouraging landlords to invest in business, creating a new base of industrialists. They instituted universal elementary education as the first step to ensuring a steady supply of human capital to feed industry. Success built slowly, supported in part by U.S. aid during the Cold War, and by 1968 the government was ready to mandate nine years of schooling, rather than the current six.

But this solution led, in turn, to a further constraint: a shortage of teachers. So the next can-if was to recruit alternative teachers among recent college graduates, and train them on the job. This gave rise to a new challenge: with more education and more teachers, they now lacked enough buildings to teach in and the budget to build new ones.

The first part of the solution to the building shortage was to look beyond the Department of Education and to "target abundance" (a concept we will explore in Chapter Five) in other government departments—education was such a high priority that all departments were expected to contribute to the budget for school building. The second part of the solution was to persuade private independent schools to open and join the program, while also expanding their own school buildings to meet capacity needs.

The final challenge was that the type of education the system currently offered wasn't well suited to the way that the government needed to grow the economy—it hadn't been designed to provide a flow of skilled workers. And so they implemented a two-track system that blended the vocational with the academic: vocational high schools and junior colleges developed new capabilities and, working in collaboration with private companies, set up training courses, alleviating the cost to the government and, at the same time, creating a shared responsibility for creating the natural resources to meet the country's overall ambition.

Clearly, governing under martial law helps to mandate compliance. Yet the connected series of constraints Taiwan needed to transform in order to meet their ambition couldn't be solved by mandate alone. In finding solutions to each of the constraints, their can-if thinking included:

- Thinking of their assets in a fundamentally different way.
- Finding new ways to resource shortages.
- Adapting existing assets to fit new purposes.
- Combining different innovations in curricula and capability to arrive at a unified solution.

This multiyear process is summarized in Table 2 on the following page.

Dr. CJ Liu, Director of Education Division of the Taipei Economic and Cultural Representative Office in Washington D.C, describes the strong feeling of national pride that drove the reform of education over decades, and which remains strong to this day. Confucian societies highly prize learning and self-improvement, and the Taiwanese, so long without a clear sense of identity due to so many foreign rulers, found unity partly in the quest for education. Since the lifting of martial law in 1987, the public has demanded more reform, culminating in huge demonstrations in 1994 and further improvements thereafter. Taiwan is now looking at making twelve years of education mandatory.[6]

The Taiwanese Miracle,[7] as it is sometimes called—enjoying an average annual growth of almost 9 percent from 1952 to 1982, higher even than Korea, Japan, and Singapore, leaving a nation of just 23 million people holding the fourth-largest cash reserves of any country in the world—is clearly remarkable.[8] While not the only contributing factor, education has been a critical one; it is a good illustration of how maintaining a can-if culture is essential to addressing the problem–solution–problem–solution sequence that a challenging propelling question can stimulate.

| We Can't Because... | We Can If... |
|---|---|
| We don't have any natural resources | We think of people as a natural resource. |
| Most of our citizens only receive 6 years of education. | We introduce an increase in basic education from 6 years to 9 years. |
| We can't teach those additional pupils because we are short of teachers. | We resource it from alternative teachers—from students graduating from university and graduate school without official training. |
| We don't have time to train them. | We introduce a program that trains them in service. |
| Our department doesn't have the money to build more junior high schools. | We resource additional budget from other departments. |
| Even with that extra budget we won't be able to build enough schools. | We persuade independent schools to participate and expand, so we can use their expansion as part of the capacity that will be needed. |
| We only have higher education focused on academic subjects, rather than vocational ones. | We combine creating a strong vocational college track with partnering up with private companies to train people with the skills we need. |

*Table 2: Cascading can-if in Taiwan*

## Failing forward

Ben Knelman is the founder of Juntos Finanzas, a financial management tool that uses text messaging for cash-based households. It was designed to help first-generation Latinos in the United States develop a sense of confidence in their ability to manage their money—a considerable source of stress. The constraints were readily apparent to Knelman from the outset: little financial literacy to speak of in this community, with most of them possessing no computer, bank account, or credit card; his customers deliberately choosing to be unbanked, rightly cautious of the fees they could unwittingly incur.

Knelman is a graduate of Stanford University. There he took classes at the Hasso Plattner Institute of Design at Stanford University (known as the d.school) where, for one project, he and his class worked with nightshift janitors to get a deeper understanding of how they managed their finances. Responding to what they heard, Knelman and his classmates developed simple, paper-based tools to help the janitors record and track their finances, to gain insight into their own spending habits and, with it, a greater sense of control. The three-week project concluded, the class moved on, but Knelman felt there was a potentially important idea there to come back to. A year later, he returned to talk to some of the janitors, and was startled when one of them told him that his simple paper tool had helped her save over $2,000 during the year. He was struck not only by the amount she had managed to save, but also by the emotional impact he saw on her face: she was fiercely proud of her newfound ability to control her family's financial future. The tool had changed not only her approach to financial management, but also the story she told about herself. So Knelman started Juntos Finanzas.

Having been a d.school student, Knelman is keen to point to the role of design thinking in his process: deep user empathy to identify latent needs, strong collaboration among the team, and the ability to quickly develop prototypes to increase the quality and speed of learning.

Knelman describes it optimistically as "failing our way forward."[9] Each of his thirty failed prototypes for Juntos Finanzas guided him away from what didn't work and toward what did. A key principle for him was staying invested in solving the problem, rather than becoming invested in a particular solution. If your favorite can-if solution turns out to be a blind alley, it's too easy to get emotionally stuck, he believes, unable to kill it. Difficult challenges demand not just humility, but the ability to draw inspiration from initial failure. He was convinced, for instance, that making his tool as easy to use as possible would be the key to creating lasting engagement. But through prototyping he and his team learned that while too much work was a deterrent, too little work was, too: users needed to invest some of their own time and effort in the process in order to feel they were managing their finances. It helped them feel in control.

In 2013, Juntos Finanzas won the G20 award for Financial Innovation, which led to an invitation to work with a major Colombian bank on a new, text-based financial management tool. With 40,000 people already in that program, Knelman and team are optimistically failing forward once again.

## Ambitious crowd-control at London 2012

Failure is not the only reason for rejecting a potential can-if solution. Sometimes it simply cannot live up to the scale of the original ambition in the propelling question.

Heather McGill was the head of Spectator Experience for the Olympic and Paralympic Games at London 2012. The first games ever to have this as a formal role, it was an expression of their explicit ambition to elevate the spectator experience to a new level, and McGill and her team were charged with optimizing every aspect of the experience across every event, inside and outside the Olympic Park. Within this, the logistics alone were a considerable challenge for London, like any host city: they would have to host, in effect, 63 weeks' worth of events in thirteen days. But they had obviously set their ambition higher than being logistically flawless.

Overall, the park design anticipated the flow of spectators well, but McGill's team recognized that there would be peak-traffic moments (several big events finishing simultaneously, for instance) when unusually large crowds would be leaving at the same time, creating pinch points that would make movement slow, even impossible. The conventional way of managing these moments is through dot-matrix signage used to communicate wait times, indicate best directions to take, and reroute chunks of the crowd. But that system was too expensive for the budget at hand.

The recommendation instead was to add more stewards with loudhailers, extra barriers, and one-way directions. The proposal came with credentials: it had worked well in Sydney. But McGill felt this solution, while no doubt effective, would compromise the fun, friendly, people-centric spectator experience they were creating. It might address the problem, but it wouldn't deliver the scale of the ambition they had set for themselves. Previously tour producer for the Spice Girls, she understood the distraction value of entertainment as a response to restrictions, and her can-if thinking fitted the ambition: their eventual solution was to have live music in the stadium at the end of events to encourage some people to linger in their seats, and a secondary ring of entertainment around the stadium itself to draw large groups of the departing crowd

*Gamesmakers at London 2012*

to a different part of the park to stay and enjoy the fun. Any direct control of the crowd who still elected to leave was achieved by the "gamesmakers" (as they called the volunteer stewards) enthusiastically waving and pointing with oversized foam hands.[10] The lack of state-of-the-art signage had spurred them to create a more enjoyable, entertaining experience, but only because they refused to compromise on the scale of the ambition. 86 percent of the ticket holders at the Games subsequently voted it the best live event they had ever been to.

Overall, then, we need to recognize that few of our constraint-driven challenges will be as simple to address as finding a single solution to a single problem.

- We'll need to use the scale of our ambition as a filter (as London 2012): just because a solution can work, that doesn't necessarily mean it will deliver the full answer to our ambitious constraint.
- We'll need to be prepared to iteratively fail forward to arrive at a genuinely powerful solution (like Juntos Finanzas).
- We'll need to anticipate that one solution may well lead to a second-level problem, with a solution that may, in turn, raise a further challenge, as in the case of Taiwan.

Maintaining the mechanics and mindset of a can-if process throughout will keep the flow going.

# Part 2: Just enough method

### The different types of can-if

Struck by the simple power of Kelly's concept of can-if, we re-examined the examples of constraint-driven breakthrough we had studied to look for commonalities across the various kinds of can-if thinking they represented. To create just enough method to make it easier to answer propelling questions, we felt a number of stimulating start points would be valuable to define. We won't go into the following level of detail on all of the six tools and frameworks in this book that are designed to help find the opportunity in a constraint. However, starting to make progress looking for a potential solution is clearly such an important part of any ABC capability, that we have in this chapter and the next spent more time than elsewhere combining the analysis with laying out a tool and process that might allow us to use it productively ourselves.

We started by identifying nine different and usable types of can-if, each of which we have illustrated below with two specific examples. Some of these have already been discussed earlier in the book, but we have summarized them to be consistent with the others that we instance.

The nine types of can-if that seemed to be most common were these:

### We can if we think of it as …

This type of can-if involves thinking in a new way about something that has become very familiar, perhaps even taken for granted, and using this new frame to open up a new possibility or new way forward.

Southcentral Foundation, for example, manages healthcare for native peoples in Alaska. Twenty years ago, their population was one of the least healthy in the United States, and the relationship between the healthcare provider and the disenfranchised community was poor. The key insight that drove the transformation came when the foundation began thinking of their people not as patients but as customer–owners. This fundamentally changed the relationship between the two parties, and created a wave of innovation through introducing a service culture to their organization and an ownership mentality to the patients. Sometimes language precedes behavior change.

*We can dramatically improve the health outcomes of a disenfranchised community if we think of patients as customers and owners.* (See page 127 for more on this case study.)

All video games take time to load, and the waiting frustrates gamers. The designers of EA's soccer game FIFA 13 knew they couldn't do anything about load time itself, but they could transform the wait. Responding to the propelling question "How can we make waiting a valued part of the experience?" they introduced skill-building games during the load. Players could improve their skills while waiting for the game they were about to play, and compete for high scores with their friends in a new way.

*We can turn loading time into one of the most rewarding parts of the game if we think of it as a chance to build skills and make better players.*[11]

## We can if we use other people to …

This type of can-if involves trying to find answers to propelling questions using the skills, expertise, or willingness of other people. It challenges us to think creatively about who else we might ask for help with our constraint and why they would be willing to offer that help.

As Airbnb grew, they realized that most people made their decisions about renting accommodations based on photos. Many in their community lacked the cameras or the skills to photograph interiors at their best, but it clearly wasn't viable to employ staff photographers to travel the world to take pictures of each property. Their solution was to resource their apparent scarcity from within the Airbnb renting community, paying local professionals and hobbyists who could shoot in their spare time—a solution that enabled them to improve conversion rates and reinforce the power of community at the same time. Airbnb now employs 4,000 such photographers worldwide—which, they will proudly tell you, is more than Bloomberg.

*We can offer great photos of each accommodation without the personnel and travel overhead of staff photographers if we use other people's skills as photographers; people from within our community.*[12]

Translating the billions of pages that make up the World Wide Web into languages other than English is a daunting task for anyone to undertake—unless you can find a lot of people who will do it for free. Why would they do it for free? Because they want to learn a foreign language, and translation exercises are part of the homework: they translate web pages in return for free lessons. Duolingo's founder has 1.2 million people worldwide translating the web for free while using his free learning app, and generates revenue to pay for his development costs from the translations students do as part of their homework.

*We can translate the web into other languages if we get a million people to do it for us. And we can get a million to do it for us, if we help them learn a new language while they're doing it.*[13]

### We can if we remove *x* to allow us to *y* ...

This can-if is about the enabling power of subtraction: how, by removing something, we allow ourselves to do something else instead.

Hue is a chain of hair coloring salons in New Zealand whose aim was to offer high-quality coloring at half the cost of other salons. They could do this, they recognized, if they eliminated one of the steps of the conventional service: the stylist drying the customer's hair after coloring. Customers at Hue dry their own hair in a separate communal area, while the stylist turns to the next customer. Far from being a disadvantage, Hue say the customers get to dry their hair the way they like it, and socialize with other customers as they do it.

*We can offer high-quality coloring at half the cost if we eliminate the stage where the stylist blow-dries the customer's hair.*[14]

citizenM is a new hotel chain founded to deliver a hip hotel experience that doesn't break the bank. Dutch co-founder Robin Chadha says that when setting up, they asked themselves, "What are the things we need from a great hotel, and what don't we need?" They focused on doing four things flawlessly: the bed, the shower, reactive technology (TV, music, ambient lighting, blinds all controlled by the one device) and great design. No compromise on any of those four. They then struck a red pen through everything else: no choice of rooms, no double sinks, no robes, no slippers, no tea and coffee in the room, no minibar, no paper receipts—none of the frills. Removing those has allowed them to offer a stylish hotel experience for 75 percent of the price.

*We can offer a uniquely hip hotel experience for a low price if we do just four things flawlessly.*[15]

### We can if we access the knowledge of ...

This type of can-if involves finding and accessing new sources of insight and information to help us transform a constraint.

PHD is a global media planning and buying agency, a division of Omnicom, with a strong industry and client reputation as a thought leader in the business. They recognized, as they pitched for large global clients against the giants of their own category, that they would never be able to compete like for like with the size of the account teams and resources that these larger companies could offer. Their solution was to offer a client not the same or a slightly larger team to work on their business,

*The PHD Source leaderboard*

but everyone in the agency worldwide—over 3,000 people. They did this through the development of a proprietary technology platform called Source, which allows clients to share a brief with everyone within PHD, and motivated responsiveness in the company through gamification, including a leaderboard of the most active contributors. The innovation offered the additional benefit of developing locally relevant solutions to global briefs, thereby circumventing regional "it won't work here" pushback from the local markets. Unilever, GSK, and VW Group are just three of the clients that have given PHD large global contracts in competitive pitches since the introduction of Source.

*We can offer a service superior to even our largest competitors if everyone in our company contributes to a client's brief.*[16]

The UK company giffgaff accesses the knowledge of its own customer base. A mobile virtual network operator (MVNO), they buy bulk access to a wireless network infrastructure and resell phones and minutes directly to the customer. In an effort to keep their costs low, yet provide exemplary customer service (their propelling question), they use their own customers to answer specific questions about specific phones—who, after all, knows the real user experience of a phone better than a fan of that phone? And customers are faster and more accurate than a customer service rep browsing through a stack of manuals. In return for credits on their bills, customers use online message boards to answer such queries. In 2012, giffgaff was named best mobile virtual network operator at the UK Mobile Industry Awards.

*We can offer superior customer service at a very low cost if we access the knowledge of our customers themselves.*

### We can if we introduce a …

This type of can-if centers on introducing a new product or service dimension into the process, one that either transforms an element of the constraint into something positive (as in India's MyDollarStore below) or offers a different source of appeal and engagement, one with the ability to change the criteria for choice in our favor (like the first example here).

We have discussed the case of Surf, Unilever's value detergent, in Chapter Two. To keep its costs, and thus its retail price, low, it can't use the same expensive cleaning enzymes as the premium brands. In a category driven historically by cleaning power, Surf needed to introduce a new criterion: How could they drive consumer preference in cleaning when they weren't able to compete on cleaning power? Their insight, we saw in Chapter Three, was that the laundry experience was neverending and joyless, and so the brand focused instead on introducing a much higher level of sensory delight in every interaction with Surf, and in particular the use of fragrances to give an emotional reward and pleasure to the user beyond cleaning power alone.

By introducing a new emphasis on fragrance as an indicator of cleanliness, they changed the criterion from "see how clean" to "smell how clean," a criterion on which they could—and did—win. Surf grew 36 percent globally between 2009 and 2012, and is now the leader in the value category. They took the lack of the best cleaning power as an offer to introduce an entirely new criterion of choice.

*We can offer a more appealing cleaning promise if we introduce fragrance and sensory delight as emotional rewards for cleaning, over and above functional effectiveness.*[17]

When MyDollarStore launched in India, it included a range of American food products that neither the customer nor the staff initially understood how to eat or cook—such as pasta, for example. But, with imported U.S food as an intrinsic part of the franchised idea, the management of the three launch stores in Mumbai had to make it work. How do you persuade customers who don't understand what a food is to buy it, even if it only costs 100 rupees? And how do you help a colleague who doesn't understand what that food is to explain and recommend it?

To address the constraint, the team introduced two new practices that ended up transforming the customer experience. First, they allowed staff to break open any pack of any food in store at the customer's request so that they could see, touch, and taste the unusual new food. More than simply overcoming the lack of knowledge, this introduction, not seen in Indian food retailing before, created theater around curiosity and learning about the new foods, generating energy in store, and conversation outside it. To ensure that they could properly satisfy this curiosity, the leadership introduced training on these new foods for everyone in the store during their first week on the job. They could all cook and try the products for themselves—trying all six different pastas, for example, or tasting chocolate-covered hazelnuts for the first time. These two introductions helped transform what might have been insurmountable constraints into novel experiences, and helped the new concept stand out at launch and quickly become established. The leadership team successfully scaled the three stores to 47 over four years, before being made a buyout offer they couldn't refuse.

*We can sell Indian buyers foods they don't know if we give them a chance to try and find out about everything before they spend their money on it.*[18]

### We can if we substitute *x* for *y* …

This can-if is about substituting one apparently essential part of the product, process or experience with something entirely different.

Two designers at Lund University in Sweden, Anna Haupt and Terese Alstin, wanted to know why adults who knew the risks of cycling without a helmet continued to do so. They were surprised to hear that much of the answer lay in the way the helmets created unflattering hat hair—who knew the Swedes could be so vain? When asked what the helmet of the future would need to be like in order to encourage them to use one, the answer people gave them was invisible. Haupt and Alstin's solution, now sold as the Hövding, is a device that uses airbag technology worn around the neck, leaving the head and hair entirely free of unseemly helmets. Over thousands of crash tests monitoring cyclist movement, they refined a mechanism to instantly deploy the airbag in the event of an accident. The Hövding covers a much larger area of the head than a normal helmet, and tests by an insurance company suggests it may be three times as effective as a conventional helmet in preventing injury—while being invisible.

*We can offer better protection with a helmet that doesn't mess up your hair if we substitute an airbag for a helmet.*[19]

The food-truck movement in the United States was accelerated by the financial pressures of the recession, and enabled by the new possibilities of social media—announcing where the cart would be and what today's specials were via Facebook and Twitter, for example. Restaurateurs who'd had or wanted their own restaurant, but could no longer afford all the capital costs of opening one, switched to the significantly more affordable truck. The food-truck business was worth $650 million in 2013, and is estimated to quadruple over the next three years. Even established restaurants have joined the movement, using trucks to promote their bricks-and-mortar establishments.

*We can afford to start our restaurant business if we substitute the high costs of a permanent fixed location with the possibilities of a smaller, more mobile one.*[20]

### We can if we fund it by …

Often the issue is not finding a solution, but funding the solution. This type of can-if addresses that issue by assuming that there is always potential funding around us; it is just not yet in our possession.

Norm Brodsky, a serial entrepreneur and author of the "Street Smarts" column in Inc. magazine, set up Perfect Courier, a messenger and trucking company based in Brooklyn, in 1979. When he fell out with his investors, it became clear that it was him or them: if he couldn't buy them out, then they would buy him out and he'd lose the business. In an act of entrepreneurial chutzpah, Brodsky approached his largest customer and proposed that they give him a year's payments up front—and after some negotiation, they agreed. With the cash injection, Brodsky bought out his investors, and in 2007 sold Perfect Courier, along with another of his companies, for $110 million.

*A food truck in Portland, Maine*

*We can afford to buy out our investors without any cash reserves if our largest customer pays us up front.*[21]

BrewDog is a brewery started in the teeth of the recession and constrained by the fact that no bank would lend them money to fuel their growth (how do we grow when we can't get a bank loan?). They raised £7,000,000 from beer drinkers in four years with a crowd-funding program they call Equity For Punks, funding growth and creating brand ambassadors in the process. They are now the UK's fastest growing food and drinks brand, averaging 167 percent growth per year from 2008 to 2013.

*We can get investment without a bank loan if we fund our growth from our fans.*[22]

## We can if we mix together …

This can-if involves mixing together things that haven't been put together before to solve the constraint (such as an apparently irreconcilable trade-off).

IBM's Watson is a cognitive system that is effectively a form of artificial intelligence. As part of IBM's exploration of how Watson can help develop new ideas as well as process existing data and knowledge, they set themselves the challenge of how it could help people come up with creative new recipes with ingredients they wanted to use. Its propelling question was, in essence, "How can we develop a way of generating creative recipe solutions with a cognitive system that can't think and isn't creative?" Their solution was to combine different kinds of algorithms into an app called Chef Watson. One algorithm would produce solutions with some of the qualities associated with creativity, like surprise and novelty. But this on its own would not necessarily lead to combinations that people would like: not all novelty is good when it comes to food, after all. But if they combined it with an algorithm that filters for flavor combinations that people say go well together, then they could come up with unexpected solutions that, while a little surprising, would still taste delicious—like Thai Swiss asparagus quiche, for example.

*We can develop a way of generating creative recipe solutions with a cognitive system that can't think and isn't creative … if we combine an algorithm for generating new and surprising combinations with one that filters through combinations humans like to eat.*[23]

Audi's propelling question for their 2012 S8 launch was how to marry the consumer's desire for a faster engine with the U.S regulators' requirement to become more fuel efficient. Reconciling such opposites might naturally precipitate a knee-jerk requirement to innovate, yet the Audi team's solution was to mix together, for the first time, three technologies they already had: twin-scroll turbocharging, lightweight engine construction, and direct fuel injection. The new S8 was a full second faster from 0–60, while delivering 37 percent greater fuel efficiency in highway driving.

*We can produce a faster engine that is also fuel efficient if we put together three existing technologies that we haven't combined before.*[24]

### We can if we resource it by …

This can-if is about being creative in how we identify and access resources that we need to help us deliver on our bold ambition—resources that we don't currently have access to, such as key channels of distribution, important products or services, or internal resources such as R&D. (This capability to access new resources in new ways is so important an ability to transform constraints that the next chapter is dedicated entirely to how to do this.)

Rent The Runway was started by two Harvard Business School graduates who wanted to provide greater access to designer fashions for young women who couldn't yet afford the high price tags of couture. Their solution was to create an entirely new channel that would allow these young women to rent rather than buy an expensive dress. The start-up's founders knew they wouldn't be able to buy and hold a high level of inventory themselves (it would require too much capital and depreciate too fast), but they realized they didn't have to resource it all themselves if they could persuade a range of top fashion designers to supply the dresses for them. We'll explain how they finally convinced the designers to participate in the next chapter, but the new brand launched with designers providing all the products in exchange for a share of the revenue, and their new model of renting couture has become a huge success.

*We can create access to the world of couture for young women unable to afford the prices if we build a rental model with inventory (resource) provided by the fashion designers themselves.*

This rental model is a close cousin of the sharing economy model. France's BlaBlaCar, a ride-sharing service, America's Uber, and the global phenomenon that is Airbnb are all examples of service companies using the sharing model with this kind of can-if at the heart of their business model: *We can create large, sustainable, and profitable businesses in transport and accommodation without significant fixed overheads if we resource through owners who find themselves with spare capacity.*

Clearly this does not pretend to be a definitive list of all possible types of can-if, but nine provides a good enough variety to help us get started in the process we will describe below. There is a little overlap between some of them—giffgaff, for example, is both an example of "use other people to" and a story about "accessing the knowledge of"—but for the sake of this exercise we have teased them apart to make the starting points of the exercise as specific as possible.

### The Can-If Map: Using the clusters to approach our own constraints

This diverse range of clusters will be useful to stimulate the exploration of solutions to propelling questions in a number of new domains, beyond the ones we are used to exploring. Their utility is not only in the description, but also the prescription: forcing us to look through a new lens, creating a more open mindset, suggesting new paths— and, perhaps, helping arrive at the solution itself.

The next step in turning this approach into a usable tool was to create a map from the nine different types of can-if (see Figure 4). Each type is arrayed around a propelling question in the middle. The question is written so that the words *can* and *if* are at either side of the question itself—as they were at the end of each of the examples across the nine types.

A team can work with the can-if map to start the ideation process by applying the structure of a particular can-if solution to their own question. For example, "Think of *x* as *y* ..." asks a team to consider ways to reframe a part of their offer or process in a new way, just as SCF reframed their patient relationship. If this can-if is productive and creates the flow Kelly described, there are three lines, suggesting the need for three ideas here before advancing around the map. If this particular can-if does not seem fertile at this stage, we can move on to one of the other eight.

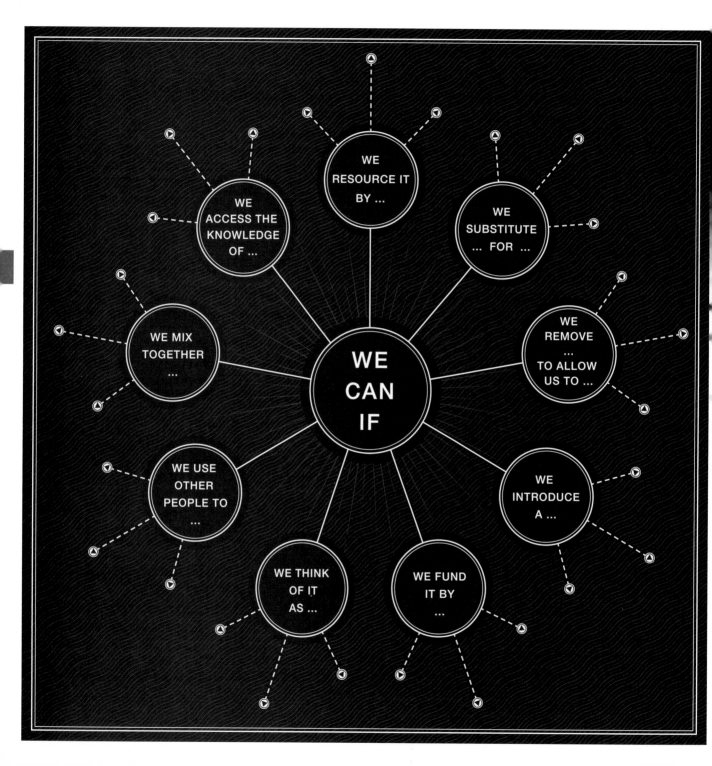

*Figure 4: The Can-If Map*

## Learning how to use the Can-If Map

Having identified a working group of types of can-if to act as launch pads, and a map that makes them visually accessible to a team and integrates the question, the final part of making this tool usable is to approach it with the right amount of structure. Using this map with clients to transform their constraints, we have learned how to make the process most productive, especially when working with large groups. It benefits from discipline in how it is approached:

**Priming:** Ask attendees to think in advance about an example—personal or professional—of when they had been able to take a constraint and find advantage in it. Ask them to share these with the person next to them as a preliminary to doing any kind of work. This is what is called priming in motivational science. It demonstrates to everyone that they have succeeded in overcoming constraints to meet an ambition before; they have that ability. They are people who can and do find solutions to questions that are hard to answer—they just haven't done it on this challenge yet.

**Legitimacy:** It is important to clearly set up the examples of where and how this has been done before, for each of the can-if launch pads on the map. This, too, is a piece of priming. It says there are other people who have found answers to difficult, constraint-centered questions like these. There is no reason why this team cannot do the same.

**A strong propelling question:** Prepared in advance with the leadership team. One genuinely critical to the business, wrapped in a narrative of why success is important, along with a picture of the implications of failing. The stakes need to be significant.

**A leader at each table:** At this stage in the learning curve, having someone who can keep the conversation a can-if one, doing some light facilitation to help maintain flow, and pull everyone into the process, is helpful. Divide the larger group into teams of 4 to 6 people, have a large can-if map handy, and use a stack of Post-It notes to capture ideas and stick them around the launch pads.

Allowing the group to go first to the exploration territories they find **most natural,** and then later forcing them to go to the ones they find **least natural.**

**Stepping back:** Difficult constraints are not going to yield easily. Persistence works up to a point—you just keep going at the problem—but sometimes you need to step away and come back with a fresh perspective. Creative tenacity—going back to the same problem in a new way—is enabled by the variety of launch pads on the can-if map. Research shows that obstacles, instead of impeding creativity, do in fact help it in this regard (see the following sidebar).

Force the group to explore **at least three** options around each launch pad. One or two early answers don't, in themselves, give an indication of the fertility of an area; the group needs to keep coming at it from fresh angles, then review this can-if area as a totality to see its potential.

**Review** at key stages, sharing experiences with the tool as well as a chance to cross-pollinate between teams. What are the types of emerging solutions? Are they strategic or tactical and, if the latter, can they ladder up to more strategic solutions? What have we learned about the constraints we are facing, and how best to overcome them?

## Methods and stimulus

We don't need to use the formality of a can-if map to access the power of this as a conversational tool. Simply using the language and establishing that this will be a can-if conversation can be enough to create flow and momentum. But the stories have value, too. It is important as well as stimulating to hear how others have been able to address constraints in creative ways; it helps keep us optimistic and inquisitive as we explore and prototype.

Reviewing the clusters here, you'll notice a theme emerging about how to create or access resources in novel ways (Airbnb, giffgaff), or create new sources of funding or knowledge (Perfect Courier, PHD). Refusing to accept the apparent resource constraints of our situation is what we will turn our attention to now—knowing how to see and access resources will be the focus of the next chapter, because it is a capability so central to transforming constraints.

We need to learn how to create abundance, and what it really means to be resourceful.

---

### Stepping Back and Global Processing

Janina Marguc and her colleagues at the University of Amsterdam studied the cognitive processes involved when creativity meets constraints. Their experiments showed that conceptual scope (i.e., the broadening of perspective) is stimulated when test subjects are confronted with obstacles. A common practice of successful problem-solving involves taking a mental step back when the way to a goal is blocked, to look at the bigger picture again and to reassess. This helps us gain perspective, spot alternate approaches, and integrate seemingly unrelated pieces of information into solutions. Psychologists call this a shift from local to global processing, and it is one of the ways constraints can catalyze creativity when we embrace, rather than avoid them.[25]

---

## CAN-IF: CHAPTER SUMMARY

- If we are to be successful in answering propelling questions, we will need to have both the right tools and the right attitude to find breakthrough, especially in complex problems that reveal systems of constraints.

- The key challenge is not simply "How do we answer this question?" It is "How do we create the conversational climate that gives us the best possible chance to answer this question?"

- Using the deceptively simple structure of starting each sentence with "We can if …" keeps the focus on *how* it might be possible not *whether* it might be possible, forcing people to find solutions rather than more problems, and keeping the oxygen of optimism alive in the process. Can-if is essential to create flow and is a critical part of constraint-driven innovation.

- We analyzed all the constraint-driven breakthroughs in our research, ranging from how FIFA 13 embraced the constraint of game-loading times to how a cellphone operator provided high-quality customer service at very low cost, and arrived at nine clusters of different types of can-if solutions.

- From these different types we have created a can-if map as stimulus for groups that have developed a propelling question and may not know how to get started.

- The chapter closes with a suggested process on how to use the map most effectively.

# 5 CREATING ABUNDANCE

How to see and access resources we don't have

1. In what ways can we gain access to other people's resources to help us overcome our own scarcities and meet our ambitions?

2. What prevents us from seeing and accessing these resources today?

3. How can we find new value in what we have, so we have more to trade and more power to create shared agendas?

# When you don't have resources, you become resourceful.

—K.R. Sridhar, Bloom Energy[1]

**If you've seen any improv theatre,** or the TV show *Whose Line Is It Anyway?* you've seen two actors walk out on stage to improvise a scene. They start with nothing, get a couple of suggestions from the audience about who they are and what they are doing, and make up a scene on the spot: "You're at a job interview at NASA, but you are a pianist. Go!" When done well, it can be astonishing to watch a richly entertaining story emerge from two people creating in the moment, with apparently so little to go on.[2]

One element of the improviser's method is accepting offers. In the scene above, job interview, NASA, and pianist are all offers the improviser is forced to accept. Rather than see these as a limiting burden, the improviser sees them as a gift because they get the story going. Every line of dialog or gesture thereafter is an offer too, and is incorporated into the scene, even the mistakes. Neither actor has everything they need to make the scene a success, but through trading offers back and forth, a co-created story emerges, one that has never been told before and never will be again, and it is usually more interesting than anything either player could have created alone.

Robert Poynton is an expert in applying the techniques of improv to the world of business and leadership. A prerequisite for success in the world of improv, he observes, is finding value in what you have. The uninitiated find this hard and might adopt the victim mindset—"What am I supposed to do with that!?" But the skilled performer finds the value in the offer, accepts it, and builds on it.

We have seem something akin to this in the way that transformers of constraints accept a constraint as an offer—an offer to think differently about the way they define what natural resources are, in the case of Taiwan; an offer to think differently about the relationship between two apparent trade-offs, in the case of those unreasonable challengers; an offer to come up with a new emotion and sensation to put into laundry, in the case of Surf. They recognized the opportunities inherent in constraints. It's this positive mindset coupled with a simple, repeatable method that gives improvisers and transformers the confidence to know that they can make something out of very little every time. They see offers everywhere.

So when faced with apparent scarcity and constraints, we need to find and build new value in what we have, no matter how meager it may initially appear to us. And we need to understand how to trade this value with other parties in order to get what we want, in the way improvisers trade offers to get a story. What can we offer them in exchange for what we need and they have in abundance? What might we do together that could have more impact than what we can do alone? How might we combine limited resources with others to create collective abundance?

In this chapter we are going to combine an analysis of how those without resource become resourceful with a structured tool that will give us the discipline to do the same.

## What does it mean to be resourceful?

If finding and building tradable value around what we have is one part of being resourceful, the other is the ability to see and access from others the abundance that they have and we need. Such resourcefulness may be championed in Silicon Valley's lean start-ups and celebrated among the Jugaadus of India, but in relatively well-resourced companies we seem to have let this capability atrophy, despite the well-intentioned rhetoric about "intrapreneurs." As the European Marketing Director of a Fortune 100 company told us:

> *If I cut the marketing budget by 50 percent, about half of my department would have no idea what to do. They would have no capability to look for other ways to move their business forward without those resources. They wouldn't know where to start.*

The way we tend to think about resources, in other words, is a form of path dependence. We see the resource available to us as only what is given to us, or is directly within our control. When that is taken away from us, we see our resource as depleted; when it is increased, we think we have more.

But those who are genuinely resourceful see available resources in a very different way. They see resources as not simply what they control, but what they can access: what the rest of the company has, what those in their network have, what their neighborhood (literally or metaphorically) has, and indeed what the big resource owners they have yet to meet may have that they can use. A key part of being resourceful is seeing those sources of abundance for what they are, recognizing that they are available, and finding innovative ways to enable them to flow in the desired direction. Resourceful people see, in other words, that if they lack something (money, time, people, ideas), and that scarcity is one of their apparent constraints, it is an opportunity to access abundance from elsewhere. And for people who want to make constraints beautiful, this will quickly become an essential capability.

With this in mind, let's be very specific about what we mean by the word resourceful here. It has tended to become diluted in use, to mean, "can get things done, whatever the circumstances," but let's return it to a more precise use. Let's define it as "able to find and deliver resources, from anywhere, that we need and can use."

In time, this will become an entirely natural way of thinking, seeing, and behaving. Initially, though, we need a tool to help us be more methodical in the way we identify more resources—both internally and externally—and get access to them. We have called this process *creating abundance* because it is in itself an act of creativity: creatively looking for sources of resources, creatively reframing what we have to maximize our own sources of value to others, and creatively trading that value to allow us to access the abundance we need.

We'll explore these interrelated parts to creating abundance:

- Seeing potential sources of resource around us.
- Reframing how we think about our own resources to create new value we can exchange.

- Understanding how to share and trade our resources to get what we need.
- Exploring how and why we might join forces to multiply our resources.

## Seeing potential sources of resource around us

There are four different kinds of relationships we need to explore for additional resources. We know some of these already, but may not have considered them as sources of resources; we will need to see their potential through new eyes. Some we may never have considered as sources of value at all before.

### Invested Stakeholders

These are the groups with which we have the strongest relationships today, because they have a stake in our fortunes and are the closest to us: our co-workers, members of the board, non-executive directors and investors, along with our most fervent and committed loyalists and user groups.

We have already seen an example of this being used to great effect: PHD developing the platform they call Source to allow a client brief to access the abundant, but previously inaccessible, talent of everybody in the company (see page 90). In Chapter Three we saw online furniture company Made.com squaring up to their propelling question: "How can we exhibit at the world's most prestigious furniture exhibition in Milan without paying for an exhibition space?" They were able to answer this by borrowing and exhibiting in the Milanese apartments of four of their enthusiastic customer base, one on each of the four days of the exhibition. They received 1,000 visitors, enthusiastic publicity, and enhanced their reputation as a brand for having a fresh and more creative perspective. In each instance, these potential resources were already within reach; they simply needed to be seen for their potential, and harnessed in the right way. Similarly, Timbuk2, the messenger bag brand, is a keen observer of the way their users customize their bags, to gain insights that drive their own product development—an example of accessing innovation resources from one's best customers.

If we are short of resources, then interrogating our relationships with all our invested stakeholders is the first place to start the search for abundance.

### External Partners

This source is made up of partners with whom we already have a relationship, but lack the same level of emotional involvement and shared agenda as our invested stakeholders: strategic partners, the broader group of users and customers, even friends.

For example, we've seen Norm Brodsky source funding from his largest customer (page 94); and Frikkie Lubbe tap SAB's network of barley farmers to source insight into water-stressed irrigation (page 61).

Our ability to tap into the extended networks of friends and colleagues has been considerably amplified by the possibilities of social networks. As Porter Gale points out in her book of the same title, "your network is your net worth."[3] For this group, resourcefulness often begins with generosity: the truly resourceful understand how to invest in their networks to build capital by giving their time, connections, and knowledge and, when faced with scarcity, are then able to draw down that capital.[4] To unlock this potential we will sometimes need to step away from our existing relationships for a moment and see them through fresh eyes. What more do they have to offer? What more do we have to offer them?

### Resource Owners

This is a group of people or companies with whom we currently have little, if any, relationship, but who have an abundance of a particular kind of resource that we need. They might have a special area of expertise, or an established route to market, for example. The NGO ColaLife draws on the might of The Coca-Cola Company's distribution system in Africa to deliver dehydration salts to children suffering from diarrhea. ColaLife exchanged the goodwill of their mission for the distribution of the Coca-Cola Company. They designed a pack that fitted neatly in the unused space between the necks of the bottles in the Coke crates, and out it went.

When Ingvar Kamprad, the founder of IKEA, stood in a market in China looking at row upon row of plucked chickens, he wasn't thinking about dinner, but wondering what the pluckers did with all the feathers. He persuaded the farmers to stop burning the feathers and sell them to him very cheaply for stuffing inexpensive comforters. The farmers made money on their abundant waste and Kamprad addressed the cost constraint of goose down. Kamprad is a master at seeing offers and resources he can use where others see only waste.

The possibilities with this group are almost endless. Every business, organization, and entity we come across could potentially be a source of abundance for us, and genuinely seeing sources of potential abundance lies in having the kind of orientation to the world that Kamprad has—open to opportunity, seeking it out, ever ready for its sometimes chance appearance.

## Our Competition

This is a group with whom we do have a relationship, but typically see ourselves as precluded from considering as a source of potential value or trade.

This is changing, though. As we saw, the actions of the unreasonable regulator are forcing Ford and Toyota to collaborate on technologies to power hybrid trucks, pooling resources to create more possibilities (page 72); Nike identifies "pre-competitive spaces" in which it shares sustainability knowledge and expertise with competitors to more quickly shift an industry in the direction everyone needs to go (its Making app, for instance, freely shares Nike data on the environmental footprint of thousands of different materials);[5] Airbus' Smarter Skies initiative imagines something similar in the airline industry, with all the players sharing resources and ideas to meet the industry goal of a 50 percent cut in carbon emissions by 2050.[6]

If this kind of resource pooling represents a win/win for both sides, the case of Dixons.co.uk in the UK is an example of what Dave Trott has called "predatory thinking."[7] As an online electronics retailer, it offered reasonable prices but little in the way of expertise. Recognizing that many shoppers wanted more education and advice on products than they could offer in their margin-constrained model, their marketing encouraged people to shop at a brick-and-mortar rival to access the full benefits of that personal advice, and then come and make the purchase with them. With a tagline "Dixons.co.uk: the last place you want to go," they were, in effect, resourcing all the expertise and advice their customer needed from their competitors—and drove a 35 percent increase in site traffic by doing so. The ability to quickly compare product and pricing via a mobile device while enjoying all the benefits of a competitor's investment is a predatory use of a competitor's resources.

Dixons aside, even the competition, with whom we may historically have had a distant, combative relationship, needs to be explored when resources are seriously mismatched with ambition. Is there a way to think about some kind of coalition?

The first place to start, then, in creating abundance is to generate a list of potential sources of the resource we need from each of these four groups. And the scale of our ambitions will mean that we need to push past the obvious here, and be vigilant against lists that reflect a historical perspective now locked-in by path dependence. This is a search for new possibilities.

## Reframing how we think about our own resources to create new value

In order to access the abundance in those sources, once identified, we need to offer them something that they value—we, who might appear to have little, need to help them see that we nevertheless have what they want. And finding this value in what we have is rarely as simple as making routine lists of our assets: we need to be as creative in how we think about these as we are about our relationships, pushing past the obvious.

Virgin America, the domestic airline based in San Francisco, was launched in 2007 with the goal to "put the glamour back into air travel." Their fleet of Airbus A320s feel like nightclubs in the sky, with hip young crews in designer uniforms, leather seats, extensive seat-back entertainment, snacks on demand, purple mood lighting, cool on-board music, Wi-Fi, and power outlets at every seat. Yet with all the money invested in what they called "the guest experience," there was limited budget left for launch, particularly in share of voice, relative to the market leader's annual marketing spend of

# We, who might appear to have little, need to help them see that we have what they want.

$200 million.[8] They had some obvious assets that would help, of course: the charismatic founder of Virgin Group, Sir Richard Branson, and Virgin's brand name would ensure some media coverage at launch. But their relative scarcity of budget, coupled with their business ambitions, demanded that they find new kinds of resources for the media coverage they couldn't afford to buy, and a level of social conversation that would establish the glamorous identity of the brand and give travelers a clear sense of all the media and technology on offer. And, specifically, they wanted the world to see images of the interiors of their mood-lit cabins, which they knew were a trigger to trial.

Looking at what kinds of value they had to offer, the Virgin America marketing team, led for the first four years by Porter Gale, recognized that their location was an asset, next door as it was to the newly minted Technorati in Silicon Valley. Who better to share news and pictures of the cabin than those who are busy building all the new social media platforms? If they could impress them with the on-board technology and give them something to tweet home about, they'd be able to generate enough buzz to sustain the brand. This proximity was a hidden asset of Virgin America—an accident of geography, but one they were smart enough to see the offer in and take advantage of. Another hidden asset was the plane itself, which they saw as a venue in the sky, complete with the most captive of captive audiences.

Combining these ideas with their notion of glamour, they partnered with Victoria's Secret to do "the first ever in-flight pajama party and fashion show" while flying the Victoria's Secret models to LA for their annual fashion show. Who could resist snapping and sharing those kinds of images? Next up was a relationship with HBO, who provided exclusive content for Red, Virgin's in-flight entertainment system, and with whom Virgin launched Entourage Class from New York's JFK airport to Las Vegas. The inaugural flight had the first-ever advance screening of a TV show in the air (the first episode of *Entourage*, Season 5) and was launched with typical Hollywood fanfare: a champagne party with the cast, and a water-cannon salute. But it was the sharing of the moment that drove what Virgin needed: more media images of the cabin.

Next to share was method, the eco-friendly, design-conscious cleaning products company. Virgin enhanced their guest experience (and bear in mind, this is economy class in a U.S. domestic carrier) by having method's beautifully packaged hand soap in their bathrooms, and method gained an invaluable sampling and communication experience among Virgin's young and influential audience. It's unlikely that either party would have shown up on each other's first list of potential strategic partners, but Virgin wasn't thinking like an airline; it was thinking like a San Francisco start-up. This in turn led them to trade with people at the Googleplex, just twenty-one miles from the Virgin America base. Google's own start-up days may be behind it, but their new Chromebook needed to find an audience with the kind of influentials working at start-ups, and who were now frequent flyers of Virgin America. Virgin guests could pick up a Chromebook, try it out, share how they felt about it via the on-board Wi-Fi, and drop it off at the other end.

Although creating this kind of relationship is obviously not a new idea—strategic partnerships are common, and business development teams routinely pursue these kinds of opportunities—it was the ingenuity in the way Virgin America framed their value, and how and with whom they sought to partner, that illustrates the kind of resourcefulness that's so valuable when faced with constraints of resources. This has more in common with the principles of open innovation (building a business model that uses external as much as internal ideas, focusing on creating the freshest ideas in the industry rather than being the sole source of ideas, using each other's intellectual property to mutual benefit) than a traditional view of strategic partnerships.

In terms of our emerging model, what we see in the Virgin America case are examples of three of our four sources of additional resources being leveraged: their invested stakeholder, Branson, to help with the launch by sharing champagne with the cast of *Entourage;* their external partners, Silicon Valley mavens, being encouraged to share and promote the experience; and a bevy of resource owners like Victoria's Secret and Google, adding their resources to Virgin America's, to drive media coverage and social buzz around their communication priorities.

We also see how redefining the way they saw their own assets was an important enabler in this process—planes as catwalks in the sky, or distribution venues for soap, or a way to sample new technology. Not only did this prompt them to go beyond the usual list of trading partners (credit cards, hotel chains) but it helped them develop that all-important relationship with Silicon Valley and its power to influence others.

So what we've learned from the Virgin America case is:

- How it's possible to create abundance where there seems to be scarcity, if we work to identify all the possible sources of resources, not just the obvious ones.
- How constraints prompt us to seek novel relationships which we would not have sought, had we plenty of resources in the first place—relationships which may be even more beneficial than we originally anticipated.
- How finding new ways to articulate the power of what we have gives us many potential ways to approach new kinds of partners with new kinds of value.

## A framework for creating abundance

Before proceeding further, we should begin mapping what we've learned about creating abundance onto a framework (See Figure 5). We can see on this map four concentric boxes that show our four potential sources of resource: invested stakeholders, external partners, resource owners, and the competition. We could begin writing our fresh, new lists of each of these onto the map, but first we need to add a little more to our understanding of how best to approach them.

Two axes cut across the four different kinds of sources. At the top of the map are those who already share our agenda (in terms of our purpose or some part of our strategic ambition) and whom we can therefore influence; at the bottom are those who don't yet share our agenda. We'll turn out attention in a moment to how we can get those who are currently at the bottom to move to the top.

On the right-hand side of the map are those who are aware that we have an abundance of something they need, and therefore are naturally going to be open to trade their resources with us. And on the left of the map are those who currently see nothing in what we have as of potential value to them.

Once we've identified all our potential sources, the map will help determine which are the easiest to access, and what the strategic challenge for us will be in accessing them.

## Our potential sources of abundance

In **Quadrant A** we'll find those that represent the Immediate Opportunity. These are potentially willing partners who both share an agenda with us and have something it would be mutually beneficial to trade. BrewDog's growth was initially stymied when it was unable to borrow from banks in the midst of the recession, but traded equity for cash from its best customers (an invested stakeholder) under its Equity for Punks crowdfunding program. Both parties wanted craft beer to succeed, and for BrewDog to be a going concern; one side represented financial abundance, the other a chance to own a bit of an exciting new company. Virgin America saw the opportunity to partner with the glamour of Victoria's Secret, but both enjoyed the exposure each other helped them achieve. The partnership was easy to arrive at.

**Quadrant B** reveals the Unmotivated Traders who would recognize that we have something of value that they would benefit from in exchange, but do not yet see us both as sharing the same agenda. Because they will have a number of potential partners also offering the kind of value that we represent, it may be necessary to persuade them that we also share an agenda in order for the value exchange to take place. So, for example, in 2008, ColaLife was just a concept in need of a single, specific partner in The Coca-Cola Company (TCCC), and their distribution resource in Africa. TCCC would recognize that the kind of goodwill that the nascent ColaLife represented—delivering life-saving medicines to communities in remote parts of Africa—would be

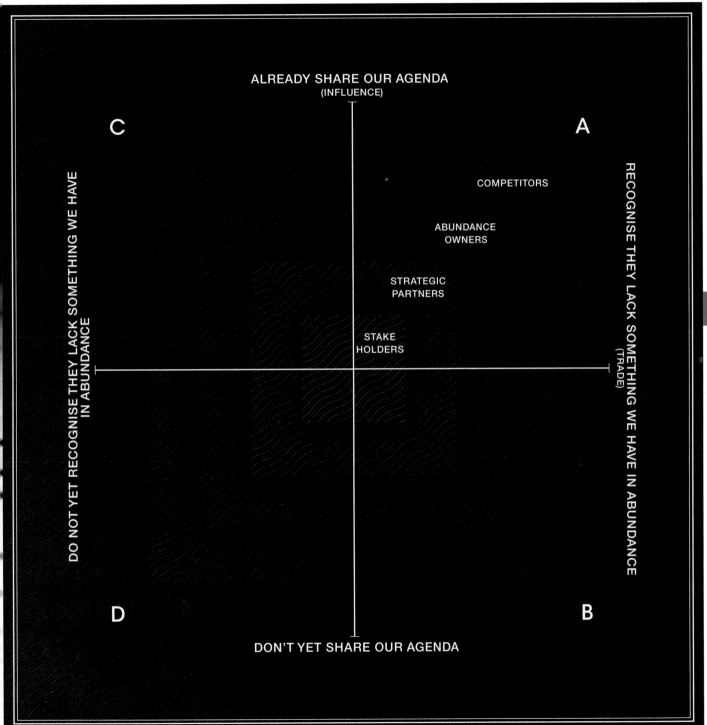

of value to them in terms of enhancing their corporate reputation, particularly in the light of the obesity debate. But with so many other competing initiatives and priorities, ColaLife initially couldn't get the resource owner to notice them. They needed to get TCCC to see that they both shared an important enough agenda for the latter to open up their distribution resources to them.

**Quadrant C** is where a Coalition of The Willing resides. The parties may share an agenda but don't need to trade anything concrete in order to have a mutually beneficial relationship. By their collective contributions, they can create abundance for many, including themselves. Nike and Dove have both discovered this opportunity, as we shall see below.

**Quadrant D** are the Distant and Oblivious. Here our sources of resource neither see any apparently shared agenda or anything of mutual value to trade. This doesn't matter if we don't need their permission to use their resources (if we are stealing with pride from their publicly available insights and ideas, for example—the technique that method refer to as appropriation). But if we do need their permission, this will clearly be the group whose potential resources it will take the most creativity and tenacity to unlock here. This doesn't mean it is impossible, if that resource is essential to us—we'll look at how Rent The Runway found a way to do this below.

Seeing and understanding who the potential sources of resource are, then, is the first step. The next is to develop a very clear sense of what our assets are, and how to see the value they might represent to these potential sources. We will need to list all the assets we have, seeing every single one as having potential for trading and sharing, but we may well need to reframe how we think of some of them to redefine their value, much as Virgin America might have listed "planes" and then reframed them as "catwalks in the sky," for instance. Table 3 on page 119 provides a way to organize this process: list as many assets as you can think of in the column titled Assets and then use the columns to the right of this to reframe those assets in new ways. On the right is a brief story of how Charles Schwab Investment Management explored their assets and how they reframed them to create new kinds of value.

## How Charles Schwab Investment Management Created Abundance

Charles Schwab Investment Management (CSIM) group is the fund manager for Schwab Funds, Laudus Funds, and Schwab ETFs. They manage over $250 billion in assets out of their San Francisco base, are growing fast, and hunger for more. We asked them to think laterally about CSIM's hidden assets to identify new sources of abundance to use or trade. We looked around the room. What could we see?

Colleagues, of course, and specifically, well-educated ones with PhDs—an asset for publicity as well as for running an investment firm, perhaps? How might we use that asset to give CSIM more geek chic in this town, where the talent wars are fierce—did we have more PhDs than Twitter up the street? And, then, where did those PhDs come from? Might their alma maters be a source of strategic partnerships and distribution? What might we be able to trade there? What

about all the data generated by the millions of daily transactions, week in week out? We're sitting on large wells of unrefined data—if we were Google, we'd anonymize that data and crunch it for patterns and insight.

What about the hundred or so vendors the firm does business with, and their collective pool of tens of thousands of employees who might have a little more interest in hearing more from one of their biggest clients? And this huge building, with a tower visible from the freeway—is that not advertising space? And the many eyeballs inside and outside the firm that see CSIM paperwork: Could this space be traded?

Within an hour, we had a list of all kinds of abundance that had been hidden in plain sight.

## Creating shared agendas: how best to share and trade resources in order to get access to those we lack

In conventional strategic partnerships it is obvious from the outset what each party gains, which is why the default list of prospects is so easy to generate—and potentially so limiting. And we've seen how an intelligent and creative reframing of value in our assets can create new offers to make to new kinds of partners. But there will be cases where the value is not apparent from the outset, and work needs to be done to convince a new partner to trade with us.

We saw above that ColaLife initially was just a concept in need of a single, specific distribution partner in The Coca-Cola Company. They couldn't get Coke to notice them, so they needed to find a very compelling way for TCCC to recognize that they both shared such a high priority agenda that the multinational company would open up its distribution resource to them. ColaLife mobilized a 10,000-person social media campaign, that led to an invitation from the BBC to a debate on the radio, which ultimately brought TCCC to the table and convinced them of the shared agenda between the two parties. They soon agreed to trade distribution for goodwill. Sometimes

*ColaLife: Medicine distributed in crates of Coca-Cola*

gentle pressure might be necessary to bring the parties to the table, to make the unmotivated traders ready to trade, to move them from B to A.

In early 2009, the twenty fashion designers initially approached by the founders of Rent the Runway were cautious about participation. They feared cannibalizing their own sales: Why would someone buy the dress from a designer if they can rent it for a tenth of the price at Rent The Runway? And though the start-up's founders had venture funding, they knew they would have nothing without the best inventory from designers. Rent The Runway sat squarely in Quadrant D. It wasn't clear what Rent The Runway had that the fashion designers needed, and it wasn't clear what the shared agenda was. So Rent The Runway took a step back and thought carefully about how to proceed.

With fast fashion retailers like Zara and H&M selling knock-offs of designer labels, Rent the Runway repositioned the value of their business as a way to reverse the trend to commoditization in the industry, by creating a direct channel between designers and customers, and not as simply switching fashion buyers into renters. The designers would, in fact, get exposure to a new user group—often younger than their historical base, many of whom might end up then buying from the designer once they'd tried a dress—and, crucially, the designers would also get data on what styles, fit, colors, and fabrics appeal most to this core group. In exchange, Rent The Runway gets wholesale pricing, quantity discounts, and full-size runs (sizes zero to twelve) of the newest dresses from leading designers. In this way, Rent The Runway moved the fashion designer community from Quadrant D to Quadrant A. They created a shared agenda around the need to combat Zara and H&M, and created a new abundance for them—a powerful data-driven insight engine about their future customer base—to win the trust of designers and gain access to the resources Rent The Runway needed to succeed.[9]

These cases demonstrate just two ways to create shared agendas: understanding the partner's needs and meeting them, as Rent The Runway understands fashion designers; and using the pressure of public opinion, like ColaLife. A genuinely inspiring and important purpose can clearly also provide a powerful bridge to others who would like to help deliver that purpose, and open up their resources to a shared agenda.

When creating lists of new partners we therefore need to start with a keen assessment of how willing the partner will be to share, and then we need some creative can-if thinking around how to make that happen if they are not initially on the same page.

## Sharing an agenda, multiplying resources

Trade is not the only way to access resources, or the only kind of value we can offer. The top left quadrant (C) is about a shared agenda, or shared purpose. When the World Association of Girl Guides and Girl Scouts (WAGGS) gives to Dove its resources of people, communication, and access, it does so because it believes that Dove's ambition—of reaching fifteen million girls with its self-esteem programs by the end of 2015—is one that it wants to help succeed. Dove is not offering WAGGS a value of a different kind of resource in return; it is offering the opportunity to help deliver an impact that both sides believe to be important. A strong purpose makes forging such alliances considerably easier.

When Nike released its Making app (which cataloged and scored 75,000 materials by environmental impact and long-term sustainability) they gave away intellectual property to all their competitors because they know that, as big as they are, they cannot

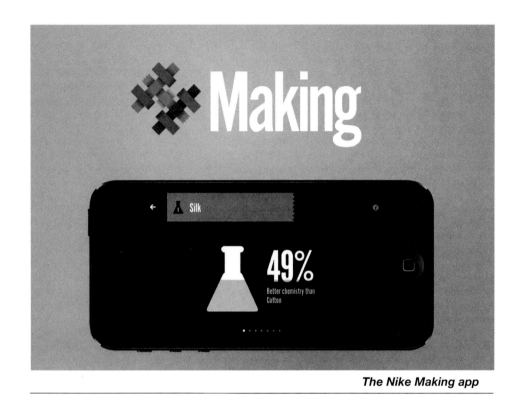

*The Nike Making app*

move markets alone. There's no direct swapping of value, as there is in a strategic partnership, but Nike has identified what it believes is, or should be, a shared agenda.

Nike now talks about pre-competitive spaces, such as the quest for waterless dyeing techniques, where the shared need is so great that it will collaborate with anyone, including competitors. This is a common practice in the world of pharmaceuticals, where companies share the expense of basic research. In a world where resource scarcity brings major challenges too big to solve alone, we believe we'll see much more of this kind of collaboration between competitors in the next few years. In these situations the addition of pooled resources to a common agenda, too expensive for any one player to crack, can create more partnerships between competitors in Quadrant C.

## Using this framework

Let's recap how this framework helps us see all the ways we can create abundance:

First, we need to be clear on what kind of resource we are focused on finding in this exercise, and what we need that resource to allow us to do.

Then we need to be disciplined in how we work through the four sources of resource, represented by the concentric squares on the framework; the closer to the center of the map, the more familiar to us they are at the moment.

These four relationships are divided in turn into quadrants by considering two further aspects to this potential relationship: to what degree the other parties already share—or might share—our agenda (the Influence axis), and how clear the complementary value of what we have to offer is to them (the Trade axis). We'll sort our potential prospects, group by group, across these quadrants. This gives us an early overview of which will be the easiest to access—prospects in Quadrant A are obviously going to require less work to access than prospects in Quadrant D.

We will need to be inventive in how we think about what value we have to offer, reframing it in different ways to meet the needs of new partners. Table 3 is there to prompt that process.

And we need to be equally inventive in how we seek to influence partners to share our agenda. This will come from a combination of understanding what is important to the partner (what their agenda and purpose is), and how they might come to see it as linked to ours.

| ASSETS<br>What do we have in abundance?<br>What can we trade? | REFRAME<br>How can we reframe these assets to give them<br>more relevance and value to others? |
|---|---|
| | |
| | |
| | |
| | |

*Table 3: Identifying and reframing our assets*

### How to feed a blue chicken

Let's leave this chapter with one last story, because it illustrates everything we have been discussing here. It concerns the chicken farmers in a rural district in Kenya called Nakuru.

If you are a smallholder farmer raising chickens in Nakuru, the most vulnerable time for your hatchlings is the first ten weeks, when there are two dangers for the chicks. One is disease, but this is preventable: for five Kenyan shillings (about five cents) you can protect a chick with a vaccine. The other danger is the aerial predators—Nakuru is famous for its eagles and hawks—and it's this second threat that stops a farmer from protecting against the first: what's the point of spending money to immunize a chick, if you're just fattening it up for an eagle in six weeks' time?

Paul Seward runs an NGO in Kenya called Farm Input Promotions Africa (FIPS-Africa), dedicated to increasing the productivity of the local smallholder farmers, many of whom have just a quarter-acre of land. Seward discovered that if you paint the chicks blue, the eagles and hawks don't realize what they are, and don't try to eat them. The biodegradable paint washes off in ten weeks, by which time the chicks have enough yard-smarts to run for cover when they see a shadow overhead.

Because the farmers are losing fewer chicks to birds of prey, it is now more worthwhile for them to inoculate the young birds against disease. Through both of these measures, they have gone from a survival rate of 20 percent to close to 85 percent. Because the farmers have more chickens, they are eating more chicken themselves— and better nutrition means a healthier family. And because it is now a better business, more people are taking up chicken farming. Oh, and the idea has created an entirely new profession: chicken painters, who charge three Kenyan shillings to paint each chick. A fascinating example of the cumulative benefits of a simple idea across an entire ecosystem.

This higher survival rate, however, has brought with it a new challenge: how to feed all those chicks. Chickens are natural free-range scavengers, but now there are more of them, so there is less food near the house to keep them going, and they are forced to forage further afield. And the further away they get, the more prone they are to being taken by terrestrial predators such as mongoose, who seem happy to breakfast on chicks of any color at all.

So the question now is: How do we feed the chicks close to the house? For free? These are not farmers who can afford to invest in poultry feed.

Insects, Seward realized, were a potentially abundant food source, especially termites—there are estimated to be a ton of termites under each acre of local soil. But that presented another challenge: they are under the soil. How could FIPS give the farmers a way to catch them easily?

Seward recognized that he didn't have to invent a method himself; all he needed to do was find someone who had already discovered a way to do it. So he traveled to a part of Kenya where people ate termites, and learned how they caught them using bundles of waste crop stalks soaked in water. He brought this method back to Nakuru, and now the farmers have an abundant source of free food for their multiplying blue chicks.

Seward had seen a potential source of abundance in the termite nests around him, but initially couldn't access it. His resourcefulness led him to recognize that accessing other people's knowledge would allow him to create abundance for his smallholders.[10]

## Resourcefulness and the mutually beneficial hustle

If we are resource-constrained, we need to be much more inventive in how we think about accessing more resources, and we need to redefine how we think about being resourceful.

Whether we're schoolteachers struggling to find the funds to run that extra class experiment, or managers in large corporations with insufficient headcount to get our projects done, if we open up our sense of availability, there are more resources accessible to us than we think. Stopping to take a fresh look, considering all the sources beyond those we would normally approach, and thinking again about what we might be able to offer and what we might gain in return, might reveal surprisingly abundant resources within reach. The discipline and structure in the framework in this chapter will be useful in overcoming the kind of path-dependent behavior that may once have rendered us blind to where new opportunities lie.

Embracing this kind of inventiveness takes us beyond the "value in kind" relationships of the past, toward the more ambitious, impatient, and mutually beneficial hustle of the 21st century, with all kinds of new value to exchange (Rent The Runway's data) in all kinds of new ways (Nike's Making app). Enabled by professional and social networking tools, accessing abundance is easier than ever before. It's a capability no longer confined to a department, but part of the planning process for any team that needs to deliver results within the limits imposed by a hyper-competitive, resource-constrained environment. The sale of the virtual reality headset company Oculus Rift, funded via Kickstarter in 2012, to Facebook for $2 billion less than two years later, was a symbol of re-evaluation (for better or worse) for the potential of crowdfunding.

The success of organizations such as Proctor & Gamble, with open innovation, and Mozilla's Firefox, with open source, shows the value of being, well, open to the outside. But in our experience, companies and brands outside the NGO space tend to fall between two stools: they are either still locked in a system where they try to do it all themselves (except for a couple of high-level, long-term strategic partnerships managed by someone in a division called Strategic Partnerships) or they rely on the wisdom of the crowd for nearly everything. That may be one way to access abundance, but it isn't the only one.

We will all need to become a great deal more disciplined and inventive in how we see and access abundance, if we are going to be truly resourceful.

**CREATING ABUNDANCE: CHAPTER SUMMARY**

- We nearly always have more resources available to us than we initially think.

- Our habitual ways of thinking about resources blind us to opportunities within easy reach. If we can learn to look around us and see it that way, available abundance is everywhere. The key is to stop thinking of resources only as those we control, and start thinking of them as those we can access.

- There are four sources of resource for us to access: our own stakeholders (who nearly always have more to offer than we have historically drawn on), external partners, resource owners (people or organizations who have a lot of what we need and may also need what we have), and even our competitors.

- Once we have identified the potential sources to access, we need to think afresh about our own assets, and reframe what we have to create new kinds of value with which we can trade.

- And we need to define an agenda that we share with that abundance owner which makes it in our mutual interest to combine resources.

- This chapter calls for more mutually beneficial hustle, the kind that has helped organizations as diverse as Virgin America, Rent The Runway, and ColaLife multiply their resources many times over.

- And it calls for a redefinition of resourcefulness: to be less about an ability to get things done, whatever the circumstances, and more about being able to find and deliver resources we need, from anywhere.

# 6 ACTIVATING EMOTIONS

How to fuel tenacity on the journey

1. Why are mindset and method alone insufficient to make constraints beautiful?

2. Why is emotion such an important motivator, and how does it help?

3. What is the range of emotions that seems to be most prevalent among people transforming constraints, and how do they differ in their power and effect?

**Military special operations** are carried out by teams of elite soldiers with very specific, targeted missions. The teams are small (U.S. Navy SEAL platoons consist of sixteen soldiers operating in eight-man squads, or four-man Fire teams) up against much larger conventional forces, and operate in highly constrained situations—having very little time to complete an operation, for instance, far from base, without backup.

Admiral William McRaven, Commander of the U.S. Special Operations Command, has led at every level in U.S. special operations, including leading Operation Neptune Spear, which led to the death of Osama Bin Laden. His thesis at Naval Postgraduate School was *The Theory of Special Operations*, which later became the book *Spec Ops*.[1] In it, he developed the six core principles that make special operations successful, illustrating them with case studies ranging from the sinking of the battleship Tirpitz to the rescue of Mussolini from a hotel atop the Gran Sasso Mountains in Italy.

One of the six principles is the concept of purpose (bear in mind McRaven was writing long before the word became fashionable in the business world), and he makes an important distinction on what it means in his context. For McRaven, purpose in special operations has two levels: first, a clear and specific sense of what the ambition is ("Sink the battleship," for example); and second, the explicit need for personal commitment to that ambition.

It is the leader's role both to communicate a clear sense of the ambition and to elevate the emotional commitment to it within his team. This is exemplified in the refreshingly direct approach of Lt. Colonel Henry Mucci of the Sixth Ranger Battalion before a special operations mission to rescue prisoners of war in the Philippines, when the Colonel shouted at his men:

> *You had better get down on your knees and pray! Damn it … don't fake it! I mean … PRAY. And I want you to swear an oath before God…. Swear you'll die fighting rather than let any harm come to those POWs![2]*

Far from handicapping elite soldiers, who we might assume would work better as detached professionals, McRaven believes that emotions are an essential part of mission success: "In an age of high technology and Jedi Knights, we often overlook the need for personal involvement, but we do so at our own risk."

We have all come to understand the value of purpose in our organizations—Gallup research has demonstrated the value of giving meaning to the work people do.[3] But over and above meaningful connection to the company and its ambitions, emotional engagement, as McRaven showed above, has a particular value in how we perform against more immediate challenges. We can see this in Yves Behar's reflections on what fueled his team's tenacity in developing the original One Laptop Per Child computer: "The reality on a project like this is that you hit a million snags, and a million people tell you 'it can't be done like this.' And every time you are presented with one of these challenges you say no. You go back to the big idea. You go back to the belief. You go back to what got you to work on this in the first place."[4]

In this chapter, then, we will look first at the particular importance and benefits of emotional engagement in realizing the beauty in our constraint, and then what types of emotions seem to work especially well to drive this, and their connection with our overall purpose. We'll conclude by looking at how to elevate emotional connection in our team and ourselves.

## The value of emotional engagement

Angela Lee Duckworth received a MacArthur Genius grant for discovering that what she calls grit—the ability to maintain commitment to a goal despite obstacles, adversity, or failure—turns out to be a bigger predictor of success in life than IQ. Stick-to-it-iveness is not just important, it seems: it might be the most important thing. Duckworth's work has now turned to understanding whether grit can be taught to children, so she can increase their chances of academic success. Though she has yet to conclude her work, her start point is that it can indeed be taught. We can learn to persist.[5]

Realizing a potentially beautiful solution to our constraint is going to bring stimulating challenges all its own; persistence will be as important a traveling companion here as ever. But the work of Janina Marguc at the University of Amsterdam, as well as the real-life experience of many of those discussed in this book, indicates that it is a very particular kind of persistence that will be important to us. Marguc's research into the effects of constraints on creativity,[6] as we saw in Chapter Four, found that coming up against a significant constraint that they didn't immediately understand how to address often caused her subjects to step back and rethink the way to move ahead. Their

cognitive processing shifted from local (focused on the particular and on details) to global (looking more generally at options available), enabling them to find a different way forward. Persistence in overcoming constraints does not lie simply in our banging our heads over and over again against a wall; it consists as much in a stubborn adaptiveness, continually stepping back and finding a new way forward. And key to this kind of persistence, Marguc found, was the level of emotional engagement and motivation to follow through with that particular problem. If the participants didn't care so much about the problem, they were less likely to solve it. While she had expected this to be largely a matter of nature and character—whether the test subjects were the kind of people who typically followed through and finished projects in other areas of their lives—the key variable actually turned out to be the degree of emotional connection.

Let's look at an example of this in practice, in what is surely one of the most challenging sets of constraints we have discussed yet.

### Transforming the health of Native Alaskans

Southcentral Foundation (SCF) provides healthcare for 55,000 Native Alaskan people. It was four years old as an entity in 1987 when Katherine Gottlieb, just 22, walked into the shabby office to take up her new job as the receptionist. "One of the first things I did was replace the dinged-up old metal reception desk with a nice oak one, and started dressing nice," she says. She felt it was time to show more respect toward her people, who at the time were being poorly served.[7]

Her community (she is half Aleut) was suffering due to a confluence of broader cultural changes. The loss of traditional ways of life, including warrior traditions and fishing as a livelihood, had disrupted native culture to the point where depression and stress among the tribes were at high levels. Obesity, alcoholism, diabetes, and violence against women were on the rise, with little hope for improvement. This, Gottlieb says with understatement, was hard to watch.

She worked to understand every aspect of how the foundation ran. Remarkably, within four years she was the President and CEO, with an ambitious new agenda. Under a new deal with the government, SCF had agreed to take on more responsibility for health outcomes, and to shift from a fee-per-treatment system to a fixed sum per person. While this deal gave SCF the impetus and freedom to innovate, it also brought with it a pressure to change: with healthcare costs spiraling across the United States on the one hand, and a local population with growing needs on the other, Gottlieb had to become very ambitious in the face of some big constraints. Her propelling question was as challenging as any: "How can we dramatically improve the health outcomes of a community that is highly disenfranchised?" In the same people she wanted to help were the roots of the very constraints she would need to embrace.

That embrace began with six months of deep listening. The first epiphany to come out of this was that SCF had been treating symptoms, not people. By their reckoning, 75–85 percent of all healthcare expenditures were related to long-term lifestyle factors of the patient. If SCF were to improve the health outcomes of the community, they would need to tackle an entire system of constraints surrounding their people's current relationship with their lifestyle and culture.

The first can-if reflected this shift in focus: they would redesign their system around the whole person "and their messy, human, longitudinal, personal, trusting, informing, respecting, and accountable relationships."[8] They called this the Nuka system of care ("nuka" is a native word meaning strong living things) and it would address the lifestyle and cultural causes of illness—a hugely ambitious mission, requiring the implementation of multiple initiatives over a decade.

At the outset, Gottlieb's team faced a host of apparently impassable obstacles: treating the whole person would take a level of time and effort that they couldn't afford, requiring specialists they didn't have, deploying a cultural sensitivity they'd need to develop, among people who might well resist it even if it could be implemented in this way. Just think about the perseverance it would have taken for Gottlieb and her team to push through the doubts and skepticism they encountered.

The second can-if had to do with the nature of the core relationship between SCF and their patients, and the language used to describe it: the Nuka system would change patients into customer-owners. As customers, the community would expect high-end service by the staff, which would be accountable for it; and as owners, people would be in charge of both their own health outcomes and the system itself, redesigning it to meet their needs. This language shift, and the relationship it embodied, forced changes to both the services offered and the behaviors of the people in the system. While healthcare professionals recommend prevention and treatment options, the customer-owners take responsibility for choosing what's best for them, and learn to see themselves not as victims of an imposed system, but as people in control of their own future—and in doing so, change the story they tell themselves about their ability to influence their situation.

The next can-if was to set up integrated care teams to treat the whole person: tribal doctors, traditional healers, acupuncturists, massage therapists, and psychologists were integrated with conventional medical staff for the first time—a considerable feat in itself. A new hospital was then built around a radically different floor plan and operating procedure. Everyone was asked to give up their offices to create collaborative workspaces and talking rooms to meet with the customer-owners in teams, and all of this coordinated by a nurse, whom the customer-owner could call directly. They would build real trust between SCF and their customer-owners by removing barriers of space, attitude, language, and time, with an 80 percent ability to deliver same-day access. Enabling systems were put in place, staff retrained, and performance data shared widely to create accountability across the system.

While all of these moves were difficult to plan and complete, reaching into the community to address the highly sensitive cultural issues affecting healthcare was when Gottlieb had to be at her most creative and tenacious. She initially failed, for example, to persuade native leaders to support a project tackling the issue of child sexual abuse: they were not even prepared to have the conversation. In the end, Gottlieb's winning can-if was to reframe the role of the warrior in native culture, and ultimately create the Family Wellness Warriors Initiative, one of her favorite projects:

*This time, I said "I need you as tribal men like you were in the old days, when you were willing to risk your lives for your wives and children and willing to step forward to defend and protect us." You could feel it—everything changed. They said, "What do you need?"* [9]

Taking the constraint—a disenfranchised community, with no motivation or sense of control over their own lives—and resisting the temptation to simply neutralize it, but rather make it the stimulus to a series of transformational programs, has generated extraordinary results. Customer-owner satisfaction levels are at 91 percent; wait lists have fallen from 1,300 to almost zero; urgent care and emergency room visits are down 40 percent due to the same-day access system, saving millions of dollars. Treatment quality has measurably increased, and third-party assessments show the staff are happy, knowing they are making a difference. Southcentral has been able to do all of this on a budget that increases just 2 percent a year while their customer-owner number grows at 7 percent a year. In 2011, the U.S. Commerce department awarded Southcentral the prestigious Baldridge Award to honor the scale and nature of their success.

Though young, Gottlieb had ensured she was well-qualified for the challenges of SCF. She had made time to study for her MBA early in her role as CEO, and was disciplined in combining the tools of modern management with creating an environment in which native people would feel more comfortable. Her relentless focus on survey data and accountability leaves no one in any doubt about what matters, and total transparency ensures that underperformers know who they are and how long they have to pull their socks up.

But that's not the whole story. The personal commitment that this twenty-five year journey demanded comes partly from her background. She's half Aleut herself, with roots in the community whose plight was once very much her own. Her mother was an alcoholic; she herself was pregnant at sixteen and fled an abusive first husband; few challenges faze her after that. It would be too glib to attribute Gottlieb's success, or that of any other person who triumphs over a difficult past, to a theory of "desirable difficulties" (the notion that there can be advantages in disadvantage).[10] But Gottlieb's struggles clearly made her who she is, and she channels all the emotional intensity and

## Tenacity and Emotional Connection at Leadership Public Schools

Scot Refsland, part-time CIO of the Leadership Public Schools discussed in Chapter Two, also needed to be tenacious, though not over twenty-five years. Time was in fact one of his constraints: he had just a few months of low-budget, high-stakes, one–chance-to-make-it, trial-and-error intensity to get ExitTicket to work. This required hacking together a usable product while working around the schools' poor quality Wi-Fi, overnighting code back and forth with India for speed, and sourcing new tools (used iPods) in late-night sniping sessions on eBay. Without his creativity and relentlessness, ExitTicket would not have made it.

Scot has a PhD in robotics and is based in Silicon Valley. He could do far more glamorous things than sit at the back of a threadbare classroom, hacking code to make used clickers work for student tests. What drove him to get this right? While Scot describes himself as "a problem-solving guy" who just wanted to figure out how to solve the intrinsic challenges; he also says Louise Waters reminds him of his mom, and they'd really connected. And, in particular, how helping these children change their self-story became important to him. Being so up close and personal with the students and seeing how well they responded to ExitTicket connected him to the cause more than coding in an office somewhere off-site would have done. Besides taking pride in making ExitTicket work, being in among the children and the reality of their lives and learning made him loyal to them and to Louise.[11]

As we saw in the case of Ben Knelman and Juntos Finanzas, developing deep empathy with the end user (when relevant) is one way to ensure emotional engagement is high, which is why design thinking rightly places so much emphasis on this.

toughness acquired into setting a high bar, finding solutions in her constraints, and making those solutions happen when others might blanch.

If this strong emotional connection is so important to success, then are there particular kinds of emotion that seem to be especially important? And, if so, how do we tap into them and draw from their strength?

## When a strong emotion meets a propelling question

We have seen that making our constraint beautiful demands the ability to repeatedly step back, rethink, and go again with something new, just as Katherine Gottlieb did with the Wellness Warriors initiative. We need a particular kind of persistence—a creative tenacity, full of willing and adaptive experimentation. Talent and capability alone can't guarantee success with constraints, and an intellectual impetus isn't enough. A strong emotional desire to solve the problem is essential. Purpose can clearly supply much of this emotional connection in certain cases, provided that it has a real meaning and value, rather than simply being a flag of convenience.

But it is unlikely that purpose alone is going to provide all the emotional impetus we need, because it defines us simply in terms of our connection to our organization. And while that is ideally an important part of the meaning in our lives, it isn't the total expression of who we are and what motivates us. As individuals, we have a much broader range of emotional drives that push us forward and hold us back than the relatively narrow range of positive ones that make up the typical canvas of purpose (the desire to improve the world in some way, to give joy, to connect people, and so on). And we see that broader sweep in the range of different human emotions, dark as well as light, in what drove many of our interviewees to find the opportunities in their constraints.

Consider South Africa's First National Bank, for example. Voted the world's most innovative bank, FNB has launched its own online currency (ebucks), created the country's first banking app, launched a Telco, given FNB customers free bandwidth, and become Africa's largest iPad retailer—all this in a category in which most financial service clients claim it is almost impossible to truly innovate. How has it done this? By creating an enabling culture, and offering a considerable financial incentive to anyone inside the organization who comes up with an innovation that makes an impact in market: the annual prize fund started as $100,000 in 2004 and has now grown to seven times that. When we asked then-CEO Michael Jordaan, who had himself set in place this cultural revolution and the innovation program within the company, what he thought were the most important emotional drivers of innovation success, he answered, "Fear, laziness, and greed."[12] It is hard to find any of those in most contemporary purpose statements, or indeed to find greed in the literature that extols intrinsic rather than extrinsic motivation.[13] Yet it is difficult to argue with the results of FNB's financial incentive, and Katherine Gottlieb would corroborate Jordaan's view about the motivational power of fear. When asked what motivated her at the beginning of the SCF journey, she said, "Imagine you are going to take it over—you, right now, personally—now you are responsible for life and death." Point taken. It was, she emphasized, "very scary."

Dan Wieden loves the power of anxiety, a less extreme form of fear, but one he finds addictive: "Crisis does a pretty good job of rewiring synapses … you can get addicted to anxiety because it is extremely helpful. If you can remain insecure, yet optimistic, you've got a pretty good chance of changing the world."[14]

In some of our transformers, the emotion moves closer to anger. When Tim Martin started his chain of pubs in the UK in 1979, he called his fledgling company J D Wetherspoon. The surname had a particular meaning for him: it was that of the teacher who had told him at school that he'd never

*A point proved*

succeed in business. There are now 900 outlets across Britain bearing that teacher's name.

Judd Apatow, the writer and director behind hit movies that include *The 40-Year-Old-Virgin* and *Knocked Up*, says that spite fueled his success. After his TV show Freaks and Geeks was cancelled by NBC in 2000, Apatow went into a deep funk and channeled the resentment he felt into his revenge plan. To prove them wrong about his show and every single member of his team, he used all of them in the movies he subsequently made. Each movie grossed more than $100 million, and made a star out of Seth Rogen along the way.[15]

Many challengers are born from dissatisfaction with their category. BrewDog's feeling about what is wrong with mainstream lager is a loathing that takes seven contemptuous adjectives to fully convey: they want to show the world there is an alternative to the "mainstream, industrial, monolithic, insipid, bland, tasteless, apathetic" beers that dominate the market.

A related form of dissatisfaction is frustration. Dr. Waters of LPS spoke about the deep frustration that had motivated her throughout her career at never being able to untangle the variables to establish what was working in education. It was this frustration that led her to accept the role at LPS and define the ambition she set for it. Sugru is a self-setting rubber designed to help people modify and repair objects that are important to them; it was started because founder Jane Ní Dhulchaointigh was frustrated with a world geared to making people feel they needed new things all the time. And much of what drove the people behind citizenM hotels was their frustration with the way the category behaved: Why does it take so long to check in after a long journey? Why does breakfast have to stop at 11:00? Why should I pay for Wi-Fi on top of my room bill?

Alongside the emotional drivers often defined as negative are the more conventionally positive ones. Frikkie Lubbe of SAB wanted to improve the lives of the local barley growers, as well as deliver SAB's corporate objectives. If the project made them more profitable and sustainable, it would improve the sustainability of the entire barley industry as well as SAB.

The Surf team's desire was to put delight into their user's day. They make the distinction between understanding your users and liking them. Knowledge is useful, but genuinely liking them enough to want to champion their interests is a significant part of their success. This closeness helped drive the design of packaging, fragrance innovation, grassroots marketing, and point of sale display.

Sometimes these positive emotions are those that surround a noble purpose, such as Unilever's Sustainable Living Plan. And sometimes the emotion is a simpler one of joy and excitement. Biz Stone, one of the co-founders of Twitter, described what he found engaging: "Twitter, even in this prototype phase, was something that was making me giggle and making me realize I definitely want to keep working on this."[16]

Anxiety, fear, greed, anger, vindication, loathing, frustration, desire, excitement, joy. All human emotion is here. And to classify the first few of these as negative is misleading; it suggests they are destructive. In reality, they can be hugely productive and important sources of emotional engagement for us. A 2010 study confirms the value of both (see sidebar). Negative emotions can help drive persistence, commitment, and focus. Positive emotions help stimulate cognitive flexibility and the ability to see new kinds of connections.

Imagine what we can do with both.

## The Power of Positive and Negative Emotions

In 2010, academics studied two different creativity paths: the flexibility path, which uses a broad range of stimuli (such as those suggested in the can-if start points), and the persistence path, consisting of a smaller range of stimuli but persisting with them. And they saw that the most successful problem solvers toggle back and forth between the two paths.

What the study also explored was the value of different emotions in helping propel people down these paths. Positive emotions—such as happiness and elation—correlate well with increased cognitive flexibility. Positivity releases neurotransmitters (dopamine and noradrenaline) which increase the flow of information around the brain, networking disparate pieces of information together. And those same moods increase feelings of safety and freedom from problems, which lead us to explore new possibilities more actively.

Yet they also saw that so-called negative emotions have value, too. Anger and fear, in particular, caused participants to knuckle down, do more work, and work through to the end. Other studies conclude that anger can act as a set of blinders, keeping us more focused on reaching the reward; and that there is an anxiety sweet spot where we are sufficiently aroused to act, but not paralyzed by fear.[17]

## The power of positive and negative together: The science of mental contrasting

Jack Dorsey, co-founder of Twitter and founder of Square, has talked about the value of tension in helping to create his two businesses. Twitter was created while in a funk at Odeo, a business that was failing, and Square during the heat of the financial crisis of 2008. (It is interesting to note how different his emotion about Twitter was to Biz Stone's.)

> *I thrive on tension. If I had a relationship where nothing was ever wrong and we were never debating or arguing, I don't think we would ever grow. There's no change.*[18]

Professor Gabriele Oettingen, a German by birth, but now "almost a native New Yorker" in her role as head of the Motivation Lab at New York University, mostly agrees with Dorsey. Not for her the unbridled positivity of the self-help literature, which she doesn't believe will help any of us get what we need. Professor Oettingen brings a "get real" view of motivation, founded in the lab and tested in real world settings.[19]

Her research suggests that the sweet spot for motivating people is in the tension between positivity and negativity. A person must act to resolve the tension, and this is what powers behavior change. The strategy Oettingen has developed is called mental contrasting, and it has proven to be the most effective strategy when trying to lose weight, battle addiction, or improve academic performance, each of which require considerable tenacity.

Oettingen distinguishes between three approaches when considering how to reach a desired outcome. The first is indulging: a mental state achieved by creating a vivid picture of what the future looks like when you have achieved your goal. Most of us tend to go to this place of fantasy quite readily; it is a quite seductive place to be. But it's easy to get stuck in fantasy, partly because our brains find it hard to distinguish the fiction from the reality. The fantasy gives us some of the psychological rewards of having done the thing itself, and so our motivation to act is reduced.

The second approach is called dwelling, which consists of creating an equally powerful and fully realized picture of all that could go wrong along the journey. If you're naturally inclined to pessimism, this can be a seductive place, too, because it tells you that there is really no point in the whole exercise. It can be very difficult to get out of the dwelling ditch and on to the road to change. This is where the victim resides.

The third, more effective approach is the active contrasting of indulging and dwelling: going back and forth between the two, tying together the promise of future rewards with the constraints and threats of today. The cognitive dissonance this sets up for people turns out to be the most effective driver of change. Because we can't easily live with that tension, it stimulates us to do what's necessary to move us toward resolution.

It was striking how most of the people we interviewed were living in this place of mental contrasting, between the possibilities of success and the constant negotiation of difficulties that could spell setback or even disaster. (One of them talked very candidly about his uplifting mission to help people live more healthily for longer, on the one hand, and a sense of impending doom on the other; he was, at the same time, a man who had doubled the size of his business in eighteen months). This is why creating a propelling question is not only useful strategically, but psychologically. A visceral understanding of what it will mean to fulfill our ambition without shrinking from the challenges in the constraints is the best form of preparation for what's to come.

Finally, Oettingen makes the point that mental contrasting, while critical, is just the emotional preparation for what comes next: the plan of action. The tension must be harnessed to action, which

# Creating a propelling question is not only powerful strategically but also psychologically.

is what the psychologists call implementation intention. Making specific, concrete plans for what you will do, and then doing it, begins to resolve the tension and starts the ball rolling. Success is never letting our indulging or our dwelling get the upper hand, but keeping the tension between them high and using it to drive action.

In fifteen years of researching and working with challengers, we've seen a version of mental contrasting play out in the driving narrative that underpins a challenger culture (and sometimes public stance) many times. Challengers can be mission-driven idealists with a positive view of the future and, at the same time, express a competitive desire to rid the world of a powerful enemy or some other cultural evil. And often their narrative combines optimism about the future with a secondary strand where the clock is urgently ticking, or barbarians are at the gates, or the future of their community is at stake. They create a narrative in their brand, and their organization, that combines the motivating benefits of positive and negative.

Consider the mix of emotional drivers that Ravi Naidoo says led him to start Design Indaba—the design conference and exhibition that has, in the twenty years since it began in Cape Town, become the largest in the world. In 1995, Naidoo was inspired by the possibilities for South Africa following Nelson Mandela's election, and haunted by a fear for the future of his country if there was not the economic progress to match the political breakthrough. He felt that unless South Africa could go further up the value chain, and become less dependent on commodities, that progress would not be achieved. His excitement about the idea that design and creativity in South Africa ("the resources between our ears") would be the source of this transformation fought with a real frustration at the insularity and parochialism of the country at the time. His vision was to bring "an alternative army of creative people," the best from around the world, and ask them to help reimagine Africa. The design conference would attract the world's greatest talent and clients to the country, while the concurrent exhibition would showcase the best of South African creativity to the world. It was a huge ambition, and one without a budget—we'll see in Chapter Seven ("The Fertile Zero") how the tension between the ambition and the constraint led Naidoo to create new forms of value to make it possible. But the mix of those emotions impelled him—telling this story and why it mattered to him, two decades later, he still talks passionately about frustration and excitement, inspiration and fear. It is a richly engaging, emotionally driven narrative, full of powerful contrast.[20]

Equally, the angry disdain for industrial beer that BrewDog co-founder James Watt displayed earlier in the chapter is only part of what drives them. The other part is a mission "to make other people as passionate about great craft beer as we are." They have, he says, "a punky ethos … we like to think that our beers have the same attitude towards the incumbents of the beer market that the original punks had to pop culture." In other words, what drives Watt and his team is a complete story, with different kinds of emotion, shades of light and dark.[21]

The combination of positive and negative emotions is powerful because it allows for greater personalization—each individual can draw from the emotions that they find most motivating, ensuring that the team as a whole is at the optimal state of activation, and this ensures durability. When one type of emotion fades for a while, other emotions kick in, so persistence is undimmed.

Oettingen's findings, however, are also about contrasts in potential outcomes. Where drivers and outcomes come together is in the narrative we need to wrap around our propelling question. If necessity is the mother of invention, she is not the only parent. We need to weave an emotional narrative that is true both to the challenge and to us, full of rich, contrasting emotions, and we need to keep it close and vivid as long as we are working on it. This is how we will enlist and reinforce the emotional engagement that we need to drive the stubbornly resourceful, step-back-and-look-at-it-differently creative tenacity that will bring us success.

## Creating the emotional narrative

We can embrace smaller constraints without an emotional narrative, but the bigger the constraint, the more motivation we will need to power us through the inevitable rounds of exploration and initial failing forward. Senior scientists and engineers at IBM are taught narrative techniques to help them engage a broader group within the company around the value of a project, and we'll need to do something similar. And while we won't provide a story structure here, we will provide a piece of stimulus to help you think through how to get the right kind of emotional content into the story. Purpose may provide some of this, but in all likelihood it will be relatively one-sided in its positivity. You will, at the very least, have the opportunity to complement it with a richer, more personally involving story if you use the following guidelines.

### Where are you in this?

Figure 6 is a map adapted from Robert Plutchik's *Theory of Basic Emotions*. Our version does not pretend to be more than a qualitative capture of the range of emotions we have explored in this chapter and elsewhere in the book; it is a piece of stimulus, not a gift to science.

The map shows eight core emotions around the outer circle, and three levels of intensity for each emotion as you move toward the middle: annoyance becomes anger becomes rage when intensified, empathy becomes care becomes love, and so on. As we saw above, it's not helpful to characterize some emotions as positive and some as negative here. They are from different parts of the emotional spectrum, but both are valuable in different ways.[22]

Think about the propelling question you face, and the constraint at its heart that you are looking to make beautiful. Why is it particularly important to you? Use each of these areas as prompts: you are not looking to create an emotion that isn't really

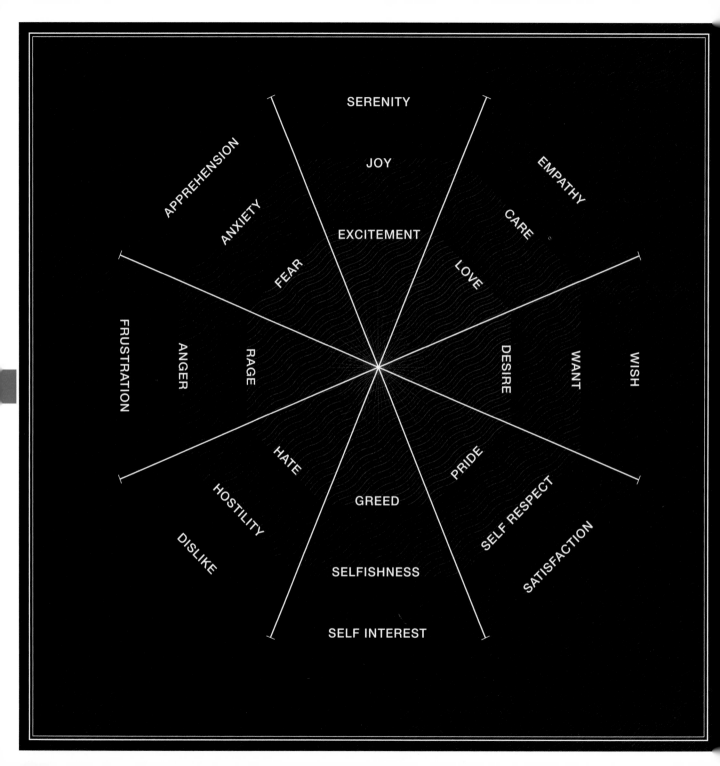

there, but using it to prompt reflection and articulate different facets of your emotional relationship with the nature and implications of the challenge. Be disciplined about it. Start anywhere you like. What excites you about it, for instance? What could be exciting to you about it? Try three different articulations of this. Which feel closest to you? Then move to the next: what are you afraid of if you are not successful here? What should we all be afraid of? Try three different articulations on this. And so on.

Then leave it for a night. What are the three you feel most strongly connected to in the morning? Why?

### Lean into range and contrast

Building on your three areas of emotional connection, try to make sure that at least one is a positive one, and at least one is a negative one. When you put them together, what kinds of emotional narratives do they start to create around why answering this ambitious constraint is so important? What narrative, personal or organizational, reflects how you feel and gives a space and role for the emotions you want to emphasize? Think about three different members of your team—where do you think they will connect most to this emerging narrative? How might this range be valuable in helping different people connect in different ways? The emotions that work hardest for you won't necessarily be those that work for them.

You might also want to explore mental contrasting: indulge yourself in the fantasy of what it will feel like to succeed and note the emotions that surround that; dwell in the horror of failure, too, and note those emotions. Rehearsing this scenario before you start is powerful. How might you intensify the emotion, moving closer to the middle of the wheel? As leaders, we will need to be skilled at creating the tension in the story around what the team is trying to achieve, in the way Oettingen describes—tying the promise of the future to the threats of today—and effective in making that a genuinely motivating part of our story.

### Keep it vivid

Everyone needs to find ways to keep these emotions as vivid as possible throughout the journey. Dan Wieden used a picture of Lasse Viren taped above his desk to evoke Phil Knight's warning, and remind him just how high the stakes were for his fledgling

---

*Figure 6: Eight kinds of activating emotion (with apologies to Plutchik)*

agency. Ben Knelman of Juntos Finanzas could conjure up the look on the face of his transformed janitor when he needed, because that epiphany birthed his company. Scot Refsland came face to face with his emotions whenever he sat in the classroom, which he did often. Individuals like Ravi Naidoo and cultures like IKEA tell stories which keep the most powerful emotions easily accessible and present.

## Harnessing emotion at the d.school

Design for Extreme Affordability is a hugely popular two-quarter course offered by the Hasso Plattner Institute of Design (the d.school) at Stanford University. It is a multidisciplinary, project-based experience that asks a team to design products and services that will change the lives of the world's poor. Many of these problems come with constraints. There are issues of time (the course is just two quarters long), knowledge (while the students are masters in their discipline, they are not professionals in the field) and money—as the name of the course implies, the goal is extremely affordable solutions. And the students work in teams of just four.

But Stuart Coulson, one of the Extreme teaching team members, a lecturer at the d.school, and a seasoned entrepreneur himself, pointed out that there's value in having a small team, "In my opinion, [people] resource constraints are a good thing. What looks like a constraint often isn't; [in a small team] there's no bureaucracy, no decision-making chain, no politics. It's completely freeing."[23]

Some of the work of the course is done in the field, rubbing shoulders with the locals, experiencing the problems first hand, using the principles of design thinking to work out solutions. Among their many successes is the Embrace infant warmer (which looks something like a sleeping bag, is designed for areas with limited access to electricity, and has reduced infant mortality at a fraction of the cost of a typical incubator). The Extreme story is impressive for how routinely the students seem to be able to transform constraints into solutions.

One aspect of the approach used by the Extreme course is, as one of the course leaders Professor Jim Patell put it, "to step away from the partner's pre-conceptions of what the solution path looks like … chances are their path is worth looking at, but let's not presume that."[24] In the case of the Embrace infant warmer, for example, the partner wanted a better hospital-level incubator, but when the students went to Nepal, they discovered that the overwhelming majority of premature babies weren't born in hospitals, and would never make it to a hospital. So the solution would need to work outside a hospital in a rural environment. They challenged one of the fundamental assumptions of the partner by asking a different question: not "How do we make a cheaper incubator?" but "How do we improve a premature baby's chances of survival?" Starting there led them to a different path and a more effective and far cheaper solution.

Quite apart from some of the inventive solutions they have found, one of the most fascinating aspects of our conversation with the leadership team there was about the psychology of the students while on the course.

Stanford is one of the most difficult schools to get into on the planet, with less than 6 percent of applicants accepted; its students are very smart. But being smart enough to get into Stanford is no guarantee you will get into Extreme; the course is heavily oversubscribed, with applicants selected as much on temperament as smarts. They look for self-aware team players who collaborate well, are passionate, adventurous, and resourceful (which they define as being "inspired, not discouraged, by constraints"). Smarts may even be an impediment to a student, making it hard for them to use the inevitable failures productively.[25]

The way the students on the team relate to each other while trying to solve the difficult issues of their brief is an essential part of success: working together for the first time, under pressure, and in emotionally charged environments—like rural hospitals in India, where their solutions are literally a matter of life or death—can be intense.

"We deal with situations that make you cry," says Professor Patell, a situation made more acute by one of the principles of design thinking: to build deep empathy with the user. Pamela Pavkov, one of the students working on a low-cost breathing device for babies with pneumonia, spoke of her firsthand experiences with mothers and their very sick children in a Bangladeshi hospital:

> I would describe the impact as "the moment." The boundaries completely collapsed, they fueled my motivation. I don't care if I'm hungry, sick, tired, lonely—I'm going to be there, I'm going to keep working.[26]

The ability to manage and productively channel all of the strong emotions that occur on these projects is another quality that the d.school selects for. "Cool under pressure" is a criterion they define as "you can channel stress and emotions toward focus and progress." At the outset of the course, the students are coached in how to have difficult conversations with each other during the design process, and how to channel the empathy they will develop with their users into a productive process. "It's highly valuable to be intentional about the emotional state of the teams," says Jim Patell.

So the work the Stanford designers are doing in the field represents an acid test for the rest of us: principled, intelligent people working iteratively in highly constrained environments, with consequences that are at once high-impact, physically proximate, and very visible to them. Far from suppressing the negative emotions that come from that, we need to recognize that they can be very productive in fostering the tenacity necessary for success. We must learn to harness emotions of all kinds to drive our ambition. We must find a way to make it personal.

## ACTIVATING EMOTIONS: CHAPTER SUMMARY

- When confronted with a truly unreasonable brief, we may try multiple approaches, uncover layers of constraints, and fail often. The kind of perseverance required can exhaust talent and professional commitment alone. It will require personal motivation.

- Scientists have found a strong link between success in working around obstacles and having an emotional connection to the goal. To make constraints beautiful, we need to identify the activating emotions able to fuel more creative tenacity.

- An organization's purpose may provide some of this connection, but we want to go beyond that to personalize the emotions. We'll want the full range: fear, greed, and frustration as much as excitement, love, and desire. And we'll want individuals to find the tug of both the negative and positive emotions around the project.

- Emotions are at their most potent when they contrast. The science suggests we should spend time indulging in the fantasy of success and dwelling on the realities of what failure would feel like—the tension between them prompts us to make a plan and act on it more than positive thinking alone.

- Once team members have found their emotional connections to the brief, team leaders can build an emotionally charged narrative around them to energize the team when necessary.

- When making constraints beautiful, motivation is method. Breakthroughs happen when a propelling question meets strong emotions. Without activating the right emotions, it will be too easy to regress to the victim mindset.

# THE FERTILE ZERO

Learning from people who succeeded with next to nothing

**THIS CHAPTER FOCUSES ON:**

1. What can we learn from people whose constraint is that they have very little or nothing of an essential resource?

2. What kinds of new capabilities and ways of thinking will that demand of us?

> **Mick ... was natural. It was electrifying the way he could work those small spaces, as a singer and a dancer; fascinating to watch and work with ... the spins, the moves.... And he's still good, though to my mind it's dissipated on the big stages. Somewhere ... he got unnatural. He forgot how good he was in that small spot.**
>
> —Keith Richards[1]

**The Resource Curse** is a term coined by the economist Richard Auty to describe the tendency for countries that are rich in natural resources to perform worse economically than countries that have none. While this is not inevitable (those prudent Norwegians), the possession of such resource wealth all too often leads to economic and political behaviors that, in fact, limit the sustainable growth potential of the country, rather than accelerate it.[2]

The apparently counterintuitive idea that less wealth leads to stronger performance is illustrated by the journey made by the McLaren Formula One team after the EU banned tobacco sponsorship in 2005. Tobacco had bankrolled the business and the lavish lifestyle its eleven teams enjoyed—the private jets that flew the teams to the races, the best hotels, the abundance of resources. And the concomitant mindset in Formula One, at the time, was that money bought performance.

The announcement of the ban was greeted by many in the business as a death knell. How could they possibly replace that income? Even if Formula One survived, they reasoned, it would be in a vastly diminished form, with a reduced number of teams. But Ron Dennis, the leader of McLaren, took a different view. He asked the entire McLaren team to examine everything they were doing, in minute detail, and see how they could be better. Their focus was now on making the car go faster and making themselves as competitive as possible in securing a new sponsor; everything else went. They had to cut where appropriate, but also change methodology and invest in new people, technology, and practices where it would improve performance against one of these two objectives.

A newer generation, without the same hunger, sense of high stakes, or preparedness to take risks, fall into a more measured, stable, and somehow less inventive step.

But surely a complete absence of a particular resource must be a disadvantage that can't be overcome. It must make us a victim—how can one transform nothing?

This chapter is going to explore how and why zero can be fertile. We'll consider the Zero Constraint—the complete (or nearly complete) absence of a critical resource—in one particular field (communication and marketing) as an acid test for *A Beautiful Constraint*. One need not be a marketing professional to gain insights from this: whatever our professions, we all need to communicate and engage, inside or outside our organizations.

We'll focus on six key themes:

- **Drama and surprise:** How lack of budget (and a naturally engaged audience) forces us to look for greater impact when and where we do communicate.
- **Being interesting on the inside:** How, if we can't afford to tell our story ourselves, it pushes us to build a brand that makes others want to talk about us on our behalf.
- **Making a secondary medium your primary idea platform:** How, if we can't use or afford primary marketing media, we find the opportunity to elevate the role of secondary ones.
- **Alliance to scale:** How, if we can't afford communication scale on our own, it pushes us to develop new kinds of partnerships and build a new kind of brand neighborhood.
- **Using other people's money, time, and resource:** How scarcity of the resource we need most forces us to access it in the resources of others.
- **Commercial innovation:** How the need to secure those resources pushes us to create new kinds of value and currency in these key relationships.

## Drama and surprise

Industrial theatre is a form of theatre used to communicate critical messages in the mining business in South Africa. Their management needs to inform and educate the miners about subjects that range from life-and-death issues (safety procedures) to the merely very serious (financial management), while facing significant constraints in doing so. Language, for instance, is an unreliable currency here: mine workers are typically drawn from nine different ethnic groups with different languages, not including foreign workers. And the unionized audience is not there voluntarily; they have been bussed in to hear these messages from their employers, and are often cynical about what they might be about to hear as they take their seats.

Faced with these constraints, industrial theatre has developed as a powerful, hard-working medium for disarming and engaging this kind of audience. It offers a number of advantages that informational video, for instance, cannot: creating a visceral rather than an intellectual involvement with the issue, letting the audience see their peers engaging with and warming up to a character and topic, and powerfully prompting the audience's own participation by stimulating their imaginations to complete a scenario that is only half-sketched on stage in gesture and sound.

Nick Warren is one of the foremost creators of South African Industrial Theatre. Previously a writer for *Sesame Street*, where he found himself working on challenges such as how to use the program to tackle child abuse, he has learned that there are a few essential rules for success in industrial theatre. You have to warm up your audience very, very quickly. You need to limit language and make it an emphatically physical performance, be completely honest and true, engage the audience's imagination to complete the story themselves, make it something they weren't expecting. When what you need to get across is a matter of life and death, he notes dryly, you can't bore the audience.[4]

What is striking about industrial theatre is not only how it has evolved into a powerful communication form in the face of those apparent constraints. In many ways, the rationale for the way it works is one that many of us in business face ourselves: we need to engage around very important areas of communication (if we want to stay in business, anyway) with an audience who can be disinterested if not downright cynical, and who, even if they are fluent in our language, are offering us only part of their attention. If we think of it this way, we are most of us in the industrial theatre business today—and the use of drama is particularly important to those with something important to communicate, but little to communicate it with.

BrewDog, as we have seen in earlier chapters, is a brewery on a mission, with a fierce ambition to change the way people think about beer and to unseat what they see

*BrewDog limited edition Never Mind the Anabolics*

as the bland mainstream brewing establishment. Drama is a key strategy in delivering this ambition, and lies in the nature, name, and presentation of their products as much as anything. In the five years following their birth, alongside their day-to-day range, they've brewed and sold what at the time was the strongest beer on the planet (Tactical Nuclear Penguin), packaged bottles in road kill and taxidermy (the End of History), fermented a brew at the bottom of the sea (Sunk Punk), and made a special edition with substances banned at the London 2012 Olympics (Never Mind The Anabolics).

Why all this drama? Because they set up, co-founder James Watt says, with no money and no budget. While beer industry marketing has traditionally been all about advertising and how much one can spend in the usual channels, they didn't want to compete in that space, and in reality, they couldn't anyway, because they didn't have any money.[5]

The budget constraint forced them to focus instead on the free but highly cluttered channels that are social media and online platforms. There, Watt notes, the currency is not money, but the ability to connect through intelligent and genuinely engaging content. The drama of this sequence of launches is perhaps, in its own way, a kind of industrial theatre, offering the unexpected and engaging the imagination. The launches of their dramatically named concepts were accompanied by visual material that would travel, from the two founders vlogging in penguin suits to photos of undersea beer tanks with a pirate flag buoy.

What makes this drama intelligent and strategic for someone with no marketing budget, rather than simply an amusing flair for mild outrage and self-publicity, is the difference between drama and communication.

### Drama commands attention

If you can't spend your way into being noticed, one of your strongest strategic options is to behave your way into being noticed. Drama, and specifically being more dramatic in some important regard than anyone else in your surroundings, is the most competitive way to focus attention on you.

### Drama engages emotionally and stimulates a response

Drama engages us first through the emotions—it is the nature of drama to arouse an emotional response first, and a more rational response second. An emotional response doesn't allow us to be unaffected—we take a point of view of some kind in response to it.

## Drama provokes conversation

Humans are drama junkies. The dramas of our day, big and small, and our reactions to them, make up much of our social conversation. Feed it.

## Drama creates a memory and an association

Drama's brief intensity leaves a memory and an association. A brand—and anything of lasting impact—succeeds through building memories and associations.

So drama is not a poor brand's media budget. Drama is a strategically more powerful way to behave, but one that brands with the resource curse seldom feel compelled to employ.

Drama is, of course, contextual. One is not obliged to stuff road kill with beer bottles to create it. The online photography store Photojojo's breathlessly enthusiastic personality is one of the qualities that sets it apart as a brand, and it infuses that into every contact with its user: our first receipt had six excited exclamation marks splashed across it, for example; we have yet to receive a receipt from anybody else with even one. Even a little drama can make a receipt memorable as a brand touch point.

Closely linked to drama is surprise. The two are different: small surprises are not dramatic, and high drama may not be surprising on repeated viewing. For instance, we may no longer be surprised by what Air New Zealand does in their safety videos, though we still find them engagingly dramatic. But surprise, like drama, is an efficient way to create greater impact with fewer resources.

Substantive research has been done on the effect of surprise in marketing. Overall, it has the effect of emotional amplification: unexpected gains bring more pleasure than expected gains (when you order a smartphone lens from Photojojo, they send you a small plastic dinosaur to give you something fun to take a picture of straightaway, for example), and unexpected losses cause more pain than those that were anticipated (unusually high overage charges on your cell plan, perhaps). People who were surprised evaluated the same product attribute more positively than when they weren't. Surprise can focus attention and improve memory. It can enhance customer loyalty and positive word-of-mouth.[6]

Warby Parker's Neil Blumenthal, beginning, like any start-up, without a lot of money to spend on communications, talks about how the inclusion of surprise into an annual report turned it into one of the eyewear company's most effective pieces of marketing:

*We launched an interactive annual report—and you might be thinking "Who would want to read an annual report?" Well, instead of boring financials, we talked about the inner workings of the company. What are our highest call volume hours during the day? What are common misspelled keyword searches? What is the beer that we drink during Happy Hour? We gave our customers a look behind the curtain and what it's*

SUNDAY · DECEMBER 29, 2013

What we know: we've sold 574 monocles this year to date.

What we don't know: how many monocles were used in service of Halloween costumes like Mr. Peanut, Karl Marx, British statesman Joseph Chamberlain, or Winona Ryder in *Heathers*.

What we're fairly sure of: Dogs and monocles go together like spaghetti and meatballs.

SHARE: **f** 🐦 | data, culture, collections

*An excerpt from Warby Parker's 2013 annual report. Photo: Noel Camardo.*

*like at Warby Parker. We thought this was a neat way to engage with our customers. It ended up being this great marketing tool, because it was shared, and led to our three highest consecutive days of sales.*[7]

We can see drama and surprise coincide in the case of Professor Sir André Geim, now perhaps best known for his role in the breakthrough development of graphene. Earlier in his career, the two-time Nobel Laureate found himself unable to interest the scientific community in his discovery of an unexpected effect of electromagnetism: in certain conditions, it could levitate water droplets. Frustrated by the lack of response from his peers, Geim realised he needed to do something more dramatic and surprising: he needed to levitate something living. It was only when he levitated a tiny frog that he finally got the attention from his peer group he had been looking for. Even in science, you need a wow factor, Geim remarked.[8]

In their own ways, Photojojo, Air New Zealand, and Geim each aimed for wow and delivered it. The combination of a big ambition and a zero constraint drove them to seek more impact from their actions than they would have using a conventional resource.

## Interesting on the inside

Sailor Jerry rum is one of the hottest spirits brands in the world, and yet it didn't start advertising until it was shipping over a million cases a year. Its creator, Steven Grasse, is a serial creator of brands that lean into the zero constraint: besides Sailor Jerry, Grasse has created Hendricks Gin for William Grant, launched a wine (Spodee), relaunched a beer (Narragansett), and a spirit that deliberately defies all the conventions of spirits (Art in the Age of Mechanical Reproduction). Like Nick Warren, he emphasizes the importance of being true to the tribe you want to engage, and the intimate understanding and empathy that demands.

Grasse's company, Quaker Mercantile, was originally an advertising agency working for other clients. A natural entrepreneurialism, coupled with a frustration about how much of their advice his clients would follow, led Grasse to launching his own brands with a clear point of view, in which conventional advertising has a very small role, even when selling hundreds of thousands of cases. Grasse is the first to acknowledge that it is supposed to be impossible to build a brand in a market as competitive as spirits without advertising. "Sailor Jerry was not supposed to work," he reflects. "You're not supposed to be able to go up against Captain Morgan, spend nothing on advertising, and win, and we did."[9]

So how do you build to a million cases a year in an advertising-driven business without an advertising budget? Sailor Jerry's constraint was an impasse between Quaker Mercantile and their distributor: the latter wouldn't invest in advertising because Grasse insisted on complete creative control. So the Sailor Jerry clothing brand, which the rum was originally launched to promote, became the lifestyle brand that promoted the rum, accompanied by grassroots support of the punk bands whose ethos was at the brand's heart. "I didn't know rums were supposed to behave in a particular way," says Grasse, "so I made mine behave more like Jack Daniels." He realized how large it had become only when William Grant told him that, since it had grown to become their biggest brand, they couldn't continue to distribute it unless they owned it.

Grasse emphasizes "being interesting on the inside." If you don't have the budget to talk about yourself to others, you have to get others to talk about you for you, and this means that you have to make every aspect of what you offer interesting, inside and out.

> *When we create a product, it needs to be as interesting inside as it is outside, to give people lots to write about … so if you look at Hendricks, the bottle is interesting, the liquid is interesting, and the whole story adds up. It can't just be window dressing.*[10]

The day Grasse sold Sailor Jerry to William Grant, he came up with the idea for his next brand, which he called Art in the Age of Mechanical Reproduction, based on the idea that the more art is reproduced, the more it loses its aura. And the same was true of us, he felt: the more we as human beings buy "reproduced crap from Wal-Mart," the more we lose. So he wanted to create a genuinely original spirit, one that wasn't in the legal categories of gin, vodka, or rum, which you had to know to look for. The four variants to date are Root, Snap, Rhubarb Tea and Sage, all based on pre-industrial American folk recipes, most of which, he says, he got from his mother:

> *Root is based on a root tea recipe, and root tea is what evolved into root beer. Sage is a colonial garden gin; back in the day, they used to make gin out of whatever was in*

*the garden, and it's a gin without junipers, so it's not technically a gin. Rhubarb Tea is based off the fact that Ben Franklin brought rhubarb seeds to America and gave them to his friend, John Bartram, who was the King's botanist, and they experimented and made a herbal tea that was medicinal, called Rhubarb Tea. So, they're all very strange, very different, and they've created more buzz than anything else I've ever done.*[11]

Each variant is not a flavor, but a good story. People don't tell each other about flavors, they tell each other stories.

Grasse notes that his model is not supposed to work, especially in such a fiercely competitive market, but he is not the only one pursuing it. Betabrand sells clothes with a funny story woven in—most famously their Cordarounds, a range of corduroy pants with ridges running horizontally instead of vertically. Integrating the story to the product is so important to their success model—to get people to talk about them for them—that they define their motto as "99 percent fiction, 1 percent fashion." More recently, they have incentivized their 40,000-strong consumer base to post pictures of themselves wearing Betabrand clothing, as part of their "Model Citizen" initiative. Many brands offer this kind of opportunity, but as a supplement to other marketing initiatives. For Betabrand, though, it was a primary awareness driver. Their solution was a piece of technology that allowed Betabrand to respond to anyone who submitted a photo with a unique URL that turned them into "Model Number One" on the Betabrand

site: their photo is the main photo, they are the main model, and they have a buy button over their head. By elevating the photo—at least at that URL—to humorously make the photo-sharer the main model, however bad the photo, they created something those photo-sharers in turn shared with all their friends. To date, over 20,000 photos have been uploaded and shared. Many of these are glimpses into stories in themselves: a man with a megaphone outside an Arkansas record store, yoga on office desks, a cat with a bow tie. Betabrand is still small—it has grown to a turnover of $6 million—but has a customer demand that is usually three times what's in stock.[12]

> # The point is not about earned versus shared—the point is what you have to focus your energy on to make it shared.

Categorizing this kind of strategy as earned media is to miss the point here. The point is not about what makes it shared—the point is what you have to focus your energy on doing to make it shared: making the product interesting, the packaging interesting, the variant interesting, and the marketing idea interesting. And not just interesting—so interesting that people want to share and talk about them with their friends. Brands and businesses with communications budgets don't have to do this; they can pay to do the talking themselves. Without an urgent need to do it, it receives less commitment and focus from senior leaders—and the results are consequently less vital; it is a side effect of the resource curse. But when you can't spend money to do the talking yourself, you have to spend your time, instead, making sure that what you produce is worth talking about. And you focus the most senior and talented people in the company on making that happen, as Grasse and Betabrand founder Chris Lindland are doing themselves.

The Australian beauty brand Aesop has grown to 43 stores worldwide, with a turnover of $82 million, without advertising. Known for using quotes from Mies van der Rohe and Camus to illustrate its desire to put intelligence into beauty, Aesop actively prohibits any part of the brand experience from being less than interesting. Store staff are not allowed to make small talk about the weather as a way to strike up conversations with customers, for instance. "Customers do not benefit from benign and obvious staff commentary," they observe. "If it's raining, it's evident to all that it is, and it doesn't particularly require further discussion."[13]

Their stores are obliged, it seems, to be always interesting on the inside.

Which brings us to the third effect of the zero constraint: finding the real potential in secondary media because you are forced to make them your primary platform for news and ideas.

## Making a secondary medium your primary idea platform

The Loi Evin is a law passed in France in the mid-1980s, restricting the nature and channels of alcohol advertising. Advertising for any kind of alcohol was no longer permitted on television or cinema, and where used in static media like print or posters, it could be used only under very restricted terms: all they could show other than the brand name was a bottle, a glass, ways of serving the drink, and the means of distribution. Anything else, including the use of people, was forbidden.

In France, at the time, Heineken was a distant challenger to the market leader, Kronenbourg, which was roughly ten times its size, although Heineken commanded a 30 percent price premium over its rival. Not content with the status quo, the French marketing team developed a twofold strategy to grow. While apparently neutered in advertising, and with the most effective media lost to it, the Heineken team and their agency nevertheless found a witty way to use a corkscrew with two outstretched arms to playfully convey the spirit of beer refreshment in the static media that were still open to them (the corkscrew appeared to relax in an ice bucket of beer as if it were a swimming pool, for example). The creative constraints around how they could advertise precipitated a more memorable idea than the one that preceded it before the law was passed.

But perhaps the most interesting effect of the advertising restriction was the effect on their structural packaging—an area in which they had, like most beer brands with advertising, previously been relatively sleepy. Heineken France began by rethinking the way they segmented their beer range, and offering a range of beer bottle sizes and shapes much more carefully tailored to each type of beer occasion. Beyond occasion-specific sizing and long-necked bottles, they then moved to use the physical pack as a primary canvas for news and creativity. The non-reclosable aluminium beer bottle designed by Ora Ito took a familiar pack size and product and gave it an entirely new kind of desirability. Every two years, new editions of the bottle were accompanied by a stylish, limited-edition aluminium bottle that was sold only in the high-end city outlets. They took a mainstream premium beer, if you like, and gave it the codes of an upmarket spirit brand like Absolut.

Since the Loi Evin was passed, Heineken has grown 600 percent in a finite French market, deposing Kronenbourg as market leader in both volume and value by 2013, while maintaining its profitable 30 percent premium. Kronenbourg was subject to the same communication constraints as Heineken, over the same period of time, so clearly not everyone finds zero fertile. Perhaps the market leader simply lacked the mindset and motivation to find the new kind of solution so powerfully developed by its challenger Heineken. It found itself guillotined as a consequence.[14]

Brands with a significant marketing budget focus their creativity within the frameworks of the usual channels. A brand unable to afford or use those channels still needs to be fresh and innovative, so their creativity is forced to find a different medium. Structural packaging, an annual report, the in-flight safety video—the constraint pushes them to unlock potential in assets which, for the resource-cursed, remain overlooked dullards of necessity and hygiene.

## Alliance to scale

Sir Lawrence Freedman is the Professor of War Studies at Kings College, London. In *Strategy: A History*, his magisterial review of what strategy has come to mean, from chimpanzee colonies to Robert McKee via the Trojan Wars and Henry Ford, one of the central and common strategic capabilities he emphazises is the ability to form coalitions. Genghis Khan's empire was founded on his initial ability to unify the disparate Mongol tribes. It took alliance with the Prussians for the British to defeat Napoleon. Churchill's key focus, on becoming Prime Minister, was to get the United States into the Second World War to help the Allies.[15]

The apparently modern form and appellation of the collaborative economy has its roots in a core strategic idea which is surprisingly underused in modern business, but critical for the fertile zero: if you have a scarcity of a particular kind of resource that is important to you, you need the capability to form a coalition with someone else who has a tradable abundance in it, a discipline and tool for which we explored in Chapter 5.

As we saw in that chapter, Virgin America did not technically have a communications budget of zero at launch, but they had such a relative deficit of it compared to the competition (they estimated Southwest had an annual communications budget of $200 million) that they were forced to look for new ways to get in front of the consumer. They formed all kinds of surprising alliances, from Victoria's Secret, with whom they did on-board fashion shows, to Google, with whom they debuted the Chromebook, and method, with whom they provided a little glamour in the bathrooms of economy class. Each of these partners willingly shared their resources for access to something Virgin did have: planes and passengers.

citizenM, the budget hotel with luxury aspirations, had very little in the way of any budgets at launch—building hotels is as capital-intensive as buying planes—but a partnership with the Swiss furniture company Vitra turned their lobbies into living showrooms and furnished them for free. And Vitra now has showrooms in some of the most stylish cities of the world, simply for the cost of furnishing them. As Robin Chadha, the CMO of the hotel chain, says, a hotel lobby like theirs, where guests linger to drink wine, is a very different experience from a furniture showroom, where you might sit in a chair for ten seconds. A similar partnership with the Dutch book company Mendo encourages guests to leaf through some of the best photography and fashion books in the world. And a Vitra catalogue is available in the lobby of every citizenM hotel, in the event that you get so comfortable that you just have to have the same chair at home.

Faced with their own zero constraint following the passing of the Loi Evin, the French Heineken team forged a different kind of alliance—not with another kind of business, but within Heineken, with "the center" (or global headquarters) in Holland. In many companies, the central-innovation function can have a difficult time implementing globally, finding that the regional businesses are not always as open, ready, or cooperative as the center might like. But Heineken France made a strategic decision that if they were constrained in television and cinema advertising, then innovation would need to be a primary growth driver for them, and they would grab with both hands the big innovations the center was working on—reciprocally feeding their own thinking and ideas into the center by way of exchange. France was the first of Heineken's markets to launch the centrally developed beer-keg packaging format, for example, and more recently the BeerTender, the home delivery device engineered in partnership with Krups. This closely forged relationship proved a critical source for the flow of the different kind of news and innovation that drove Heineken's share gain against Kronenbourg within the constraint of the Loi Evin in France.[16]

## Other people's resources

Central to the fertility that the zero constraint forces is development of the capability to draw on other people's resources to...

- Promote our brand and business for us.
- Give us a crucial capability or resource that we lack.
- Do some or all of the work for us in a key area at a scale we are unable to achieve on our own.
- Do some or all of the work for us in a key area at a speed we are unable to achieve on our own.
- Enable us to offer something to another partner that will make them more likely to partner with us, and deliver an enhanced, more attractive offer and experience.

… and all in a way that is open, or mutually beneficial, rather than exploitative. Far from being a victim to the constraint, we can develop a way of overcoming it that may well also lend a scale and impact we could not have achieved on our own.

The world of the zero constraint is full of examples of people and teams working through how to use other people's resources—be they time, money, work, or ideas—to promote the agendas of both parties. There is an important difference between this and what we mean by an alliance. Alliance means explicitly linking with another brand, in part to benefit from the image, scale, and reputation that brand and business brings to our offer. Using other people's resources, on the other hand, means accessing value that we need, without its source being necessarily visible to the outside world at all. Eric Ryan of method, for example, used to take photographs of all the innovation, across a range of categories, that he saw on what he called his foreign "strategy safaris" abroad, and reviewed them upon his return with a small, cross-disciplinary team. "Let's use the world as our R&D department," was his budget-constrained insight. "Each of those innovations has had hundreds of thousands of dollars of other people's money spent proving the insight and testing the concept; all the innovation we could ever want is already out there—we just need to find it and work out how to make it relevant and powerful to our market." Elsewhere in this book, we have seen that giffgaff uses its customers as its customer service department, Duolingo its users as translators, and Threadless its community as its creative department and chief buyer, in effect.

We discussed the concept of accessing other people's resources in the previous chapter, along with a tool and structure for thinking about it in a more disciplined way. We saw there that inventiveness in finding the source of a resource has to be complemented by inventiveness in persuading that source to allow us to access it. The next section, then, focuses on a particular kind of innovation and value creation that this requirement demands: commercial innovation, and the creation of new kinds of mutual value.

## Commercial innovation

We tend to think of innovation as the domain of product or experience engineers, with support from the insights and marketing team. Yet at the heart of seeing, creating and cementing the relationships that allow access to other people's resources, as well as formal alliances or coalitions, is an entirely different form of innovation: commercial innovation.

Vitaminwater's innovative commercial relationship with rapper 50 Cent, in which he became a significant shareholder in return for promoting the brand and allowing himself to be used on the packaging, is famous for making both of them wealthier; Vitaminwater traded what they had (equity) for what he had (fame, appeal, and a loud mouth) and made it legal. Before the 2011 World Cup, England's Rugby Football Union, wanting to motivate their team to win, calculated that they needed a pot of £2.5 million to offer the right level of incentive for the team to share. Not, unfortunately, having £2.5 million, they had to commercially innovate: they placed a bet of £250,000, spread across several bookmakers, that England would win. The ambition of this commercially creative masterstroke was undermined only by England's lamentable performance in the tournament itself; the bookies were never required to reach into their pockets. When Steven Grasse sold his brand to distiller and distributor William Grant, the deal came with an embedded contract that paid his company, Quaker Mercantile, to be their key marketing partner for the next ten years.

In 2007, Yves Behar (designer of the One Laptop Per Child computer) became the Chief Creative Officer of Aliph, now makers of Jawbone and the UP band. Behar's design company, fuseproject, had been designing products for Aliph for a number of years in a fee-for-service relationship and, despite some stellar design work, the company was struggling and about to lay off staff. CEO Hosain Rahman faced a dilemma: how to retain the services of the star designer to improve the products, without a budget to pay for it. The solution: make fuseproject an equity partner, a deal that has paid off many times over.[17] This kind of relationship has become quite common in Silicon Valley, where cash-strapped start-ups use equity to attract top talent. For Behar's firm, this commercial innovation launched a new, on-going business model, too. They continue fee-based relationships with corporate clients, develop equity-based partnerships with start-ups, and use the returns to continue to fund their on-going commitments to civic projects (like OLPC), which are very often constraint-driven. Their latest project is a partnership with the Mexican government and Augen Optics to provide free, cool, customizable eyewear for a half a million Mexican school children who can't afford or won't wear glasses.

But perhaps the most interesting example for us here comes from Cape Town. We saw in Chapter Six Ravi Naidoo's motivations and emotions around the founding of Design Indaba—at once inspired by the possibilities for South Africa following Nelson

Mandela's election, and concerned for the future of his country if there was not the economic progress to match the political breakthrough. And we saw that his ambition, while considerable—to create an ideas exchange that would transform the world's relationship with South Africa as well as South Africa's relationship with itself—was also an ambition without a budget. As such, a key issue in the early days was how to be able to afford to attract the world's best talent—people accustomed to flying business class on international flights—despite a poor exchange rate between the local currency and the dollar or pound sterling. And Naidoo recognized that there was a second, related challenge of funding: how to fund it in a sustainable way, so that he could be confident that his idea exchange would not grow vigorously in the first year or two, only to wither as the money dried up.

He commercially innovated in two key ways. The first was in creating economic value for each party involved, to enable them to donate their services or resources while feeling they were benefitting economically from doing so. For his international speakers from the world of creativity and design, this meant the chance for local commissions, besides the chance to network and see what their peers were doing. Alongside, he offered them the best of South Africa as an incentive—accommodation in the luxurious Mount Nelson Hotel and the experience of the Blue Train, for example. These, in turn, he persuaded to donate rooms and seats for the opportunity to host some of the world's most influential opinion leaders, at a time when South Africa was opening up to a new world of global tourism. He negotiated, in other words, real value for both sides at no cost to himself and his project.

The second piece of commercial innovation was to bring the commercial logic and discipline of sports sponsorship to design event sponsorship. South Africa is a country of sports fanatics, and big sponsors understand the strategic rationale of long-term sponsorships in sport, so Naidoo recognised there was an opportunity for him to apply a sports sponsorship model to a design event. He proposed and secured three-year sponsorship deals with blue chip sponsors that would cover the conference and exhibition costs. He reinforced this strategic rigor, and the language that his sponsors felt comfortable with, through commissioning an analysis of the economic impact of each conference by the head of the Economics Department at the University of Cape Town Graduate School of Business, and creating a virtuous circle that would help the sponsorship renewal when the time came.

Held over three days in February every year, Design Indaba is now the largest design conference and exhibition in the world. Consistently sold out, even during the economic downturn, it has put South Africa, and the creative talents within it, on the global creative map. It and South Africa are, says Naidoo, proof that even the most intractable problems can be neutralized by the will of people.[18]

## The benefits of zero

This chapter set out to ask two questions: Can even zero (or almost zero) of a particular kind of resource be fertile? And, if so, in what ways? We have looked almost entirely within the world of business and enterprise here, and well-networked teams with adjacent resources and available partners, because that is the situation that most of us are in. And we deliberately focused on one particular sphere—communicating and engaging with a desired group—because even if we are not all in the business of marketing, we are all in the business of communicating and connecting with people with too much information and not enough time. While there is a significant skew to the territory we have chosen, the findings may have a broader relevance.

We can see from these examples that, yes, the zero constraint can be enormously fertile, but doesn't start to be so until there are consequences that matter to the team facing it. While these may not be as literally life-or-death as those necessitating industrial theatre or MacLaren's root and branch re-examination of all their processes and practices, the

## We have no money, so we will have to think.

—Sir Ernest Rutherford[19]

combination of a big ambition and the consequences of failure are the preconditions for new life here. For these are not brands and businesses that are somehow surviving in spite of their zero. They are brands that are determined to grow, and are growing. The fertility in their lack of budget comes through the tension between what they are determined to achieve, and what they have with which to achieve it.

Coupled with that ambition, this kind of constraint seems potentially to have a range of beneficial impacts:

- The first is a propensity to use ways of communicating that achieve greater impact, particularly the use of drama and surprise, which heighten levels of attention, emotional connection, degree of response, memorability, association, and word of mouth.
- The second is playing out the ruthless logic around how to get people talking about you, if you can't afford to tell them about you yourself (or don't, like Steven Grasse, believe that is the best way to genuinely engage). If you want to get people talking about you, you have to be interesting on the inside.

Everything is an opportunity here, from the direction the cord runs around your pants to the story behind the seeds that your flavor is made from. If you can somehow work the King's botanist into your origin story, this seems to be a plus.

- The third impact is being forced to promote secondary or entirely overlooked channels (such as an annual report) as a primary piece of communication, and unlocking the hidden potential within it to communicate your news and ideas.
- The fourth impact is being pushed to link up with other partners from completely different categories, who could use their resources to help you achieve the impact you need.
- The fifth impact is the accompanying impetus to develop new forms of mutual economic value around the collective potential benefit from the joint venture, to secure those partnerships.

Perhaps the ghost in the machine impact of the zero constraint is also that of forcing an unflinching honesty. In a company with large budgets, the development of marketing and communications is full of small dishonesties: "Yes, this is our very best work," "Yes, I think this time we've really nailed it," "We think this promotion works very hard for the brand," "Those four would be great additions at this meeting," and so on.

But if our ambition is high and our constraint is almost absolute, it forces a different level of truthfulness on us; small dishonesties start to carry very high penalties.

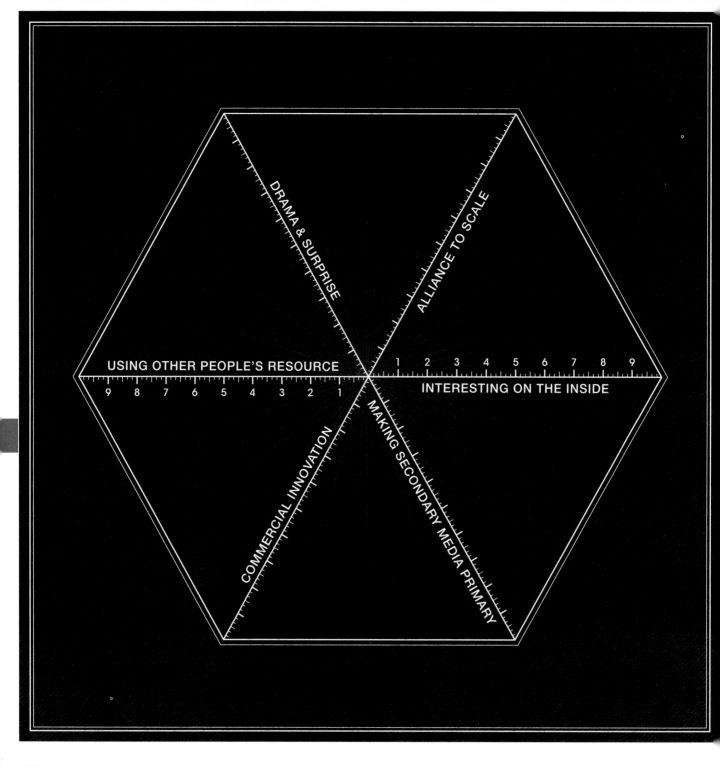

## Mapping ourselves against the learning from this chapter

Let's use this chapter as stimulus. Look at Figure 7—it will be most relevant to you if you are in the business of marketing or communications.

- Each of the six axes represents one of the dimensions we have discussed in this chapter: strategic behaviors stimulated by having very little communications budget.

- Each of the six axes has a scale from 0 to 10. How much are we actively using each of these in our approach to marketing and communication? Assess each individually and then join up the assessed scores on each of the axes to show the overall shape we currently represent.

- Where on this map are we underperforming and why?

- Is it the size of our ambition or the current limits of our inventiveness around the constraint that is holding us back, for instance?

- Where is the biggest opportunity—and what is the shape we need to be to succeed?

- What would it mean for us to build some or all of these dimensions more explicitly into the DNA of our next marketing or communications plan? Of our next innovation?

- What would be the three key differences in how we would think and behave?

*Figure 7: A tool for assessing marketing and communications behavior on a zero budget*

## When Ambition Is Greater Than Resource

There are endless ways to engage audiences without communication budgets, if we are honest about what it will take to do so. People have short memories: there was a world before any of the forms of modern media, when nobody had a TV budget because there was no TV, so all the world was a showman or showwoman.

Elizabeth Arden designed red lipstick for both the suffragettes and the U.S. servicewomen in the Second World War. Sir Thomas Lipton, known now for the tea brand, but who started as an entrepreneurial grocer, was in the habit of importing giant cheeses for his shops' Christmas displays that were so large that, on one occasion, they had to be hauled to the shop through the streets by an elephant. Tabasco used to tour America with a show called "The Burlesque Opera of Tabasco." In 1784, Joseph Bramah, who gives his name to the building that houses our London office, designed a lock that was so hard to open without the right key that he placed it in the street window of his shop and offered a prize of 200 guineas (roughly $60,000 in today's money) to anyone who was able to open it. It wasn't cracked until the second half of the following century—by which time, of course, the lock had long since become famous.

Even zero, then, can be fertile if the motivation, mindset and creativity are there. Pier Luigi Sigismondi tells of his experience working with C.K. Prahalad on the board of Hindustan Unilever, and the great business strategist drawing a simple equation on the pad in front of him:

$$A \gg R$$

When ambition is exponentially greater than resource, said Prahalad, that's when real innovation happens.[20]

## THE FERTILE ZERO: CHAPTER SUMMARY

- This chapter represents an acid test: In what ways can having next to nothing of a key resource be fertile?

- It explores brand and businesses with significant ambition but a negligible communications budget, and how this combination led them to think and behave.

- It outlines six behaviors and capabilities this zero stimulated in them:

  - Drama and surprise. Lack of budget (and audience engagement) forces us to generate greater impact when and where we do communicate.

  - Being interesting on the inside. If we can't afford to tell people ourselves, we must build a brand that makes others want to talk about us.

  - Making a secondary, overlooked medium your primary idea platform. How, if we can't use or afford primary marketing media, we need to elevate the role of—and find the hidden potential in—secondary ones.

  - Alliance to scale. If we can't afford communication scale on our own, this pushes us to develop new kinds of partnerships and a new brand neighborhood.

  - Using other people's money, time, and resources. Scarcity of the resource we need most forces us to find it elsewhere.

  - Commercial innovation. The need to secure those resources pushes us to create new kinds of value and currency in these relationships.

- We do not need to be a marketing professional to learn from this: whatever our professions, we all need to communicate and engage, inside or outside our organizations.

# 8 CONSTRAINT-DRIVEN CULTURES

How big companies have learned to love constraints

1. Are there examples of large companies that now routinely embrace constraints...

2. ... even if they have little history of doing so?

3. Are their methods replicable for those without experience in doing it?

**This book is neither** a paean to brilliant mavericks nor a buffet of hacks for cash-strapped start-ups. It describes a way for everyone to progress, regardless of size, including large companies.

But so far much of the discussion has been about individuals and teams, albeit sometimes as part of bigger organizations. So can this really work at a more systemic level in a large organization? More particularly, can one teach a large organizational dog new cultural tricks—if a company has not behaved in this inventive way historically, is there any evidence that these behaviors can be acquired and embraced late in life, and with real impact?

In this chapter, we are going to look at three large companies which are not simply embracing the constraints they encounter, but actively seeking them out. They are doing this partly because they have seen the power of constraints to repeatedly spark invention and business advantage, and partly because they have seen the future and the pressure for change it will bring. They see that the scarcity we discussed in the introduction is impacting their businesses now, and that the abundance they seek is, in large part, reliant on the transformation of not only their own businesses, but also the systems of which they are a part. They are—they have had to become—ambitious change agents.

We'll start by looking at IKEA, a company whose desire and ability to embrace constraints are in its DNA, and how that still drives its culture 70 years later. We'll look at how Nike, always an innovator but not always comfortable with constraints, made a shift from victim to transformer, and is now fully committed to the virtuous cycle of benefits that has resulted. And we'll look at Unilever's hugely ambitious journey to double their size and halve their environmental impact by 2020: how they are approaching it and how they are succeeding. We will close by looking at collective will: what it means, and a simple model for driving it through a company.

## Transformers by upbringing: IKEA

Everyone who works at IKEA knows where its founder, and the company, were born. Småland is a region of Sweden that was historically agricultural and poor, with stony soil. Småland farmers had to make a little go a long way: they used the rocks they cleared from their fields to make the walls that divided them, for example. They turned the constraint of poor-quality soil into the benefit of stone walls.

We have come across farmers at several points in this book: the Boer farmer who, in the Afrikaans expression, "makes a plan" (works around a setback) when things go wrong; the jugaad farmers of India, who find a way to put an oxcart and an engine together to make a truck; and Ernest Rutherford, the father of nuclear science, who ascribed the roots of his own celebrated approach ("We have no money, so we will have to think") to his hardscrabble upbringing on a New Zealand farm. But the farmers of Småland are perhaps the first to have gone on to inspire the culture of a leading global business.

For Ingvar Kamprad, the stone walls of Småland were such an important symbol of the way IKEA needed to think that, in many stores around the world, there is a large image of a stone wall somewhere. It means nothing to the customer; how could it? But it is not there for them, it is there to remind IKEA coworkers of a mindset at the heart of the way the company behaves. IKEA's name is an acronym that is itself a story of origin: the founder's initials, followed by the first letter of the name of the farm he grew up on, and then the first letter of the name of the Småland town where it lay.

Kamprad is famous within IKEA for asking questions, throughout his life, about making a little go a long way. In his twenties he was visiting sawmills, observing what the most regular shapes of their offcuts were and asking himself what he could make out of this waste timber and sell. Fifty years later and in his seventies, he was standing in an open-air food market in Beijing, looking at rows of plucked chickens, asking himself what happened to all the feathers—and turning a food waste product into the stuffing for more affordable duvets. Making expensive things is easy, he would insistently tell his company. Making affordable things that also work and last—that's the real challenge. And it's a challenge IKEA must constantly rise to in order to meet its purpose of championing "the many"—ordinary people who deserve the change a well-designed home can make in their lives.

The constraint IKEA is most known for working within is price. Earlier, we saw the IKEA practice of framing the question around the desired price of a table in a way that is impossible to answer, forcing entirely new kinds of approaches and solutions. They even celebrate this approach of starting with a price constraint in mind in their consumer communications. But there are other kinds of constraints that are equally important to both their values and their business. Their commitment to bamboo fiber (starting with the blue carrier bags you pick up at the beginning of your trip around the store) is driven

**The stone wall of Småland—a key symbol
IKEA uses to communicate its values**

ways to design the living spaces themselves, including apartment blocks. What would it mean to construct housing in a way that turned the space constrictions into advantages? If there isn't space for a dining area in an apartment, for example, a more communal, shared dining area in the building would free more space in the apartments, while also helping to address the isolation and loneliness that are among the challenges of big-city living. IKEA champions the many whose lives are constrained—they have big dreams and small resources—and it is up to IKEA and its inventiveness to help all of them achieve those dreams in the face of their constraints.

IKEA has a culture that has always thought and behaved like this, because their founder has always thought and behaved like this, and because they are very careful to nurture a culture that continues to behave like this. Their journey is not one of moving from victim to neutralizer to transformer; it is one of moving from a transformative individual to a transformative global culture of 140,000 people.

## The stories IKEA tells about itself

Michael Hay had both global strategy and creative roles at IKEA in his fifteen years there. If you are a designer, Hay notes, it starts with the interview. On the interview table might be an IKEA coffee cup and spoon, and designers are asked to look at both of these and discuss what they notice about them. Do they pick out the four grooves on the underside of the cup, which help with stacking and minimize the space they take up when packed? Are they interested

by the need to face up to the sustainability issues with cotton. And, like Nike, they are an investor in DyeCoo, the company that has commercialized waterless dyeing.[1]

Perhaps as important for the future of IKEA and its customers, though, are the space constraints of living in large cities. They initially approached this by creating units for small rooms (a kitchen in a cupboard), but are now thinking about different in the shaft of the spoon, which isn't solid but made of two separate, narrow shafts to use less plastic and reduce heat transfer? Are they naturally driven, in other words, by an interest in how to be more inventive in saving materials and transportation costs, as well as designing products that work better and look good?

Once employed, you are introduced to the company's purpose, and you are told the stories. Storytelling is an important part of the IKEA Way program, in which everyone participates when they start and then again for a week every year. The stories are usually apparently small ones, but with a bigger significance, their aim being to communicate and reinforce mindset and culture. Being celebrated in the in-house magazine, *IKEA Ideas*, as part of the team who was involved in a breakthrough project, is considered an honor.

As you spend more time at IKEA, you observe the less formal, but no less important aspects of the company mindset, all of which have their roots in Småland. One story about the bumblebee theoretically being unable to fly, but doing it anyway, symbolizes what Hay calls an underdog spirit within this huge global company: a sense that to do what they want to do, they're probably going to have to throw out the textbooks and find a completely different way of doing it. They have institutionalized the practice of breaking path dependence. And this desire to look for entirely new ways to arrive at answers is part of a cultural sense that "it is more fun when things are really hard to do."

> *When it's easy, then you're just coasting through life; you go into autopilot mode. We don't pat ourselves on the back, because the next challenge is going to be even harder, but we're going to do that and we're probably going to do it with less people and definitely a lot less money than anybody else has ever done it before. This goes through the whole company.*[2]

IKEA knows that we are the stories we tell ourselves. And we are the questions we ask of ourselves—the answering of which become new stories and a fresh part of the fabric of a fiercely prized, self-reinforcing culture of constraint-driven inventiveness. A culture that grew net profits 8 percent to $4.29 billion in 2012, while continuing to drive costs down.[3]

IKEA has this inventiveness in its DNA, along with a founder whose influence is still very much felt. Their challenge is about preserving the culture in a large and growing company, rather than creating it. And part of the brilliance is in avoiding path dependence by constantly introducing new levels of constraint, asking impossible questions that nobody knows how to answer, and consistently finding new ways to answer them. IKEA operates at that threshold level right below transformer that we noted in Chapter One, driving breakthroughs in everything from the design of a plastic spoon to how the constraints of small living spaces can be made beautiful.

But can a company make the journey to constraint-obsessed culture if it hasn't always had one?

Nike has.

## From victim to transformer: Nike's journey

Nike has always been an innovative company. From the very first time Coach Bowerman poured molten rubber into Mrs. Bowerman's waffle iron to see if he could create a shoe sole that would offer more traction, Phil Knight, a runner on Bowerman's University of Oregon track team, knew that he could build a business around the innovation. Nike was then, and still is obsessed with understanding the needs of the athlete and how to innovate for them, an obsession that has paid off. Today, revenues approach $30 billion and Nike is one of the most well-known and best loved brands in the world.

But Nike hasn't always had a productive relationship with constraints. Back in the mid-1990s, they became the poster child for the poor conditions of workers in factories across Asia. Global Exchange had decided to single out Nike, one of the hottest brands of the moment, as a way to make a splash and raise awareness of the serious issues of worker treatment in these sweatshops. And it was working. With activists around the world calling for a boycott of Nike, the company was feeling the heat, and its brand was being damaged.

At first, CEO Phil Knight was furious and Nike's public posture defensive. The 1997 Annual Report contained this statement:

> *We are not here to eliminate poverty and famine or lead the war against violence and crime. Our critics say that the world is going to hell in a Nike sports bag. Then again, our critics, for the most part, aren't athletes.*[4]

But under constant pressure to change, with consumer boycotts and a shareholder meeting disrupted by activists, Nike realized it had no choice but to engage. The complexity of the issues was daunting. Southeast Asian shoe factories were as much Wild West as Near East. Any standards Nike tried to impose, no matter how many competitors came on board, or how strong the endorsement of NGOs, would be hard to enforce.

In 2004, Hannah Jones, newly appointed VP of Corporate Responsibility, realized that policing compliance to the new standards at hundreds of factories in many countries was practically impossible. As described briefly on page 49, workers had to wear face masks to protect themselves from the fumes that came with gluing soles to uppers. When the inspectors were watching, compliance was easy. When they weren't, standards slipped. Standing in a contract factory, staring at the masks, Jones had an epiphany.

"I realized that you can either solve the worker's rights issue by monitoring every single factory, 24 hours a day, for whether they're wearing personal protective equipment. Or you innovate a new glue that removes all the toxics so you don't have to have the personal protective equipment."[5]

Jones was asking a propelling question: "How do we ensure 100 percent compliance to health and safety practices at all Nike factories, when we don't have the people to police every factory, every moment?" And her can-if thinking answered at least one aspect of the question: we can if we invent a solvent that negates the need for face masks in the first place. The way to fix the compliance problem was to render it unnecessary. Nike's new water-based adhesives reduced worker exposure by 95 percent. And the new glues performed better. This was perhaps the larger epiphany for Nike. By starting out to address a constraint in neutralizer mode, they transformed that constraint into something beautiful: a better-performing solvent that would ultimately perform better for athletes—and that always gets Nike excited.

The journey to a new form of Nike Air took longer. In 1992, Nike received its first angry fax about sulfur hexafluoride (SF6) from a German environmental group, which Tom Hartge, who had spent a good deal of his career developing Air, described as "a kick in the gut." But there was no denying the impact of all that SF6. When Nike was at peak production, it was the equivalent of putting one million additional cars on the road. It may have been the lightest, most durable cushioning on the market—and a key brand differentiator—but something had to be done.[6]

Nitrogen was the preferred alternative, but had smaller molecules that broke up and leaked out. Years of work by a team of sixty went nowhere, each new idea ultimately proving to be a dead end. Target dates were missed and the pressure mounted. "We knew this would be difficult, but we underestimated the challenge," said Hartge.

There was to be no epiphany this time, just a series of small breakthroughs, each building on the other. Sixty-five wafer-thin layers of plastic film were used to hold the nitrogen in place. This required Nike to abandon the old blow-molding process (where air is blown into a plastic part, a little like glass-blowing) and refine a technique called thermoforming instead (where separate sheets are molded under heat).

Then the team realized that the seal created by thermoforming was so strong that an air bag for the whole foot, not just the heel, could be developed. The result was Air Max 360: more comfort and less weight for the athlete, and one of the best-selling Nike running shoes of all time. Commenting on the success of the 360, *Business Week* said, "Hartge brought a marathon runner's tenacity to the task."[7]

While the Nike Air journey was underway, Hannah Jones had kicked off a scenario-planning initiative. Concerned that Nike had "missed the weak signals on the labor issue," her team began exploring a host of global trends—population growth, water scarcity, energy shortages, climate change, the Internet, health issues, governance. They began planning for them before they became crises, staying ahead of their competitors into the bargain. Water shortages alone could soon constrain the cotton crop, hydroelectric energy generation, garment dyeing, and even the laundry habits of athletes. There was much to think about. It was clear to Jones that "doing less of something wasn't going to cut it … big goals are needed to realize big achievements."[8]

Buoyed by recent successes, Nike proceeded with more intention. The Nike Considered Design Ethos, launched in 2006, details the sustainability index of all the materials Nike uses to design products—a massive undertaking, involving Nike going deep into sourcing and supply-chain issues. Using the list, designers are able to make smarter choices at the beginning of the design process. They can see which materials come with the greatest environmental impact (or constraints)—and perhaps, therefore, with the greatest potential to spur innovation. Nike has published the indexes with their Making app, so that other designers can benefit, too. (See Chapter Five: Creating Abundance.)

**RUN ON AIR.** Introducing the new Air Max 360. Our lightest, most cushioned, most flexible, most durable Air Max ever. And the first running shoe to put air under every inch of your foot.

*The 2006 Nike*
*Air Max 360*

Over the course of the next few years, Nike would emerge as a full-blooded transformer. Where once unwelcome constraints had been resisted, then reluctantly wrestled with, they were now embraced for the opportunities they provided. What began as risk mitigation became opportunity creation. A series of one-offs, an insider at Nike told us, "has now crystallized into a core competence, a journey from individual moments to a way of thinking, where we go hunting for constraints."[9]

To tackle the water problem, in 2012 Nike entered into a strategic partnership with DyeCoo, a company that has created a remarkable waterless dyeing machine using recyclable carbon dioxide. Two years later, CEO Mark Parker announced a manufacturing revolution as he unveiled a water-free dyeing facility in Taiwan that reduces energy consumption by 60 percent. It also reduces dyeing times by 40 percent, meaning faster speed to market. And what is more, "the most saturated, intense and consistent color we've seen."[10]

Last, the Flyknit shoe. For serious runners, the best shoe has always been one that you don't know you're wearing; the constraint that needs transforming is the shoe itself. Shoes have been shaped and shaved and made lighter year after year, but the manufacturing process for shoes was still very wasteful, with extensive offcuts left behind on the floor. So another multiyear mission saw Nike having to forget everything they knew about how uppers were made.[11] The solution was to knit a single-layer upper, like a sock, with an ultralight thread. In a "messy, beautiful burst of creativity and pure force of will,"[12] a featherweight, form-fitting, virtually seamless shoe was born. It reduced weight by 20 percent and waste by a staggering 80 percent compared to the previous lightest shoe. Best of all for the athlete-obsessed company, it is a shoe that fits better, breathes better, and is faster.

Nike is not done. One of the best lines Wieden+Kennedy ever gave them was "There is no finish line," and it applies as much to the constant need to invent better as it does to the mindset of the athlete. They continue to look for constraints in their system and in the wider world that they can use to create more of the kind of transformative inventions that helped them grow revenue in double digits the last five years. In a shift both strategic and symbolic, Hannah Jones' department has been renamed Sustainable Business & Innovation, is at the heart of Nike, and is sponsored by the CFO.

Athletes have benefited from the company's repeated ability to take lemons (a ban on SF6) and make lemonade (Air Max 360), a knack they believe is now a long-term competitive advantage. Nike's relationship with NGOs is stronger now, too. Responding in the way they have has built bridges and created alliances. And while investors remain indifferent to Nike's sustainability plans, the company remains resolute about its goal of decoupling growth from constrained resources, striving for a closed-loop system that generates no waste and in which sustainability is synonymous with performance.

The third example we will look at is Unilever, another enormous company looking to uncouple growth and resource use, whose journey might be more ambitious yet.

## Unilever: Transforming industries and a culture

In 2010, Unilever's CEO shared a new vision with his company, one that was about to have a profound impact on the way they thought about everything they did. The board had decided that Unilever would double its size, while halving its environmental impact, by 2020. Ambitious growth coupled with a significant constraint would require them to challenge all the paths on which they had become dependent.

The vision had been born in an Executive Board meeting some months earlier. Pier Luigi Sigismondi, Unilever's Chief Supply Chain Officer, was new to the board at the time. The vision, he says, happened "like any innovation—by coincidence." In the morning, board members had aligned around the growth ambition. In the afternoon they went on to discuss sustainability. Unilever has been a leader and catalyst on environmental issues for many years (helping found the Round Table for Sustainable Palm Oil and the Marine Stewardship Council for Sustainable Fishing, for instance), and wanted to do more to reduce its environmental impact and make a more positive social impact. With the morning's conversations still fresh in their minds, they all saw that growth could be at odds with their desire to reduce their footprint. They needed to explicitly link the ambitions: doubling size while remaining neutral in the terms of resource use, effectively halving their environmental footprint. They wanted to grow and be a force for change; and they wanted to stimulate other companies to adopt a similar agenda. (We'll look more at why Unilever is so committed to positive environmental and social impact in Chapter Nine.)

The response from the company to Polman's announcement was hugely positive, inspired even. Yet Sigismondi, on whose shoulders much of this would fall, confesses to rational doubts as much as emotional excitement even as it was announced. How could they sustainably source 100 percent of their agricultural materials if the industry wasn't prepared for it? And what if Unilever's leverage with the growers of a particular crop was insufficient to get them to change their practices? He—and all of Unilever—had put their hands up to answer a question they didn't know how to answer.

Sigismondi distinguishes between the logic and the emotion of his reaction:

> *The logical thinking took us to a concerned place, but the emotional intent was so high that we said "We don't have all the answers; we need to work with others. We announced this as a multi-stakeholder effort: please help us get there, and if we join forces we can find a way."*[13]

The Unilever Sustainable Living Plan (USLP) has three key components. The first is to help one billion people take steps to improve their health and well-being through hygiene and nutrition. The second is the reduction of the company's environmental impact. And the third, called Enhancing Livelihoods, seeks to help smallholder farmers make a better living, and provide fair and equal-opportunity workplaces. Unilever's challenge in delivering the Sustainable Living Plan is, in an important sense, a steeper one than Nike's. For Nike to succeed, they needed to behave differently themselves and influence their own industry; Unilever, a larger company with multiple product lines across many different categories, would need to influence multiple industries and persuade their consumers to behave differently as well. For example, in laundry and personal care, they would need to get their consumers to reduce their own water use.

The leadership realized very early on that there were some key enablers they needed to put in place:

**Sacrifice some relationships in order to fully commit to the rest.** They used the USLP as a filter for every relationship they had. Reviewing how wide their involvement had become with forums, associations, and initiatives all around the world, they realized their impact had become diluted. They now focused only on those associations and initiatives that would help deliver their vision, and cut those that wouldn't.

**Make it every executive's agenda.** While they had a Chief Sustainability Officer, they recognized that this vision would not be realized if it were simply delegated to her. They needed to explicitly build this part of the ambition into the business plans and strategic agenda of every executive in the business. (Compare this integration with Nike changing Hannah Jones's group's name from Corporate Responsibility to Sustainable Business and Innovation and linking her function more explicitly to the design team.)

**Make an ongoing commitment.** Executives are used to change and evolution. And there would be setbacks, minor failures, and doubts as the vision began to be delivered. This needed to be a plan that remained boringly committed to do the same, year after year, even when results came slowly.

The supply chain team at Unilever is responsible for delivering key components of the USLP, including the sustainable sourcing of all their agricultural materials. This challenge has made this the most ambitious job Sigismondi has ever had, he observes. Success depends on changing not just the way Unilever does business, but the way whole agricultural industries behave—industries over which he has limited control.

Let's look at the very different ways they have tackled two of the most important industries, and what we can learn from each.

Palm oil presented a particular challenge. As of 2010, the palm oil industry paid little attention to traceability, and there was little segregation of palm oils. Buying 100 percent GreenPalm certificates helped Unilever make progress quickly, but to get a true picture of sustainability, they would need to start tracing oil back to the sources, track it through the various mills, and evaluate their labor practices, transportation systems, and so on. This would require some significant changes for the industry. And while Unilever was a substantive buyer of palm oil in terms of volume, it accounted for less than 3 percent of the industry's output. How much leverage did they really have?

Unilever was clear, though, that palm oil was one of their biggest levers if they were to meet the goals for the USLP. They couldn't flinch; they would have to find a way through. They set themselves the target that by 2020, every drop of palm oil used in Unilever products would come from certified, traceable sources through a segregated supply. And then they worked out how to have that conversation with their suppliers.

At a meeting in Singapore, they brought together the five palm oil traders who represented 80 percent of the world's production: successful, hard-nosed businesspeople from China, Indonesia, and Hong Kong. Explaining Unilever's vision to them, Sigismondi painted a picture of the future that contrasted the opportunity to create a better world and leave a proud legacy with the threat of consumer activism against unsustainably harvested palm oil, even the prospect of European regulators imposing more stringent rules on imports. As shapers of the palm oil business, they could change it so that they could tell their families that they were doing something good for the world, or they could change it to ensure they would still have a healthy business in ten years' time. What did they want to do?[14]

When Sigismondi finished, some of the traders left, uninterested even in talking. Others stayed and talked, but prevaricated, reluctant to commit.

But the largest palm oil producer in the world identified with the picture that had been painted and wanted to hear more. After further conversations, this producer agreed to a strategic alliance with Unilever, in which they both publicly and formally committed to no deforestation, no development on peat land, and no exploitation of local communities, starting in 2015. Although Unilever is only a very small customer, the long-term commitment they were prepared to make as part of the deal was significant. They had collectively taken a huge step forward. This was a symbolic as well as significant moment for the supply chain team, a move towards meeting their environmental goals while also securing the future of their own supply.

As big a step forward as this undoubtedly was, palm oil is only one of the crops Unilever buys. To succeed with the USLP, they need processes and alliances that will drive this level of change across a broad range of industries, each of which presents different challenges, even within the same crop. We saw in Chapter Two, for instance, the challenging of path dependence in those geographies using mechanized tomato harvesting, and how early progress came about. But in many important markets tomatoes are not grown on large, mechanized farms, but by smallholder farmers, which demanded an entirely different approach.

Take India, for example. Up until 2011, India was importing all the tomatoes used in processed food; Unilever, with a large local tomato-based brand called Kissan, was no exception. Tomatoes were being grown locally and used when cooking from scratch, but the upwardly mobile Indian buyer increasingly wanted convenience food: to meet its ambitions with the USLP Unilever needed to create a way to source tomatoes that could be processed for this growing consumer need.

There were several challenges in doing this. Indian farming was made up of smallholders, growing tomatoes that were low yield, with an unreliable final market, and of a variety unsuitable for processing. In other words, they weren't very committed to growing tomatoes, and were growing the wrong type when they did. To succeed here, Unilever had to set up a new kind of partnership that would create a secure and sustainable market for the farmers. It included an alliance with a local partner to set up the first large-scale tomato processing facility in India, an innovative public-private partnership with the local Maharashtra government who helped with loans and education for the farmers, and other specialist partners who would help with agrochemicals and drip irrigation. Unilever built, in effect, a new ecosystem of support around the farmers throughout the value chain from farm to factory. At the same time, they still had to persuade the farmers to change to a new variety of tomatoes, and help make tomatoes a more profitable crop for them; they solved this partly by establishing a guaranteed buyer in the local processor, but also by introducing an innovative practice called intercropping, where the two-foot gaps between the tomato plants could be filled by another crop, such as guava or grapes. This would mitigate the risk to the farmers and increase their income.

Around 3000 farmers are now part of the scheme. For those farmers tomato yield has increased 50 percent through better farming practices, and their income has tripled through the addition of intercropping. Water consumption has been cut through the introduction of 100 percent drip irrigation, and chemical use reduced through better education. And Unilever has gone from importing all its tomatoes in India to being entirely locally sourced in three years.

So the USLP constraint of reducing resource impact is clearly turning out to have a range of beautiful dimensions to it: across Unilever as a whole, 55 percent of agricultural inputs are now sustainably sourced—up from 14 percent in 2010; a million tons of $CO_2$ emissions have been eliminated across their system; 85 percent of their factories send zero waste to landfills; one million smallholder farmers are now involved in sustainable development practices. In a business such as tomatoes in India, we can see that the USLP has precipitated an entirely new model and ecosystem, which is better for the farmers and their families, better for local government, better for Unilever, and better for the planet. And while investors have been slow to embrace all that the USLP involves, Unilever's overall business performance has been strong since Paul Polman became CEO in 2009. The stock price has doubled, and 2013 sales were up 4.3 percent and margins 40 basis points.[15] There are still challenges ahead: persuading their consumers to change their behavior will require entirely new kinds of solutions again. But it is impressive progress.

Sigismondi is very open about the fact that, like Unilever, he has been on his own journey over the past few years; he was not initially the confident transformer he has become. One of the qualities he has most come to prize, in others as much as himself, is commitment: a willingness to uncover and challenge long-held assumptions and to have difficult conversations. He has employed a Royal Marine Brigadier to help develop the personal discipline and commitment of his 250 factory directors who look for the business opportunities in the USLP. Echoing the words of Admiral McRaven, he notes, "You have to get the organization emotionally attached to what you're trying to do."

## Success factors across the three cases

Far from being the domain of just a few brilliant individuals with insights applicable only to a few, the principles described in this book are a vigorous force for growth in some of the world's largest companies. Illustrating this with examples from IKEA, Nike, and Unilever proves that some of the very best use of constraints is happening inside corporations.

For Unilever and Nike, embracing constraints has become an engine of growth and transformation, while IKEA works hard to ensure that it remains that way in their organization.

The three began the journey for different reasons. For IKEA, it is simply who they are and who they will continue to be as they do more to champion "the many." For Unilever, it is about becoming a more responsible global citizen, making their ambitious

**Far from being the domain of just a few brilliant individuals with insights applicable only to a few, the principles of making constraints beautiful are a vigorous force for growth in some of the world's largest companies.**

growth plans both more acceptable and possible. And Nike, initially forced to respond to outside pressure, has come to realize the wisdom in this way and the competitive edge it gives them.

For each of them, embracing constraints unlocks solutions that achieve at least two of the following:

- Enhance profitability.
- Create competitive advantage.
- Create better products or lower prices for consumers.
- Benefit business partner profitability.
- Strengthen ties to communities.
- Drive the sustainability agenda.

Their ways of doing this are very consistent with the themes and principles around transforming constraint discussed in the book so far.

It's in the DNA of IKEA, for instance, to ask challenging questions that harness ambitions to constraints of price, materials, or space. That they create these challenges themselves as a matter of routine helps them avoid becoming dependent on the paths and processes that led to previous success, forcing them to find new ones. Rather than flinching from the challenges, they consider them part of the forward energy in a culture where those who meet the challenge are lauded.

At Unilever a very big propelling question at the corporate level drives a whole series of smaller ones, deep into their supply chain and beyond. Finding answers means interrogating all legacy assumptions, entertaining all kinds of can-if propositions, including forming ambitious alliances with powerful partners to change industries. The commitment required to succeed there is as personal as it is professional.

And Nike, having had no choice but to form propelling questions about externally imposed constraints, now imposes constraints on itself. It has rethought pretty much everything in its quest to serve athletes better and uncouple its own growth from scarce resources.

The success factors appear to be:

- Big ambition and strong intent: propelling questions that are specific, and have authority and legitimacy.
- Start from the top and empower key people to drive it deep into the organization.
- Make it central to the business—part of every executive's agenda, not a siloed initiative.
- Be consistent—boringly consistent: resist the temptation for a new year to demand a new objective.
- Be willing to challenge and interrogate every partnership, process, and assumption to discover what's no longer relevant or legitimate.
- Know that the benefits and virtuous circles will emerge; accept that you can't predict what they will be in advance.
- Be a storytelling culture: change the narrative about constraints, define success through simple stories, make successes easy to pass on. Celebrate your transformers.

Note that not everyone will rush to join; not everyone will be inspired to act. Michael Hay believes that within large organizations there is a different flavor of victim that he calls the martyr—individuals who gain a kind of status from the apparently insurmountable constraints that they have to deal with on a daily basis. It is, he believes, a type of defense mechanism against change of this kind. Sigismondi noted that there will always be cynics waiting to point to the inevitable failures as proof of the impossibility of the initiative: leaders must draw on the strength of their conviction and intent, and celebrate the early victories. Marc Priestley of McLaren admits that most of his team, including himself, initially thought what Ron Dennis was asking for was "a pain in the arse," and getting them past that required leadership. Not everyone can lead the kind of programs that our three corporations have in place: challenging long-held conventions, leading can-if thinking sessions, living with ambiguity creating abundance, and developing a larger narrative around the exercise—these demand strong, open leadership. Most people are happy simply managing; but management doesn't make constraints beautiful.

We'll return to the implications for leadership in our last chapter.

## Collective will

Airbus' Smarter Skies initiative is a five-part plan to deliver a 50 percent cut in $CO_2$ emissions by 2050. The ideas that make up the plan are as boldly innovative as one might hope: ways to create an eco-climb as planes take off, for example, lead to flocking flight paths to reduce drag and save fuel, and finish in gliding descents which use the kinetic energy created in the landing to deliver the onboard power requirements. But Airbus' EVP of Engineering, Charles Champion, is clear that delivering these will not come from the technology and talent of Airbus alone. It will also need to come from the leading actors of the industry genuinely cooperating between each other with "a strong collective will."[16]

One could regard collective will as powerful but intangible. We might think of some of the notions in Chapter Six about how we can create determination, tenacity, relentlessness. But Michael Hay helped give this far more tangibility in the diagram on the following page, and it has proved a valuable tool in forcing the right conversations at the outset and throughout any process that requires change.

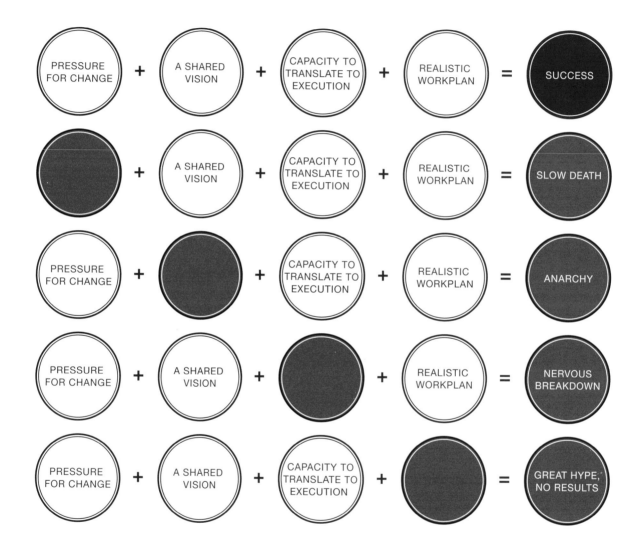

*Figure 8: The elements needed for successful change.*
*Source: Strategy&; adapted by Michael Hay[17]*

Look at the top line of the chart. The four boxes describe the essential elements of success for any shift in strategy. To create the will to change, we first need the pressure to change. Without a strong, clearly articulated business case for embarking on a new direction, the initiative will stall pretty quickly when the going gets tough. We need to feel the heat.

Then we need a view of where we want to go, and why, which everyone needs to buy into. Third, we need some confidence that we have the capability and capacity to do what is being proposed—we may not know precisely how we are going to do it yet, but we know we have those kinds of capabilities. And finally we map out the practical steps it will take, with realistic expectations in timing and outcomes. From alignment and concurrent movement against each of these four factors, in turn, comes collective will.

The brilliance of Hay's summation is in the four rows below the top one. Each row lays bare what happens if one of these four factors is not present. Without pressure, we move without urgency and run out of steam. Without shared vision, we run off in different directions—the very best outcome of which is that nothing gets done. And so on.

Unilever, IKEA, and Nike take very deliberate steps to ensure that the conditions for success across these four boxes are in place. As the U.S. Army notes, hope is not a method.

## Constraints and healthy cultures

In the modern world we don't need to run to catch food, but we impose exercise on ourselves for our health. If we succeed as organizations, we grow beyond the reach of the constraints that initially helped define our decisions, but perhaps we still need constraints for our continued organizational health. Is Yahoo!'s failure over the last few years in part a failure to understand which constraints it needed to impose upon itself to succeed and grow? Can Facebook flourish if it imposes no constraints upon itself at all? And how will it know what kinds of constraints will most benefit it?

At the moment, we see leaders in successful organizations preserving the health of those companies by maintaining the kinds of constraints that took them to their current success. Mojang, for example, is the game-development company behind Minecraft, the low-tech computer game that has sold 54 million copies, earning Mojang $120 million in profit in 2013. As they look to develop a broader portfolio, CEO Carl Manneh is deliberately restricting the size of the development teams. Keeping the teams small, he notes, not only makes them more agile and faster in making decisions, but also means they have to create games that are less development-heavy, and won't require 200 to 300 people to bring them to life. Just like Minecraft.[18]

But what if we were able to be more precise than this, in time? What if we were able to link specific kinds of constraints to specific kinds of organizational health, so that they became, if not exactly corporate vitamins, still part of a more precise and disciplined way of preserving the right dimensions of health in any organization?[19]

It may be a healthcare company that is one of the best examples of this. South Africa's Discovery Group is now market leader in South African healthcare, with over 50 percent of the market. Their Vitality program is at the heart of their healthcare offer; its success driven by the insight that the way to lower healthcare costs is to keep people healthy. They then ally with partners to give members big discounts on activities that benefit their health, such as gym memberships and preventative screenings. One of the most successful of these partnerships has been encouraging their members to eat healthy food. If one of their members walks into one of the two largest retailers in South Africa today, there are around 12,000 items which they can get at a 25 percent discount—flagged both at point of purchase and on the till receipt—because each represents a healthier way to eat.

Global CMO Hylton Kallner says they keep their edge by deliberately introducing constraints into the questions they ask themselves.[20] The deep discounts created for members on healthy food, for instance, owed much to the way that they framed the initial question: they didn't ask "How can we encourage our members to eat more healthily?" but "How can we give our members healthy food for free?" It was the constraint-driven stretch in the framing of this question that helped them arrive at the partnerships and at the impact of the solution. They make a habit of "setting impossible goals and settling for mildly impossible solutions" even now; if they don't continue to retain an insurgent mindset, says Kallner, they risk both losing relevance and failing to progress for their customers and for society.

## CONSTRAINT-DRIVEN CULTURES: CHAPTER SUMMARY

- Finding opportunity in constraints isn't solely the preserve of brilliant individuals operating outside the strictures of the corporate world. Some of the best examples can be found inside the three very large companies we explore in this chapter.

- From inception, IKEA has made the most of very little, reflecting the values of its founder. With a habit of asking "impossible questions," Ingvar Kamprad ensures that IKEA never forgets that making expensive things is easy, but making things that last and are affordable is hard. IKEA was born of constraints and has embraced them ever since.

- Nike, though one of the world's most innovative companies, initially responded as a victim when forced by NGOs to examine its practices. Then one constraint after another prompted a better solution than before, and Nike began proactively seeking out constraints as stimulus for innovation. Nike now sees its capability to do this as a long-term competitive advantage.

- The Unilever Sustainable Living Plan seeks to reinvent the model of what a major corporation must be in a future of scarce resources. To do so, it is challenging long-held assumptions in its business, creating bold new alliances, reshaping industries, and creating virtuous cycles that benefit farmers, producers, and Unilever alike.

- These three different businesses had different start points and different journeys, yet have all ended up operating at the threshold of transformation. It is possible for big companies to create constraint-driven cultures.

- Success factors include strong direction from the top, to lend authority and legitimacy to challenge paths; big ambitions and specific constraints integrated into core business strategies; responsibility among all leaders who stick to the task over time; preparedness to live with ambiguity; culturally embedding compelling stories around constraint-driven success.

# 9 SCARCITY AND ABUNDANCE

Why this capability is so important to all of us today

1.  Will the future be characterized more by scarcity or abundance?

2.  Why will constraint-driven problem solving be an inevitable part of the future?

3.  Why is it so important to develop this capability more broadly and not just leave it in the hands of a chosen few?

**These are, to echo Dickens,** the best of times and the worst of times.

On the one hand, scarcity is, for good reason, at the top of many political and business agendas. The pressures of an increasing population and developing economies on finite or diminishing resources have led some to dub this the Age of Scarcity.[1] While the field of economics has long been said to be, at its heart, the science of scarcity, the very real constraints the world needs to address give this a new emphasis. Indeed, they are largely constraints to which we are already too slow to respond (if they can be solved at all). As such, they threaten to become the definers of individual, national, and global progress—or regression—for the next twenty years.

Abundance, on the other hand, is a post-scarcity mindset that some suggest is now within reach. Abundance is about multiplying opportunity and ambition with new capabilities emerging today, such as the immense power of technology, and the global networks increasingly connecting people and ideas. You may have experienced this yourself, in ways big and small—faster transactions enabled by massive computing power, or a wealth of insights from the far-flung corners of your organization, like PHD's Source, for instance. The Age of Abundance insists on grounds for optimism, and the possibility of more for everyone. We are, they say, looking at this the wrong way round.

While the nature and consequences of the scarcity–abundance debate are being articulated most energetically at the global level, as we saw in the brief discussion in the introduction, it is also a lens for personal and organizational progress as well. Do my 300 new Facebook friends represent abundance, a thriving, valuable community, or a squeeze on the time I have to spend face to face with the two people who matter most? Do the plethora of new channels connecting me to customers represent an exciting opportunity, or are they the overload to be sacrificed in order to implement this year's initiatives? Are all the educational programs available on my tablet a wonderful tool for me to help my daughter with her Mandarin, or one more way to add to our already overscheduled relationship?

This bigger picture is a critical context for our exploration of constraint-driven inventiveness. Whichever of these two worldviews we assign more significance to, they will, in the very near future, have a profound effect on us personally, on our organization, and on the planet we share. And they will also be a critical context for whether, where, and how we intend to be a transformer, neutralizer, or victim.

But making a choice between the two at all is, of course, too binary. We'll make the case here that all of us live at the nexus between scarcity and abundance at each of these personal, professional and global levels. How we manage that nexus, and in particular how well we develop the capability to make constraints beautiful, will determine how well we progress.

But first let's explore the arguments on each side of the scarcity and abundance debate, focusing primarily at the global level.

## Scarcity vs. Abundance: Examining the arguments

### Are we in the Age of Scarcity ... ?

To read the news today is to sink into an abyss of torturous limitations: wars and political instability over scarce resources, overpopulation, mass unemployment, food and water shortages, climate crisis, bankrupt education systems. These concerns are becoming central to our thinking in boardrooms, schoolrooms, and parliaments around the world. Our continued prosperity, and possibly even survival, depends on our ability to address them.

The scarcity worldview argues that we once had abundance in the developed world, but those days are gone. As the developing world aspires to the same standard of living, it puts even more pressure on already scarce resources. So the Age of Abundance is over, and we are now living in the Age of Scarcity.

Paul Polman, Unilever's CEO, declared definitively in the pages of the Harvard Business Review:

> *We have reached the end of the era of abundance ... we are already consuming 1.3 times what the planet can replenish this year—and the forecast for net global population growth of two billion by 2040 will only worsen the situation.*[2]

The World Wildlife Fund claims that if everyone on earth consumed like Americans, we'd need the resources of three planets to feed the demand. And because the rest of the world is starting to do just that, the price of those resources is dramatically on the rise; after a steady decline over the last hundred years, almost every commodity has doubled or tripled in price since 2002 alone.[3] Eighty-five percent of the world's fisheries have been pushed up to or beyond their biological limits.[4] In a 2012 report, the U.S. security establishment suggested that water shortages will "contribute to instability" in states important to U.S. National Security.[5]

Can we come back from this? Saul Griffith, a material scientist and MacArthur Genius, says that even if we built what he calls Renewistan (an area of land half the size of the United States that, when covered in renewable energy sources, could power today's global economy), "It is not accurate to say we can still stop climate change … we are now working to stop worse climate change, or much worse than worse."[6] The impact of climate change on agriculture will be profound, with the prospects for huge and chaotic displacements of populations due to famine. More scarcity lies ahead.

Scarcity scenarios are chilling. Table 4 gives an oversimplified but digestible at-a-glance view of how scarcity is shaping today's world, creating serious impediments to our ability to prosper and progress. In recent years, commentators have started moving beyond the sustainability narrative to discuss resilience: it is no longer about sustaining what we have, they argue, but about our ability to adapt to changed circumstances while fulfilling our purpose—an essential skill in an age of unforeseeable disruption and volatility.[7]

### … or the Age of Abundance?

The more optimistic worldview of abundance can be glimpsed in venues like TED, PopTech, and *Fast Company* magazine, offering the belief that we can and are fixing our messes—that we are on the threshold of a new era of technology-enabled transformation. The high priest of this view is Peter Diamandis, who, with Steven Kotler, wrote the book *Abundance*, in which they detail all the ways we will soon be able to exceed the basic needs of everyone on the planet, much of it enabled by technology:

> *Progress in AI, robotics, infinite computing, ubiquitous broadband, digital manufacturing, nanomaterials, synthetic biology and many other exponentially growing technologies will enable us to make greater gains in the next two decades than we have in the previous two hundred years.*[8]

In this future, the story goes, we'll turn algae into global fuel, lend a fiver to each of the world's poor, turning them into wealth-creating entrepreneurs, and make ocean water

# Scarcity Scenarios

**Population:** We'll be nine billion by 2040. How will we feed, house, and educate everyone? We already have resource wars and populations displaced by huge infrastructure projects. People will retrench into ethnic and tribal groups, and be prepared to fight for what's scarce.

**Food:** Bio-fuel crops squeeze agricultural land use just as growing populations need it for homes; increasing use of fertilizer ruins already depleted soil; biodiversity and crop yields collapse.

**Energy:** Cheap oil is getting harder to find. Emerging economies bid to grab what's left, driving up prices. Fracking is a short-term win with devastating environmental impact; renewables have yet to deliver on their promise.

**Climate Change:** Burning more carbon hastens our demise. A disturbed climate creates massive agriculture failure, displacing people due to famine and rising sea levels. The world experiences refugee problems on a huge scale.

**Water:** Population growth drives huge demands for water; producing more food and more products, along with a warming planet, creates droughts. Water wars break out.

**Economy:** Stagnation drags on in mature economies. It's structural, not cyclical. No new jobs. Wage pressure increases. Workers struggle to lift themselves out of poverty. Retiring boomers strain underfunded social services. Underfunded schools limp along. Unrest develops.

**Health:** In the global north, pressure to create cheap calories as food demand increases creates more ill health. Heavy pesticide use drives incidence of cancer higher. Strained healthcare systems are stressed more. Costs spiral. In the developing world billions still don't have clean water or mosquito nets.

**Connection:** We exhaust ourselves working longer, harder; multitasking makes us dumb as we try to do it all. We become disconnected from others and ourselves.

# Abundance Scenarios

**Population:** Violence is already in decline and will continue as civilization pacifies and prosperity spreads. The web democratizes education, and the educated have fewer children. Population stabilizes. Better-connected people understand and share more. More solutions emerge from connected minds.

**Food:** Genetic engineering, hydroponics, aeroponics, and agroecological practices create leaps in productivity. Vertical farming solves distribution issues, is immune to weather, and powered by local feces. Meat is grown in-vitro.

**Energy:** Renewables and smart grids pay off. Solar decouples from silicon, becomes more efficient by powers of 10. As does wind. Algae and Gen IV nuclear in the mix, too. Non-carbon power is cheap and plentiful, powering breakthroughs in other areas.

**Climate Change:** A cooperative and resilient population leverages breakthroughs to mitigate the worst consequences of climate change. We squeak through, adapt, and endure.

**Water:** The planet is mostly water. De-salinization plants driven by cheap energy turn salt water into fresh water. Portable distillers help make wastewater potable, too.

**Economy:** Distributed manufacturing (3D printing, robots) creates a new industrial revolution, thousands of start-ups, and local jobs. Education gets Khanified, hacks multiply effectiveness, creating a supply of inventors to sustain abundance. Developing countries develop mature, stable economies. The bottom of the pyramid prospers.

**Health:** Scientists produce food that heals. Genome sequencing leads to customization of medicine. Robo-nurses take care of the elderly. Fitness hacks yield impressive results. Cleaner water and better distribution of meds make progress against disease, and SMS use prevents spread. Polio and malaria are eradicated.

**Connection:** The hyperconnectivity of the web serves to bring us closer to each other, working on the issues that count. A global mindset emerges; we choose to pursue abundance together.

*Table 4: Scarcity and abundance scenarios*[9]

fresh enough to irrigate plants in giant greenhouses in the desert (see page 202: Transforming a Desert). And the case for abundance is underpinned by the immense power of exponential growth in technology. Moore's law, for example, (see page 47) has driven the remarkable breakthroughs we've seen in personal computing and the development of the World Wide Web, and, the disciples of *Abundance* claim, we are about to see similar exponential growth in other technology-related domains. The price of DNA sequencing is falling in line with exponential growth in processing power, opening up the prospect for more timely, accurate, and personalized medical interventions, making healthcare vastly more efficient. Or look at energy. Solar power costs have been steadily falling 5 to 6 percent a year, while capacity has been increasing at 30 percent a year; at some point soon, some experts suggest, both of these factors will drive explosive exponential growth in solar, which could see us source all our energy needs from the sun within two decades. By that account, energy abundance and a carbon-free future are within reach.[10]

Developments like these may seem far off. But it's in the nature of exponential growth to surprise us—at first the constant doubling of growth is off a small base, and trends appear linear. And then, boom!—the doubling of larger and larger numbers results in the classic hockey-stick growth curve; seismic change will come sooner than we think.

Once something like that happens in energy, this argument says, the knock-on effects could be genuinely world-changing. With abundant cheap

## Developments like these may seem far off, but it's in the nature of exponential growth to surprise us.

energy, water scarcity becomes less of an issue, thanks to lowering the cost of desalinization. Abundant salt water becomes fresh water. This leads to better hygiene, helping solve a broad range of health issues, which brings stability to societies and a base from which to progress. Cheap energy reduces the burden on children in developing countries to collect wood for fuel and brings light for their studies at night, which improves education, which relieves poverty, which reduces the birth rate, which frees women to join the workforce, which empowers millions and builds economies. Entire systems of constraints can be transformed once that first domino falls. If that first domino is cheap, renewable energy, then we will create the kind of abundance that cheap, abundant oil once created.

As the above example shows, the forces of abundance aren't only a developed-world phenomenon. Even basic connectivity can have a huge impact on a farmer today if they can call ahead to find out when milk was last delivered to a village, and hence how high a price they might be able to get there. In Kenya, the ability to make payments using the simple technology of a feature phone through M-PESA has made a huge difference.

A system introduced to enable cashless micro-financing in rural villages, where the SIM card acts, in effect, as an ATM card, it has also reduced robberies in Nairobi slums, for example. With Kenyans finding all kinds of new value in even this simple form of financial connectivity, 60 percent of Kenya's electronic financial transactions are now through M-PESA.[11]

All around the world, people are arming themselves with the knowledge they need to solve problems. Empowering what has become known, colorfully, as "the BoP" (the one billion people at the bottom of the pyramid) in this way, allowing them to participate in the economy more productively by identifying and solving their own problems, will be a further driver of abundance.[12] This group can be resourceful, creative entrepreneurs as well as potential consumers, and a whole new world is opening up for them with access to knowledge through technology. Professor C.K. Prahalad has argued that we must stop thinking of people in the developing world as victims and join them as they transform their world for the better. And as we saw earlier, the notion of reverse innovation proves that not only are people in the developing world helping themselves, but their ideas help the developed world, too.

Diamandis puts huge faith in the entrepreneurial spirit to solve the problems of today. As the founder of the X-Prize—a series of high-profile, public competitions intended to encourage technological development that could benefit mankind—he points to the relatively short eight years it took from the announcement of the Ansari X-Prize to seeing the first-ever private space flight as proof of a powerful do-it-yourself ethic that is energized and enabled by exponential technological change.

Such audacious private missions simply weren't possible a few years ago. Yet now a group of highly motivated, maverick inventors and entrepreneurs across the globe is taking on some of our biggest challenges (and biggest industries) and arriving at entirely new kinds of answers. With the audacious automobile start-up Tesla, Elon Musk is using his PayPal millions to prove that electric cars are not only viable, but also highly desirable; while it's still too early to declare victory, Tesla has opened the world's eyes to what is possible with zero-emissions vehicles. Richard Branson's Virgin Atlantic has partnered with LanzaTech to create jet fuel out of captured carbon, and aims to cut emissions of its fleet by 30 percent even as it grows globally.[13] And Jeff Bezos wants to deliver our Amazon boxes via drones, not diesel-powered trucks. You wouldn't bet against him.

## Transforming a Desert

From 2007 to 2008 there was a global food crisis. Droughts in many parts of the world and the commodity speculation that followed pushed prices up, and riots broke out in Mexico over the price of tortillas. It was a glimpse into a dark future. As the climate warms, droughts become more severe, the food supply less stable, and the chance of major disruptions is high.

In the most recent crisis, Saudi Arabia banned the export of poultry, potatoes, and onions to Qatar.[14] In Qatar there are no rivers, no lakes, and annual rainfall averages 2.9 inches. It is almost impossible to grow anything. Oil has made it the richest country in the world, but in 2008 it couldn't find food to buy. Constraints come even to the wealthy.

But money can fund ambition. And the ambition of Qatar's National Food Security Program (QNFSP) is to produce half its own food within twelve years. It comes with a $30 billion price tag and a lot of constraints. Average summer temperatures reach the low 40s Celsius. Officially only 1 percent of Qatari land is arable. And oil wealth has swelled the population to 1.8 million people. While there is plenty of salt water in the Gulf, burning oil to power today's desalinization plants doesn't make sense when carbon is one of the major contributors to climate change—and drier deserts—in the first place.

In a remarkably ambitious piece of can-if thinking, Qatar sees opportunity in these constraints.

All that sun is a godsend if you're thinking about the possibilities of solar, and yet the 753 megawatts required would cover the equivalent of 2000 soccer fields with today's panels. So the search for more efficient solar solutions—already underway in many corners of the world—now has a new patron. New desalinization plants are expected to be in place by 2025, providing abundant fresh water from the Gulf, powered entirely by solar.

The water produced will be used to irrigate the roots of plants engineered for maximum productivity. The QNFSP looked at 400 crops to assess which ones would work best in their conditions. The goal is to grow five times the amount of produce on the same amount of land using 30 percent less water.

Still, the country needs farmers to make the system work. To meet the need, Qatar is investing heavily in education. They also need supply-chain management skills, sewage treatment expertise, and more. If successful, the QNFSP will birth a new knowledge economy, transforming not just their energy supply, but their economy, and possibly their culture, too.

Today, 68 countries are considered too arid for agriculture, a number set to grow as climate change increases desertification in arid areas. All of them are watching Qatar.

Alongside, successful billionaire philanthropists are using their wealth to address scarcity-driven issues in other ways. The Gates Foundation is, among many other things, playing a major role in eradicating polio and malaria, diseases that seriously hinder progress in the developing world. The Skoll Foundation funds world-changing social entrepreneurs like Global Witness, who aim to expose corruption and environmental degradation around natural resources. Omidyar Networks are funding big bets in education. These entrepreneurs see themselves as change agents as significant in the wider world as they are in their own businesses. Eradicating disease, addressing corruption, and hacking education are just a few ways they hope to address scarcity and create abundance.

So these factors are driving the abundance worldview: entrepreneurs around the world, enabled by the exponential growth of technology, aided and abetted by disruptive social innovation, and funded by billionaire philanthropists, will help us leave scarcity behind forever.

## The interdependence of Scarcity and Abundance

A rather binary, pick-one-worldview smackdown is how this debate is typically presented, especially in the West, where there is a tendency to simplify complex issues into two-sided arguments. We need, though, a more integrated way of thinking that recognizes the interdependencies and the truths on both sides. Let's consider, for instance, what can happen when abundance becomes overabundance.

Look at food. Over the last few decades, we have increased supply and lowered the price of food significantly, using a combination of technologies (fertilizer, pesticides, and industrial farming) to produce cheap calories—only to find that we've inadvertently created an obesity crisis, itself a scarcity of wellness and longevity. Or look at the modern car: built by state-of-the-art manufacturing, loaded with technology, its good value has led to an overabundance, which in turn has led to congestion (making time more scarce), pollution (making air quality scarce) and suburban sprawl (making community scarce). Or consider over-parenting in affluent circles. We're learning how a child raised on excessive possessions and praise, given every opportunity, protected from failure or even disappointment, can fail to develop a true sense of self. Not knowing how to cope, some of these children develop depression, anxiety, and eating disorders. Finding that line between being intrusive and involved, between laying down the law and allowing for autonomy, defines parenting in an age of abundance. "More struggle" is one psychologist's prescription for a healthy and happy childhood: the imposition of constraints, she believes, builds character.[15]

Think of the relationship between abundance and scarcity as an infinity loop. Abundance is not a self-reinforcing virtuous cycle—it leads to new forms of scarcity. And the ability to unlock the possibility in constraints, in turn, opens up new forms of abundance.

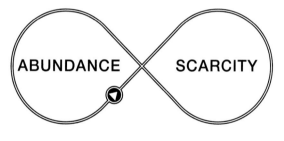

**Figure 9: The scarcity and abundance loop**

This is true in our personal lives, too. If you are anything like us, you are both thrilled and a little stunned by the abundance of the connection economy and its side effects. There's nothing new about information overload at work,[16] but *Scarcity*, by academics Sendhil Mullainathan and Eldar Shafir, discusses what happens to us when confronted by it.[17] They looked primarily at the disabling effects of poverty or dieting on people's decision making, but made the case that a mind confronted by too much work and email exhibits similar patterns to one desperately short of money: scarcity captures our attention so fully that we find it hard to focus on other things. The metaphor we're all familiar with is that of bandwidth. Lack of bandwidth may make us less insightful and less forward-thinking, the research says: scarcity of time can create tunnel vision (or tunneling) that inhibits our ability to make good decisions. There is, of course, also a benefit to time scarcity. Recall Dan Wieden's love of a deadline to focus the mind? The science supports that, too. Where the benefits of being laser-focused end and the costs of tunneling begin is not clear, as the *Scarcity* authors admit. People will have different tolerances and different preferences, though, as the authors point out, we cannot infer preferences from behavior: tunneling isn't a voluntary behavior.

Even the so-called digital native has a love/hate relationship with the abundance we have today. While we attend to our Instagram feed, and Twitter, Medium, Jelly, Tumblr, Spotify, Facebook, FaceTime, Snapchat, Pinterest, email, and texts, we squeeze out the way human beings are really wired to connect: face-to-face—it's something we genuinely need. The recent cultural phenomenon known as phone stacking—where at dinner friends place their phones in a stack on the table to prevent each other from checking them obsessively, and the first one to do so picks up the tab—is one solution to the overabundance of digital connection. We're trying to get the balance right.

And most of us know by now that we can't deal effectively with all the incoming information by multitasking. This turns out to be pure fiction as a productivity hack. It may help us feel productive—giving us lots of little hits of dopamine every time we deal with an email or a tweet—but all we're doing is inefficiently moving back and forth between tasks quickly, or splitting our attention between them and doing each significantly worse.[18] Studies show that multitasking diminishes cognitive skills more than being high on marijuana or losing a night's sleep.[19]

What's more, being able to fully disconnect periodically is such an essential part of the creative process that we may actually be making ourselves less, not more, creative with this flood of information that needs to be dealt with outside of normal office hours. We can, it seems, be victims of abundance as much as scarcity—the personal equivalent of the resource curse, if you will.

No wonder that all of this, in an era when leaner post-recession staffing is the new normal, may actually be contributing to a culture of burnout, not breakthrough. An alarming 70 percent of employees say they have no time for creative or strategic thinking at work.[20] This is something we will return to when we address leadership in the final chapter.

## Flowing the other way: what turns scarcity into abundance?

So characterizing ourselves as primarily living in the Age of Scarcity or the Age of Abundance is to misunderstand the relationship between the two. They are interrelated; we live in both. Abundance is not a smoothly self-reinforcing loop of good: it generates new, often-unintended forms of scarcity. The resource curse is one instance of this. And "problems are the answers to solutions," as economist Brian Arthur points out. Our solutions have a tendency to create new challenges for us to solve.[21]

So far we have examined only the flow from abundance to scarcity in our infinity loop. But of course an infinity loop comes back the other way, too, and the evidence accumulated in these pages shows that there is also a rich potential flow from scarcity to abundance. Constraints, and our ability to transform them, sit right at the intersection between scarcity and abundance. The ability to make constraints beautiful can be the valve that opens up the flow from one to the other.

Look at drip irrigation, such as that developed by Netafim: a response to water scarcity that increases productivity from the same finite acreage of farmland—and with it a domino effect of accompanying benefits, from food security and political stability

# Constraints, and our ability to transform them, sit right at the intersection between scarcity and abundance.

to how women can spend their time when they are not having to walk miles to collect water. Look at how the scarcity of natural resources in Taiwan led to the creation of a new kind of abundance through education, and the economic prosperity that followed. Look at how London 2012's lack of digital signage opened up the opportunity for more entertainment, a chance to add more pleasure to the spectator experience in the Olympic and Paralympic Park, with a more positive outcome for the London games overall. In each case, it was a constraint born of scarcity that started a new virtuous cycle spinning, creating abundance.

## We all need to start

The subtitle of this book proposes that transforming limitations into advantages is everyone's business now. This is a unique moment in history, with the drivers of scarcity and abundance coming together as never before, presenting us all with a unique set of challenges and lending even greater urgency to the theme of this book. We will continue to progress only if we develop a more widespread capability to make constraints beautiful. We must all learn to transform the challenges of scarcity into yet more opportunities for progress—to keep the flow going around the infinity loop.

We can't all work at the scale of the billionaires or the abundance prophets. But we can't simply wait to see if they will take care of all the issues for us, either. We can start in our own lives, in our own businesses, with our own families—changing our responses to constraints, starting to see opportunities where we might once have seen only limitations. We can start small, in our own ways. But we must start.

We should not underestimate how much intention and commitment this will take. Just as dieters tend to think about food at the expense of other things, and the poor make bad decisions because they are worrying so much about money, it's not always easy to see what's most important to work on when you already have more than enough on your plate. Given how likely people under stress are to default to the victim mentality, how likely are we to go hunting for constraints of our own volition? Perhaps our biggest constraint is ourselves.

So we will need the kind of leadership we've seen at McLaren, LPS, Southcentral Foundation, Nike, and Unilever to set the agenda and to keep us honest. And we'll need the mindset, method, and motivation.

In the next chapter, we will summarize how this all works together.

# SCARCITY AND ABUNDANCE: CHAPTER SUMMARY

- This is a unique moment in history, defined by this question: "Is this the Age of Scarcity or the Age of Abundance?"

- Reviewing the arguments on both sides at the personal, professional, and global scale reveals that we always live at the nexus between the two—scarcity and abundance are more accurately seen as an infinite loop, one side constantly feeding and stimulating the other.

- At the global scale, the Age of Scarcity is characterized by increased competition for diminishing resources from growing populations and developing world economies. Commodity prices are spiking, water is scarce, we're over-fishing the seas. We need massive changes to accommodate increased demand.

- In the Age of Abundance, however, we're more connected and share the enormous power of new technology, enabling the bottom-billion people as never before, and facilitating the reinvention of business. We could invent our way out of scarcity.

- At the personal and professional level, abundance is thrilling in the connections and opportunities it brings. But when it becomes an overabundance, it creates scarcity of time and attention in the face of limited personal bandwidth, leaving many of us too busy to be strategic or creative.

- Some believe others will solve problems for us. But this is a dangerous proposition. Given the magnitude of some of the issues, and their pervasiveness in all corners of business, we'll need a greater and more widespread capability to turn constraints into opportunity, in all ways, big and small.

# 10 MAKING CONSTRAINTS BEAUTIFUL

How to use the ABC approach

**THIS CHAPTER FOCUSES ON:**

1. What might be a simple and easy way to use what you learn from this book?

2. What would be a more formal and disciplined way to use this approach with a larger team?

3. Can we summarize the different types of benefits that constraints stimulate?

### How constraints can transform the way we think and behave

**We have come a long way** from the optimistic but vague generality of "every cloud has a silver lining." The cases we have seen have opened up a rich variety of ways in which constraints, whether externally or self-imposed, stimulate better outcomes and solutions.

Constraints are not the forces of regression or punitive restriction we tend to think of them as. On the contrary—they are liberators of new possibilities, and we need to have a completely new kind of relationship with them. Their apparent limitations force us to question, surface, and challenge assumptions that, while they might have been reasonable once, are no longer useful strategic foundations for us. They push us to think of what we do or offer in an entirely new way, offering up a fresh and fertile perspective. They impel us to behave differently—amplifying, simplifying, dramatizing. They make us search for and find primary solutions in secondary or unconsidered areas. They drive us to create new kinds of alliances, develop new kinds of capabilities. They are parameters that have the potential to expand, not constrict.

Table 5 summarizes some of the key benefits we have seen constraints stimulate in the cases we have explored. It cannot hope to be definitive, and it doesn't include, for example, the focused energy that working with clear constraints releases. But it does give some sense of the range of potential ways in which constraints can open up new perspectives and possibilities.

The virtuous reader who has read the book cover to cover, and spent some time with the cases, will point out that some of the specific examples could be categorised in more than one box; this is true. The complex sequence of can-ifs precipitated by Taiwan's constraints clearly occupy a number of these boxes, but even a single constraint (such as Formula One's loss of tobacco sponsorship), if the implications are big enough, can stimulate a number of these to be explored for potential benefits at the same time. Constraints will force us in many directions. They can work in a range of ways and open up a number of different vistas.

### Why inventiveness is as important as innovation

We have said that we want to champion inventiveness, rather than innovation. While successful innovation is obviously essential to all enterprise, it has become too elitist in

Constraints stimulate us to:

| | |
|---|---|
| **Productively question...** | ...what in our past/present is holding us back? |
| | ...what really matters today? |
| | ...whether entirely new possibilities exist? |
| **Rethink or reframe...** | ...how we think about the challenge. |
| | ...how we see what we have. |
| | ...how we define success. |
| **Find the benefit in subtraction by...** | ...making what we have work harder (efficiency). |
| | ...eliminating the unnecessary/superfluous. |
| | ...making simple better than complex. |
| **Find new ways to augment by...** | ...amplifying what we already have. |
| | ...adding something new. |
| | ...forming new partnerships. |
| **Find or create new kinds of solutions...** | ...within what we already have. |
| | ...by elevating the overlooked. |
| | ...in entirely new and unexpected places or ways. |
| **Build entirely new systems or business models in the form of...** | ...new virtuous cycles. |
| | ...new ecosystems. |

**For example:**

Unilever's tomatoes, back-end language

citizenM

Aircraft carrier, Hövding personal airbag, SAB barley

LPS and ExitTicket, Audi Le Mans

SCF customer-owners, FIFA 13 waiting, Taiwan's people as a natural resource
Nike's water-based glue

McLaren

Hue color-only salons, food trucks

Google homepage, Mojang

Jagger, Industrial Theatre

London 2012, Zappos, Mario

Virgin America, Airbnb photographers, BrewDog (crowdfunding), ColaLife

FNB, PHD Source, M-PESA

Heineken France, Air New Zealand, Warby Parker

Surf, Nike Flyknit, Air Max 360, IKEA table

Netafim, Unilever palm oil

Rent the Runway, Taiwan education system

*Table 5: Key benefits of constraints*

> # We need another way of thinking and behaving inventively that sits alongside innovation.

concept and practice to be a useful word for us here. We need a complementary concept to the "this-is-difficult-that's-why-we-have-a-special-department-of-really-creative-people-who-do-it-and-not-everyone-is-really-creative-like-them" culture of innovation. We need another way of thinking and behaving that sits alongside innovation in ourselves and our organizations, one that is more democratic, that is accessible, important, and possible for all, and that is understood as a powerful and exciting way of responding to and transforming apparent limitations into sources of beautiful opportunity. This concept, we propose, is inventiveness.

Inventiveness, and the small and big breakthroughs it generates, will be at least as important as innovation to the future of what we do and how we progress. It will be the thousand small ways in which people throughout the company find new sources of possibility in the weekly challenges they face. It will be the structured question ("What is the constraint we need to make beautiful?") introduced at the heart of the team plan for next year. It will be a leader's propelling question that prompts us to challenge our own path dependence and open up new ways of thinking about how to grow.

And if it is to work like that, it will need to be a capability that we talk about, celebrate, and actively develop, in ourselves and in our teams.

## Can all constraints be made beautiful?

In Chapter Eight, we saw that in their analysis of the psychological effects of scarcity, Mullainathan and Shafir observed how scarcity can completely capture the mind, creating a tunnel vision that leads to poorer decision making, and behaviors that make the situation worse—a vicious cycle downwards.[1] Their studies suggest this is not only true of the poor, but of people who feel scarcity of any kind. How does our emerging, optimistic view of the opportunity in constraints sit with this?

Our focus here has been on less extreme situations than are the focus of much of Mullainathan and Shafir's work. *A Beautiful Constraint* is not intended to be an answer to fierce austerity, or grinding poverty, or the isolation of extreme loneliness or locked-in syndrome. There are constraints so severe that saying that everyone has the ability to find opportunity in them would be wrong, and beauty an inappropriate word.

Yet a thoughtful optimist would, even here, note two key points:

- Even in these very difficult circumstances, remarkable breakthroughs are starting to be made, in big and in small ways: revolutions in education quality in the most deprived areas, microcredit-financed entrepreneurialism, turning waste into energy, creating free light through soda bottles, the domino effects of drip irrigation and more productive farming practices. And of course the can-do spirit of India's Jugaad sees small opportunities everywhere, and not simply in their famous diesel-powered carts. A friend in Mumbai talked of a man in the city cycling to his job as a manual laborer each day without a power source at home to come back to. By putting a small generator on his bike, he charges it enough to run a light bulb for the rest of the evening when he gets home. He uses his commute to transform his evening.[2] While no one should romanticize poverty, especially the conditions in India's slums, there is room for invention here, too. After visiting Dharavi, a slum of Mumbai, the *Economist* noted that they are "vibrantly and triumphantly alive … everyone is working hard and everyone is moving up."[3]

- The person most affected by the constraint will not always be the person best placed to see the possibility in it. Hence the importance of external groups like the d.school, who aren't directly impacted by the constraints themselves, and come with different skills, able to see the possibility as well as the constraint, even in some of the most challenging circumstances.

There are some constraints so severe, then, that they sit outside this discussion. But those are not the ones most of us face, and not the ones that will define our progress; they are not those that we currently feel victim to and most need to transform. And yet, even there, the human ability to find potential in those most straightened of circumstances remains one of our most uplifting qualities.

## A series of strategies: Working with the ABC approach

We saw that key spurs of our ability to be inventive in this way, to find fertility in constraint, were the scale of our ambition and our emotional investment. There were sequenced stages that each of us potentially goes through in response to a constraint: the victim stage (where we react to the constraint as a necessarily limiting force), the neutralizing stage (where we refuse to accept that the constraint needs to limit us, and find ways to reduce or nullify its apparent restrictions and still deliver our ambition), and the transformative stage (where we use the nature of the constriction as an offer to explore new kinds of solutions altogether, ones that take us to a stronger position than before). It is the capability to move ourselves and our team into these second and third stages that allows us to be inventive and make constraints beautiful.

Trevor Davis, a distinguished engineer at IBM, observed that creativity is simply a series of strategies. Rather just than an innate ability ("she is, he isn't, we are, they're not"), it is a series of learned approaches. Inventiveness, as a particular type of pragmatic creativity, is no different. A number of the protagonists and organizations we have looked at, after all, were not confident in their ability to answer the questions asked of them, but new possibilities opened up as they moved through the series of strategies they undertook to tackle them.

At the heart of changing our approach towards constraints is changing our core question about them. Simply having a framing orientation of "How can we make this constraint beautiful?" (or even "Where might be the beauty in this constraint?") is in itself a change of attitude that is more likely to lead us to see the potential and the opportunity in our situation or challenge.

Our ambition has been not simply to offer inspiration, but to start to derive just enough method to help a team explore the transformative possibilities in a constraint. The thinking and tools we have laid out are designed to be able to be both modular (usable on their own in different stages at different times) and able to be used at either a simple level or a more rigorous and detailed one (as part of a disciplined strategic exploration, for instance).

# Our strategic planning process for the year ahead could include a new question: What is the constraint we need to make beautiful?

At the end of the previous chapter, we talked of the importance of commitment here, and how it will take real focus and leadership to unlock the possibility in our biggest constraints. Nevertheless, there will be some kinds of lower-level challenges for which we don't have to embrace the entire ABC process in order to get some of the benefits of it. So we can take the overall approach on our own terms, and choose the level at which we want to apply it, ranging from simply reconsidering the way we see and talk about constraints to implementing much more far-reaching programs of capability development in our organization. How we apply it will depend on our starting point:

## A. A spur to look at constraints differently

*The starting point:* "I agree with the principle, but I don't need all the details: I want to use it as a basic orientation, not a process."

*How to use it in this case:* Each of us is forced to confront constraints on a regular basis. You can use the book and the stories within it simply as inspiration to look beyond the initial, natural reaction as a victim, and focus instead on the possibilities that the constraint should make you think about. Recognizing where you tend to start and stop within that sequence of stages (victim, neutralizer, transformer), and being encouraged by seeing others doing much more than this, is valuable in itself.

How we change our language can also make a surprisingly large difference. Recent learning has made all of us more aware in recent years of the value of nudges in changing behavior,[4] and how we frame questions has long been understood to be a key part of stimulating better outcomes.[5] Simply getting people accustomed to asking "How can we make this constraint beautiful?" will start to help initiate different kinds of thinking and behavior. (What it won't do on its own, though, is drive tenacity further down the road if the going gets rough.)

## B. Taking two or three simple principles into everyday use

*The reaction:* "Two or three of these thoughts really resonate; I want to explore using them and see how they land with my team."

*How to use it in this case:* If you want to do more than change your attitude, you might find it useful to take away two or three principles that can help you think more productively about constraint-driven inventiveness. We'd suggest that the ones to focus on are surfacing path dependence, linking a bold ambition to the constraint to make a propelling question (and addressing that as the challenge, instead of the apparent problem presented by the constraint in its original form), and the can-if way of framing the solution-development process. They are easy to understand, easy to communicate, and don't require the formality of the tools in order to make a stimulating difference to a conversation within a team.

## C. A tailored use of the tools underneath the principles

*The reaction:* "I've got a particular constraint I'd like to try this on. I want to try the discipline of some of the tools, without making it into a longer strategic process."

*How to use it in this case:* This involves a little more conscious effort with the tools and techniques under the two or three principles you want to apply. You'll want to pick and choose from the following list to customize your own miniprogram, based on what best suits your situation. This is probably best done with others, but can also be done alone, and is more suitable for situations where you need to respond positively to a constraint, rather than deliberately impose it on yourself, your team, or your business.

Share a summary of the book with your team beforehand (you can get one from hello@abeautifulconstraint.com), and prepare or draw large-scale versions of the maps or tools you are going to use. Give yourself two hours with each of the tools to explain, explore, use and review each in sequence. Those that seem particularly useful or fertile you can then choose to go into deeper.

Use the guidelines in the relevant chapters to help your team use the tools most effectively. And be prepared to be tenacious; if you aren't getting good enough answers the first time you do it, you may need to introduce a broader range of "intelligently naïve" people into the process and use their different perspectives to explore it more productively again.

## D. A structured program to transform a particular constraint

*The reaction:* "I have a particular constraint I would like to try this on, and need to take my team with me. It will be valuable for all of us to move together through this in a disciplined, collective way."

*How to use it in this case:* Figure 10 serves as a map to guide you and your team through the entire ABC process and key tools described in the book.

### The ABC Approach

page 16

#### 1. Victim, Neutralizer, and Transformer

Understanding our starting point, and why we are there, will help us understand which of the following tools and processes will be most important to us.

How much do we believe it is possible for us to make this constraint beautiful? To what degree do we feel we know how to begin to do it? How much do we want to do it? A low threshold in the first of these will need us to do more priming before we get started—becoming more conscious of other areas of our lives when we have done this, our organization's history of doing this, and the possibilities others have unlocked with the same kind of constraint. A low threshold in the second of them leads to focusing on the tools in the following four groups. A low threshold in the third will require getting much clearer on why this matters, and spending time with the emotional motivations around why we want to succeed, and the implications of failure.

### 2. Break Path Dependence

page 34

If we feel we may have locked-in ways of thinking and behaving that could prevent us from finding the real possibilities in this constraint, we need to surface and examine them.

The first part of this is examining our organizational biases. A simple way to start doing this is to write down the six most important words in the organization (marketing, sales, innovation, consumer insight, and so on) and discuss what we really mean by them. If what we mean by "innovation" is "functionally better products," for example, perhaps we need to explore a different way to think about innovation that would allow us to make the most of this apparent limitation.

The second part is to unbundle the core elements of how we usually approach this kind of challenge. Use the BREAK questions on pages 49–52 to unpack and question Beginning Assumptions, Routines and Processes, Expected Sources of Solutions, Associations and Relationships, and KPIs and Measures of Success.

### 3. Ask Propelling Questions

page 56

A propelling question links a bold ambition to a significant constraint. It is the tension between these two that starts to make a constraint fertile.

There are different families of constraints, and different families of ambition. If we are starting with an imposed constraint, we'll want to explore what kind of ambition might be most stimulating to pair it with. If we are imposing a constraint on ourselves, we'll want to start with the ambition and explore which kind of constraint might open up the most opportunity.

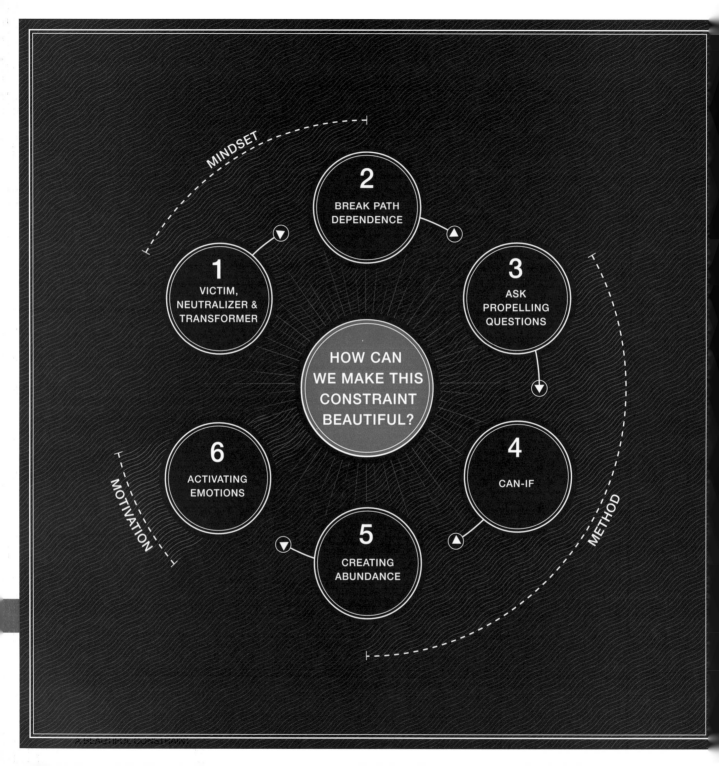

It is called a propelling question because it pushes us off the paths we have become used to—we simply cannot answer it the same way we have answered our previous three questions.

To be most useful, a propelling question needs to have specificity (precision on the ambition and the constraint), authority (it comes from someone who needs to be answered) and legitimacy (we can recognize the underlying validity of both sides of the question).

### 4. Can-If

page 78

Keeping optimism and openness in what might be a difficult, trial-and-error solution development means that how we frame the potential answers is key. Making every one of the team begin every statement with "We can if," rather than "We can't because," keeps the conversation on how the problem can be solved, and doesn't allow it to become a different conversation about whether it can be solved.

The Can-If Map offers nine launch pads to start these conversations, and two examples in each case to bring them to life. You will get more out of using the map if you follow the slightly more formal process on pages 99–100.

### 5. Creating Abundance

page 102

If we have a scarcity of the resources we need, we have to find a way to access them from elsewhere.

We are going to stop thinking of our resources as those we control or are given, and think of them instead as those we can access. The grid is a prompt to explore each potential source in stakeholders, external partners, abundance owners, and competitors, and then become clear, for each of those potential sources, how we can best trade with or influence them to give us access to what we need.

### 6. Activating Emotions

page 124

Inventiveness starts when a question meets an emotion. If we cannot connect the need to transform our constraint with an emotional reason why it matters to us, we simply won't have the stubborn adaptiveness and creative tenacity further down the road, when our initial solutions hit their first setbacks. Finding a

**Figure 10:**
**The ABC approach**

way to surface and even amplify our personal emotional commitment, over and above alignment with a corporate purpose, will make the difference between success and failure.

The map of activating emotions is a piece of stimulus to prompt us to find productive motivations, both of positive and negative emotions. Each type of emotion has a particular value to us, and we are looking for an authentic narrative about what we are trying to do that constantly reminds us of the emotional incentives both to succeed and to avoid failure.

### E. An opportunity to impose a constraint on ourselves, and stimulate us to respond to it

*The reaction:* "I am struck by the challenge represented by the Unreasonable Consumer/ Customer/Regulator/Competitor. We need to be less complacent and stretch ourselves in terms of what could be possible. We should impose a relevant constraint on ourselves that forces us to really push our thinking, and puts us in a stronger position for the future in terms of defense and offense."

*How to use it in this case:* Most of the core process here will be similar to C or D above, depending on how seriously you want your team to address the challenge. Key, though, will be understanding the right constraint to impose and why, in your propelling question. The nature of the unreasonableness may make this a very easy decision, and define it for you. If not, Table 5 in this chapter might be a useful stimulus, as you think about what kinds of constraints might prompt the lines of inquiry and thinking you feel the group needs to explore. It will be important to give the question real authority and legitimacy in order for the group to embrace it, rooting it in your purpose, and an urgency to deliver that purpose.

### F. A different way of thinking about the capabilities our business needs to develop to flourish, and the kinds of strategic initiative we may want to put in place to make sure that it does

*The reaction:* "The impact I need this to have requires more than a single process. My team or organization needs to integrate this way of thinking more fundamentally into the way we think, plan, and solve, and I need to raise the capability development of some of my team in key areas to enable them to respond to this kind of approach."

*How to use it in this case:* The final level at which you can choose to use this looks beyond responses to particular constraints, and instead to the development of organizational capabilities, the refinement of key strategic processes, and how to frame strategic initiatives.

Organizational capabilities might include, for instance, introducing resourcefulness or commercial innovation as being measurable and rewarded development ambitions; resourcefulness could be assessed at an individual and team level.

Our regular strategic planning processes for the year ahead could include a new kind of question: What is the constraint we need to make beautiful here? This may be a parameter in the open, which we have been skirting for a while, or it may be an issue that needs more surfacing and discussion. But integrating it explicitly into the way we think about developing plans and solutions for the year ahead will open up new avenues and possibilities, and spur us into fresh and possibly transformative perspectives.

## Can there really be a recipe for lemonade?

One can't reduce all the rich possibilities of inventive thinking to a table and a process. But we can get further than desire, good intentions, and all those well-worn and often misleading clichés about innovation. Necessity is the mother of invention? Well, she may be one of its parents, but only one, as we saw in the diversity of activating emotions in Chapter Six. Whether you think you can or think you can't, you're right. Henry Ford's dictum about positivity is one important strand of mindset—but mindset alone, as we have seen, will not succeed without enough methodology to guide a team trying to answer a question they don't know how to answer, and the right motivation to drive the solution around the road bumps that will come its way.

So while we can't codify inventiveness, we can infer enough about what kind of mindset, method, and motivation will be needed to derive a series of strategies that will give us a stronger chance of success. We can learn from those who have been successful here. It isn't magic, but a different kind of discipline. We can use and apply the approaches that have helped others break through to transform our own constraints as well.

## MAKING CONSTRAINTS BEAUTIFUL: CHAPTER SUMMARY

- There are some extreme forms of constraint that clearly sit outside the scope of this book; its focus is the more general ones we face in our business and personal lives.

- It is designed to stimulate a pragmatic inventiveness throughout an organization, as an essential complement to an increasingly specialized and siloed world of innovation; we need both to progress.

- There are a number of levels at which we can choose to apply the learnings and approaches in this book to our own situations.

- At its simplest and easiest, we can simply use it as a spur to see constraints in a different way. Asking the question "How can I make this constraint beautiful?" or "Where is the beauty in this constraint?" starts to move us from a victim mindset to looking for the opportunity.

- If we want to pursue it with a little more discipline, the concepts and tools around path dependence, propelling questions, and the can-if approach are three that are easy to communicate and use.

- And the chapter also offers a fuller process, for those wanting more structure and rigor to take a team through this approach on a given constraint.

# 11 LEADERSHIP & THE FUTURE OF CONSTRAINTS

The opportunity for progress

1. What are the implications for leadership?

2. Why is this more than an invitation to cost cutting?

3. Why is this capability so important to our individual and collective future?

**By 1957, Theodore Geisel,** better known as Dr. Seuss, was already a bestselling author of children's books. But it was the imposition of a stringent constraint that would lead him to pen a book that has sold more than ten million copies around the world. A 1954 article in *Life* magazine had criticized the insipid fare on offer in the American classrooms of the time, "pallid primers [with] abnormally courteous, unnaturally clean boys and girls," and recommended that some of the "wonderfully imaginative geniuses among children's illustrators" be given the opportunity to do something new. William Spaulding, then head of Houghton Mifflin's education division, invited Geisel to dinner to ask him to "write me a story that first-graders can't put down."

The added requirement came later, in the form of a list of words that Geisel was to use. Phonics was the new wave in education at the time, teaching children the sounds that letters and groups of letters make so that they could figure out unfamiliar words themselves. Spaulding wanted a story written using a vocabulary of just 225 specific words. Geisel responded first as a victim:

> *At first I thought it was impossible and ridiculous, and I was about to get out of the whole thing; I then decided to look at the list one more time and to use the first two words that rhymed as the title of the book—cat and hat.*[1]

*The Cat in the Hat* was an immediate success, praised as an exciting alternative to the Dick and Jane primers. It transformed children's books and the nature of primary education. Random House appropriated Spaulding's model, launching the Beginner Books series with Geisel in charge, and soon became the largest publisher of children's books in America. When the head of Random House bet Geisel $50 that he couldn't write a book using just 50 words, Geisel responded with *Green Eggs and Ham*, which uses 49 words of one syllable and the word *anywhere*. It became the best selling Dr. Seuss book ever.

Stories like this one, of ingenuity in the face of a constraint, are all around us. When we come across them, we enjoy the small triumphs of the human spirit that they represent. We can't help but love Dr. Seuss for rising to the challenge: the compact journey Geisel took from victim to transformer is, in its own way, a heroic one. We admire those who make the journey, and aspire to make it ourselves, because it is at the heart of what it means to be human: to create, to progress despite—or because of—

***Dr. Seuss and** The Cat in the Hat*

limitations. We impose limits upon ourselves because they make us better: they elevate our art (from sonnets to haiku), enhance our piety (Ramadan, Lent), and improve our play (the basketball shot clock).

Knowing this doesn't necessarily make it easy to find solutions, though. As we have seen in many of the cases in this book, even for those who see constraints as fundamental to defining a problem, and appreciate their value, often the initial response is that the constraint will make life harder, even impossible. And understandably so—whether a ban on advertising, the threat of water scarcity, or advancing schoolchildren three grade levels in a year, these are daunting challenges. And with a team unsure that they have the ability to do it, and that the organization will support them (and not fight them) if they try, it becomes clear that this is not a process that can be managed. It must be led.

In Chapter Eight (Constraint-Driven Cultures), we saw clear implications for leaders who want to incorporate this process into their organizations. If we are simply looking for innovative ways, say, to deal with a lack of marketing budget, we can, of course, draw on the stimulus of tools and inspiration and begin. We don't all have to hire a brigadier from the Marines to help sharpen the sword. But if we are heading into a more constrained future, then how we manage those constraints will determine how we progress, and it will be important to understand a little more about how to lead in the face of constraint.

## Leadership and constraints

Whether or not they have the seniority or the title, leaders are those who know how to influence others, to get them to work hard and constructively toward a common goal.[2] In many of the cases here, the teams involved didn't know how to answer the challenge, and were initially uncertain that an answer was even possible. So, what were the most important areas of focus for leaders in these situations, and what characteristics did they share?

### They believed transformers are made, not born

While some of those we met clearly have advantages in skills, personality traits, or personal experience, none claim an inventiveness gene, and many were solving this kind of challenge for the first time. These leaders understood that even people who don't think of themselves as capable of solving this kind of challenge can do it with the right mindset, strategies, and motivation, and it is their role to inspire and enable each of those three conditions for success.

They also knew that new habits of mind can be created with regular use. So the leader that proactively imposes constraints, as South Africa's Discovery or Sweden's IKEA does, is increasing capability as well as pushing for more ambitious solutions. The tools described here provide strategies for leaders who aspire to do the same.

### They steered their organization toward constraints, not away from them

Getting to the future first, and in the best shape to meet its unreasonable needs, is the way to develop competitive advantage. We saw Nike anticipate water shortages, and IKEA boldly plan for smaller apartment sizes. The confidence to navigate teams toward constraints tends to follow a first, smaller triumph, which is why building the capability early, with smaller constraints or lower-hanging fruit, is so important.

When Formula One's ruling body told the teams, in advance, of the 2014 rule change that would impose a 35 percent reduction on the amount of fuel a car would be able to use in a race, some teams (such as Ferrari) protested, spending time resisting the change. Mercedes, on the other hand, accepted it almost immediately. Putting their engine and race teams in the same room together for the first time (until then they had been based in two different countries), Mercedes used the months Ferrari spent denying the constraint to work out how to approach it. By the time the change came into force, Mercedes were the best prepared for it, with a breakthrough in turbocharger technology that gave them the fastest cars, and the world title. For these leaders who were thinking competitively, steering their team towards constraints sooner than their rivals was an important source of competitive advantage.

### They set a high level of ambition, and legitimized that ambition

The leaders we met understood that raising the level of ambition alongside a constraint creates the impetus to abandon current paths, assumptions, and ways of thinking. This is when it becomes obvious that what may have worked before won't work now. The clarity and boldness of the ambition energizes a team most powerfully when it is connected to the larger purpose and strategies of the organization.

These leaders also gave the ambition an organizational legitimacy. They helped the team see that this is an ambition whose solution the organization needs and will embrace. Renaming Hannah Jones' group as Sustainable Business & Innovation (replacing Corporate Responsibility), for example, was symbolic of their weaving their ambitions into the fabric of Nike's future plans.

### They knew when to reject compromise of that ambition

It's easy and understandable to settle in the face of a daunting constraint, especially when the team has worked hard to solve a problem. Though some level of compromise may be inevitable, however, these leaders knew how and when to push for more. Yves Behar's team kept going back to the driving belief of the OLPC project, again and again, when setbacks threatened to compromise it. London 2012's Heather McGill accepted their technology limitations, but didn't accept the crowd-control solutions of previous Olympic and Paralympic Games. She held the team to the real ambition for the spectator experience, and pushed for more.

### They got people to believe that it is possible

This is perhaps the most challenging of all. These leaders were able to convince a sometimes-skeptical team that, no matter how difficult the constrained ambition appeared to them, it was possible to find a good, even transformative solution, and they would find it.

There was no easy how-to for this. For some, it lay in communicating that there was no alternative: necessity (either of delivering their purpose or moving away from their current reality) was their possibility. For others, it lay in amplifying the belief that this organization had this ability at its core in some way, in the stories about its early growth. For others still, it was a personal embodiment of their own conviction that there was a real opportunity here, and they were going to find it.

### They used tension and storytelling to generate a longer-term emotional commitment

Above and beyond providing McRaven's mission clarity, these leaders were able to gain personal commitment from their team by wrapping the task in a narrative laced with light and dark emotion: vivid pictures of success and failure, creating the contrast and richness of emotional connection that will fuel the creative tenacity it will take to push through. We saw how Louise Waters combines deep frustration with care for her disadvantaged students, and a feisty brewery combines an articulate hostility to everything mainstream brewers produce with a desire to make everyone as passionate about craft beer as they are.

### They encouraged and enabled their teams to challenge the organization's routines and assumptions

These leaders were not only prepared to break their own path dependence, but actively asked for, encouraged, and supported it in the organization. It takes rigor and discipline to constructively make visible the invisible patterns of an organization, calling for a new level of candor and persistence (look at McLaren's Ron Dennis, pushing his teams to examine every process for a better way, even though they were initially skeptical). Clearly, it will not always be as root-and-branch as in McLaren's case; it may lie in questioning assumptions and processes in a very specific area, such as what it means to develop and host a good customer service experience, for instance.

### They knew how to manage the transformation threshold

We saw in Chapter One that leaders effective in dealing with constraints know that there are times to raise the stakes and ask for more, and times to allow the organization to run efficiently and effectively. Few cultures can live at a high level of transformation all the time, nor would they want to. "Small i" inventiveness that can show up every day, without any disruption to the organization, should become routine practice, though, so that when the major constraints appear, an organization will be ready. Their organizations don't run so lean that their people have no slack within which to work against these more significant constraints when they need to.

The enormous opportunity that lies in the ability to transform constraints suggests that these qualities are important for any leader at any time. But as we begin to feel the pressure of scarcity more and more, and the corresponding need to get better at creating abundance, we need to start thinking about these skills as a fundamental dimension of a new kind of leadership.

So why is this not just an open invitation to the CFO to cut budgets and position it as a spur to all of us to unearth transformative opportunities? The leadership qualities above, along with all that we've learned so far, should make that easy to answer. A constraint without an ambition, and an ambition linked to the organization's core purpose, is not going to have the legitimacy to motivate a genuine attempt to find strong solutions—it is not a propelling question. There is no attempt to elevate a team to a transformative threshold here. The lack of an emotional connection to the task will mean that initiatives will tend to run aground in the first shallows. And in such situations, the injunction tends to be "do the same, with less." The first part of that challenge offers little encouragement to break path dependence, or challenge any of the upstream assumptions the business makes about what it does and how it does it. Simply imposing a constraint of any kind on a team doesn't in itself drive transformation; it misunderstands when, how, and why people succeed in making constraints beautiful.

## Why is this everybody's business?

We knew, from the outset of this project, that our dive into the world of constraints would lead us to the issues we touched upon in the "Scarcity and Abundance" chapter (Chapter Nine). But we were struck by the strong sense of urgency with which we heard them discussed in so many places. Nike, IKEA, and Unilever, three exemplars of constraint-driven cultures, are increasingly motivated by the need to perform better against significant natural-resource constraints. Audi and Tesla are responding, in different ways, to the need to address issues of excess carbon in our atmosphere, while South African Breweries pioneers new techniques to reduce water use. And look at the ways the Qatari National Food Security Program is grappling with the many constraints around food security in the region.

As parents, it's hard for us not to be alarmed by the fragile and perilous state of the world. Our children will feel the impact of future scarcity the most, yet the causes need to be tackled by us—and some say we may be too late. The sense of helplessness this kind of narrative engenders stands in stark contrast to the more positive nature of the initiatives described in this book, and some of the more optimistic visions of the future that accompany them. Living with both simultaneously for some time, we found ourselves, as many of our research subjects did, oscillating between the positive vision of success and all the things standing in its way. Just the kind of mix, Professor Oettingen's Mental Constrasting would say, that should drive us to act.

> The real world imposes constraints of many, many kinds … Freedom, in the real world, is not utter license to do as we please; it is much closer to Robert Frost's famous formula—"moving easy in harness." Constraints are always there. It's a matter of how we move within them.
>
> —Robert Bethune[3]

Our own first action, then, is to try to steer the dialogue toward the kind of inventiveness that the world needs more of today, that can sit alongside more formal and specialized innovation processes. Second, by offering just enough process to start to approach a bigger propelling question of more profound consequence, we hope to give more people more confidence to embrace a new level of constraint, and perhaps help nudge the world toward a more constructive approach to its problems. And, third, we ourselves are committed to making this work an important focus of our own organization.

In the end, how we each define the ambitions and constraints we need to work with most is obviously up to each of us. The ABC approach can be used to win races, take share from competitors, engage with more customers, and succeed in what New York University Professor James P. Carse calls "the finite game," a game with a beginning and an end, played only to be won.[4] But Carse also talks of the Infinite Game, the larger game of life, without an end, that we all want to *keep* playing; the one not defined by one person winning and another person losing, the one that requires abundance to sustain it. Sustaining the infinite game for humanity is far from inevitable and, if we lose, the finite games end too—which is why we see what have historically been some of the world's largest, most competitive companies fundamentally rethinking historical path dependence to succeed at the infinite game. Nike needs many more of its competitors to adopt its practices around material use in order to move the entire industry in a sustainable direction; Airbus needs to pool resources with its historical enemies to allow them all to succeed in hitting emissions targets. They need their competitors to play the infinite game with them, so that we can all continue to enjoy the profit and pleasure of the finite games.

## "The beginning of a glorious age"

As we write, the media is full of the changing world order. China is due to overtake the United States as the world's largest economy earlier than predicted: five of the ten largest companies in the world are now Chinese. Apple recently lost its top spot as the world's most valuable brand (to Google), yet still has a cash pile that could halve the national debt of Russia. And, in other news, Costa Rica topped the Happy Planet Index for the second time in a row.

But it's the *how* of the changing world order that needs to be scrutinized as much as the who. The enormous questions we face as people, whether parents, business leaders, or global citizens, won't be addressed by changes in the players per se, as much as by changes in how they (and we) think and behave. It's the innovative approaches to poverty and disease catalyzed by the billionaire philanthropists that are as interesting as who developed them. It is the prospect of a third industrial revolution, driven by new forms of distributed manufacturing, enabled by 3-D printers, and powered by locally generated sustainable energy, that will create dramatic shifts. It's in how we harness the enormous power of technology to rapidly accelerate learning, to better enable minds to invent a new future. And it's in the prospects of creating a more global mindset that can come together to play the infinite game. Our hope is that this approach allows more people to participate and play a meaningful role, however small, in creating this larger shift.

In the BBC program *The Age of Invention,* aired in 2013, the engineer, inventor, and businessman James Dyson was asked if he thought everything that could be invented had been invented. His response was instant and heartfelt. No, he said, this is a wonderful moment—a very exciting time for engineers. We have got to stop using all these resources: we no longer have to build the biggest and quickest, we have to build something that uses less: less water, less power, fewer materials. The inventions that are coming, he believes, will come from new materials that answer that challenge, and from these new materials, scientists and engineers will be able to create a new generation of extraordinary products. We are, he concluded, at the beginning of "a glorious age."[5]

We like and share Dyson's optimism. In the introduction we posed the question "Are things getting better, or are they getting worse?" Surely one way to give us a fighting chance at better is if we ourselves can learn, and help others to learn, how to make constraints beautiful.

## LEADERSHIP & THE FUTURE OF CONSTRAINTS: CHAPTER SUMMARY

- Simply being able to see the beneficial effects of constraints doesn't make finding those benefits easy. This is an approach that requires skillful leadership.

- Our research revealed a number of common leadership qualities in those who successfully find beauty in constraint:

    - They believe transformers are made, not born.
    - They steer their organization toward constraints, not away from them.
    - They set a high level of ambition alongside the constraint, and legitimize that ambition.
    - They know when to reject compromising that ambition in searching for solutions.
    - They are able to create belief in their teams that it is possible to find a solution for an apparently impossible challenge.
    - They use tension and storytelling to generate emotional commitment.
    - They encourage and enable their teams to challenge current routines and assumptions.
    - They know how to manage the transformation threshold.

- Scarcity in our future will require more leaders with these qualities, and far more constraint-driven invention, to keep generating abundance.

- And, indeed, the challenges we all face mean that developing this capability is no longer just the province of creatives, engineers, and designers—it is everyone's business now.

- This book and its approach aim to help by structuring the dialogue around constraint-driven invention and by providing just enough process to give us the ability to begin to transform constraints for ourselves.

- In short, in facing our future challenges it should become second nature for us all to ask with confidence—"How can we make this constraint beautiful?"

# NOTES AND SOURCES

## Introduction

1. *Life: Keith Richards*, by Keith Richards, W&N (UK) and Little, Brown & Co. (US), 2010—Jagger is estimated to be worth $300 million today, aside from the ongoing value of the Stones as a business. While there is clearly much more to the band's success than their lead singer's performing chops, it is striking that their revenue today is largely driven through touring and performing, and the spectacle they still offer.
2. Nicola Kemp, "Tuning Out: Why brands need to disconnect and embrace the new simplicity", Marketing, March 26, 2013, www.marketingmagazine.co.uk/article/1176005/tuning-out-why-brands-need-disconnect-embrace-new-simplicity.
3. Timothy D. Wilson, *Redirect: The Surprising New Science of Psychological Change* (New York: Little, Brown & Co., 2011).
4. Eric Ries, *The Lean Startup: How Constant Innovation Creates Radically Successful Businesses* (New York: Portfolio Penguin, 2011).
5. Charles Leadbeater, *The Frugal Innovator: Creating Change on a Shoestring Budget* (New York: Palgrave Macmillan, 2014).
6. Navi Radjou, Jaideep Prabhu, Simone Ahuja, *Jugaad Innovation: Think Frugal, Be Flexible, Generate Breakthrough Growth* (Hoboken, NJ: John Wiley & Sons, 2012).
7. Malcolm Gladwell, *David and Goliath: Underdogs, Misfits and The Art of Battling Giants* (New York: Little, Brown & Co., 2013).
8. Eliyahu M. Goldratt and Jeff Cox, *The Goal: A Process of Ongoing Improvement* (Gower Publishing Ltd., 2004).
9. Jennifer Schlesinger, "10 Minutes That Changed Southwest Airlines' Future," CNBC, July 15, 2011, www.cnbc.com/id/43768488.
10. Tina Rosenberg, "A Hospital Network with a Vision," *New York Times*, January 16, 2013 http://opinionator.blogs.nytimes.com/2013/01/16/in-india-leading-a-hospital-franchise-with-vision/?_php=true&_type=blogs&_r=0.

11. www.thechallengerproject.com; Some of our recent clients include Audi, London 2012, Charles Schwab, PepsiCo, Sony PlayStation and Unilever.
12. We are also a little wary of how some of the findings from academia, with their reliance on experiments with students in labs, are some distance from the real-world problems we have encountered, and are often contradictory, and so have been reticent to rely too much on them.

## Chapter One: Victim, Neutralizer, and Transformer

1. Author's own interview with Naty Barak, Chief Sustainability Officer, Netafim.
2. W+K now has eight offices around the world, continues to create iconic communications for the likes of Coca-Cola, Old Spice, and Chrysler, and has extended its capabilities beyond communications, into programming and content.
3. Linda Tischler, "All About Yves," *Fast Company*, 2007, www.fastcompany.com/60525/all-about-yves.
4. Author's own interview with Yves Behar.
5. While 2.5 million laptops have been distributed around the world as part of the program, opinions are divided as to the success of the One Laptop Per Child initiative overall.
6. Marissa Ann Mayer, "Creativity Loves Constraints," *Bloomberg Businessweek*, February 12, 2006, http://www.businessweek.com/stories/2006-02-12/creativity-loves-constraints.
7. Author's own interview.
8. Official PlayStation magazine, UK Agenda, "10 Questions for Todd Batty, Creative Director EA Canada," April 2012.
9. Author's own interview.
10. Mayer, "Creativity Loves Constraints."
11. C. K. Joyce, *The Blank Page: Effects of Constraint on Creativity*, PhD thesis, Haas School of Business, University of California, Berkeley, 2009, www.caneelian.com/research/.
12. Author's own interview.
13. "Jerry Seinfeld Intends to Die Standing Up," *New York Times* magazine, December 20, 2012, www.nytimes.com/2012/12/23/magazine/jerry-seinfeld-intends-to-die-standing-up.html?pagewanted=all&_r=0.

## Chapter Two: Break Path Dependence

1. Paul Kedrosky, http://edge.org/response-detail/23860.
2. Kevin Kelly, *What Technology Wants* (New York: Viking, 2010).
3. Jörg Sydow, Georg Schreyögg and Jochen Koch, "Organizational Path Dependence: Opening the Black Box," *Academy of Management Review* 34, no. 4 (2009), 689–709. http://amr.aom.org/content/34/4/689.abstract.
4. The positive aspects of Path Dependence are not too dissimilar from Clay Christensen's idea of *The Innovator's Dilemma*—companies ultimately stumble not because they are badly managed, but because they are well managed. They keep doing what they have always done and do it well, but get disrupted by companies whose innovations don't work as well, or are lower cost innovations sold initially in unprofitable niches.
5. *Michael Lewis*, "Obama's Way," *Vanity Fair*, October 2012, www.vanityfair.com/politics/2012/10/michael-lewis-profile-barack-obama.
6. David T. Neal, Wendy Wood, and Aimee Drolet, "How Do People Adhere to Goals When Willpower Is Low? The Profits (and Pitfalls) of Strong Habits," *Journal of Personality and Social Psychology*, 104, no. 6 (2013): 959–975, http://psycnet.apa.org/?&fa=main.doiLanding&doi=10.1037/a0032626.
7. Ina Fried, "Intel CEO Brian Krzanich: We Missed the Tablet," Recode, http://recode.net/2014/05/28/intel-ceo-brian-krzanich-we-missed-the-tablet/.
8. Bob Schaller, "The Nature, Origin, and Implications of Moore's Law," (Paper for Macro Policy course, 1996), http://research.microsoft.com/en-us/um/people/gray/moore_law.html.
9. Vijay Govindarajan and Chris Trimble, *Reverse Innovation: Create Far from Home, Win Everywhere* (Boston, MA: Harvard Business Review Press, 2012).
10. A charter school is a school in the United States that receives public funding but operates independently.
11. Author's own interview.
12. Daniel Kahneman, *Thinking, Fast and Slow* (New York: Farrar, Straus & Giroux, 2013).
13. Nike, http://nikeinc.com/news/nike-flyknit.
14. Author's own interview.

15. Harvard Business School, "HBS Governance and Sustainability at Nike," www.hbs.edu/faculty/Pages/item.aspx?num=44895.

16. According to Millward Brown's Brand Z study of the Top 100 most valuable brands globally, Visa was the 9th most valuable brand in 2013, growing brand value by 46 percent and moving up 6 places from the previous year, www.millwardbrown .com/brandz/2013/Top100/Docs/2013_BrandZ_Top100_Report.pdf.

17. The legendary British adman's original saying was, of course, "Interrogate the product until it confesses its strengths."

18. Author's own interview.

## Chapter Three: Ask Propelling Questions

1. Steven Levy, "Google's Larry Page on Why Moonshots Matter," *Wired*, January 7, 2013, http://www.wired.com/2013/01/ff-qa-larry-page/all/.

2. Google Income Statement 2013 from their website.

3. Larry Page google+ post of January 24, 2012, quoting *Wired* magazine article January 2012. https://plus.google.com/s/Larry%20Page%20google%2B%20 post%20of%20Jan%2024%2C%202012%20quoting%20Wired%20 magazine%20article%20Jan%202012%20.

4. Driverless cars will also free up people's time and, many believe, will reduce congestion. It is a project driven by multiple constraint-driven ambitions.

5. Audi, www.audi.co.uk/audi-innovation/audi-motorsport/audi-r10-tdi.html

6. Author's own interview.

7. Miron-Spektor, Francesca Gino, and Linda Argote, "Paradoxical Frames and Creative Sparks: Enhancing Individual Creativity through Conflict and Resolution," http://francescagino.com/pdfs/mironspektor_gino_argote_obhdp_ 2011.pdf.

8. Or parents wanting twice the amount of teenage help around the house, with half the amount of eye-rolling.

9. Unilever, www.unilever.com/brands-in-action/detail/Domestos/292042/.

10. Chipotle, www.chipotle.com/en-us/fwi/fwi.aspx.

11. Wesley Yin-Poole, "We Have the Ambition to Build the Best Gaming Console for Fans," Eurogamer.net, April 10, 2014, www.eurogamer.net/articles/2014- 04-10-meet-new-xbox-boss-phil-spencer.

12. Author's own interview.

13. Three minutes was the exact amount of time that Otto Skorzeny gave himself to secure Mussolini after crashing his glider on the Gran Sasso in 1943. Source: William H. McRaven, *Spec Ops: Case Studies in Special Operations Warfare: Theory and Practice* (New York: Presidio Press, 2011), p. 180.

14. Charles Handy, *The Age of Unreason: New Thinking for a New World* (New York: Random House Business, 1980).

15. Charles Handy, *The Age of Paradox* (Cambridge, MA: Harvard Business School Press, 1995.)

16. Inspired by the brilliant Louis CK's "everything's amazing and nobody is happy" rant on *Conan*, www.youtube.com/watch?v=uEY58fiSK8E.

17. Martin LaMonica, "Stringent Café Standards Push Automakers," *MIT Technology Review*, August 29, 2012, www.technologyreview.com/view/429041/stringent-cafe-standards-push-automakers/.

18. Austin Carr, "What Hotel Operators Really Think of Airbnb," *Fast Company*, March 20, 2014, www.fastcompany.com/3027976/what-hotel-operators-really-think-of-airbnb.

19. Chris Morran, "T-Mobile Added More New Customers Than AT&T, Verizon Combined," *Consumerist*, May 1, 2014, http://consumerist.com/2014/05/01/t-mobile-added-more-new-customers-than-att-verizon-combined/.

20. John Gerzema, *Cinderellanomics,* www.johngerzema.com/articles/cinderellanomics.

21. John Gerzema and Ed Lebar, "The Trouble with Brands," www.strategy-business.com/article/09205?pg=all.

22. Author's own interview.

23. The data is not able to assign causality to this. We can only infer the relationship at this point.

24. Author's own interview.

## Chapter Four: Can-If

1. Mark Prigg, "Sir Jonathan Ive: The iMan Cometh," *London Evening Standard*, March 12, 2012, www.standard.co.uk/lifestyle/london-life/sir-jonathan-ive-the-iman-cometh-7562170.html.

2. Tali Sharot, *The Optimism Bias: A Tour of the Irrationally Positive Brain* (New York: Vintage, 2012).

3. Barbara Fredrickson, *Positivity: Groundbreaking Research to Release Your Inner Optimist and Thrive* (London: One World Publications, 2011).

4. Kelly's concept of flow is not the same as the one developed by Mihaly Csikszentmihalyi to describe the feeling of energized focus that comes from being totally immersed in an activity. Mihaly Csikszentmihalyi, *Flow: The Psychology of Optimal Experience*, (New York: Harper Perennial Modern Classics 2008).

5. Thomas Friedman, "Pass the Books. Hold the Oil," *New York Times*, March 10, 2012, www.nytimes.com/2012/03/11/opinion/sunday/friedman-pass-the-books-hold-the-oil.html?pagewanted=all.

6. Author's own interview with Dr. CJ Liu, Director of Education Division of the Taipei Economic and Cultural Representative Office, Washington, D.C.

7. Taiwan Miracle, Wikipedia. http://en.wikipedia.org/wiki/Taiwan_Miracle.

8. Friedman, "Pass the Books. Hold the Oil."

9. Author's own interview.

10. Source: Heather McGill.

11. Author's own interview.

12. Author's own interview with Christopher Lukezic, CMO, EMEA, of Airbnb.

13. Greg Toppo, "Crowd Sourced Language App Seeks to Translate Entire Web," *USA TODAY*, February 3, 2013, www.usatoday.com/story/news/nation/2013/02/02/crowdsourced-language-app-seeks-to-translate-entire-web/1885847/.

14. Author's own interview.

15. Author's own interview.

16. Mike Cooper, CEO WW, PHD.

17. Author's own interview with Sue Allchurch.

18. Author's own interview with Ajoy Krishnamurti.

19. Meghan Petersen, "Equip Your Bike for the Ride of Your Life," *New York Times*, April 26, 2014, www.buffalonews.com/life-arts/fitness/equip-your-bike-for-the-ride-of-your-life-20140426.

20. Kendra Nordin, "Restaurants Reinvent the Food Truck," *Christian Science Monitor*, August 24, 2013, www.csmonitor.com/Business/2013/0824/Restaurants-reinvent-the-food-truck.

21. Norm Brodsky, "The Blessing of Not Enough Money," Inc.com, April 2014, www.inc.com/magazine/201404/norm-brodsky/why-too-much-money-is-bad-for-a-startup.html.

22. "Equity for Punks," www.brewdog.com/media/efp/EFPIII.pdf?v=2 and author's own interview with James Watt.

23. Author's own interview with Trevor Davis.

24. *Jason H. Harper, "When Less Is More,"* Bloomberg Markets, February 2013.

25. J. Marguc, J. Förster, and G. A. Van Kleef, "Stepping Back to See the Big Picture: When Obstacles Elicit Global Processing," *Journal of Personality and Social Psychology* 101, no. 5 (2011): 883–901.

## Chapter Five: Creating Abundance

1. K.R. Sridhar, http://harikn.com/tag/k-r-sridhar/.

2. Thanks to the On Your Feet team, especially Robert Poynton's book *Everything's An Offer: How to Do More with Less* (Portland, OR: On Your Feet, 2008). And to fifteen years' experience with these principles in our own work.

3. Porter Gale, *Your Network is Your Net Worth: Unlock the Hidden Power of Connections for Wealth, Success, and Happiness in the Digital Age* (New York: Atria Books, 2013).

4. See, for instance, Adam Grant's work on generosity, http://hbr.org/2013/04/in-the-company-of-givers-and-takers.

5. Triplepundit.com, July 11, 2013. http://www.triplepundit.com/2013/07/nike-launches-free-materials-app-already-looks-ahead-next-level-innovation/.

6. "Future by Airbus: Airbus Unveils Its Vision of 'Smarter Skies,' http://videos.airbus.com/channel/d8d5814b6ccc.html.

7. Dave Trott, *Predatory Thinking: A Masterclass in Out-Thinking the Competition* (New York: Macmillan, 2013).

8. Author's own interview.

9. Thomas R. Eisenmann and Laura Winig, "Rent the Runway," Harvard Business School Case 812-077, November 2011 (revised December 2012), www.hbs.edu/faculty/Pages/item.aspx?num=41142.

10. Author's own interview with Paul Seward, FIPS.

## Chapter Six: Activating Emotions

1. William H. McRaven, *Spec Ops: Case Studies in Special Operations Warfare: Theory and Practice* (New York: Presidio Press, 2011), p. 180.
2. Ibid., 23.
3. Nikki Blacksmith and Jim Harter, "Majority of American Workers Not Engaged in Their Jobs," http://www.gallup.com/poll/150383/majority-american-workers-not-engaged-jobs.aspx.
4. Author's own interview.
5. Angela Duckworth, Christopher Peterson, Michael D. Matthews, and Dennis R. Kelly, *Grit: Perseverance and Passion for Long-Term Goals,* www.sas.upenn.edu/~duckwort/images/Grit%20JPSP.pdf.
6. Janina Marguc, author's own interview; plus see earlier source in Chapter Four: Can-If.
7. Author's own interview.
8. Katherine Gottlieb, "Transforming Your Practice: What Matters Most," *Family Practice Management* 15, no. 1 (2008): 32–39. www.aafp.org/fpm/2008/0100/p32.html#.
9. Rasmuson Foundation Press Release, "First Alaskan named MacArthur Genius, October 5, 2004, http://rasmuson.org/PressRelease/index.php?switch=view_pressrelease&iReleaseID=42#sthash.YCs6rfkM.dpuf.
10. Malcolm Gladwell popularized the concept of "desirable difficulties," using the research of Robert and Elizabeth Bjork of UCLA, in *David and Goliath: Underdogs, Misfits and The Art of Battling Giants* (New York: Little, Brown, 2013).
11. Author's own interview.
12. Author's own interview.
13. For example, Daniel H. Pink, *Drive: The Surprising Truth About What Motivates Us* (Edinburgh: Canongate Books Ltd. 2011), emphasizes the superiority of intrinsic motivations over extrinsic motivations.
14. Author's own interview.
15. Whitney Friedlander, "Judd Apatow: Everything He's Done Is Revenge for Canceling 'Freaks and Geeks,'" *Variety*, March 11, 2014, http://variety.com/2014/scene/news/judd-apatow-freaks-and-geeks-1201129436/.
16. Matt Cowan, Wired.co.uk, "Fail to Succeed," April 25, 2011, www.wired.co.uk/magazine/archive/2011/05/features/fail-to-succeed.

17. B. A. Nijstad, C. K. W. De Dreu, E. F. Rietzschel, and M. Baas, "The Dual Pathway to Creativity Model," *European Review of Social Psychology* 21, no. 1 (2010), www.tandfonline.com/doi/abs/10.1080/10463281003765323#.U9u5CPldWSo.

18. D. T. Max, "Two Hit Wonder," *New Yorker*, October 21, 2013, http://www.newyorker.com/reporting/2013/10/21/131021fa_fact_max?currentPage=all

19. Author's own interview. For more information about Gabriele Oettingen, Professor of Psychology, Social, Developmental, New York University see her website www.psych.nyu.edu/oettingen/.

20. Author's own interview.

21. Author's own interview.

22. Robert Plutchik's Theory of Basic Emotions, http://visual.ly/robert-plutchiks-psycho-evolutionary-theory-basic-emotions.

23. Author's own interview with d.school principals.

24. Ibid.

25. Professor Carol Dweck distinguishes between growth and fixed mindsets. A growth mindset understands that talent can be developed, a fixed mindset that talent is fixed. Smart students can get stuck with a fixed mindset if they are always told how smart they are, as opposed to how hard they have tried. When someone with a fixed mindset fails it can be harder for them to incorporate the learning and try again. *Mindset: How You Can Fulfill Your Potential* (Edinburgh: Constable & Robinson, Ltd., 2012).

26. Design for Extreme Affordability, www.extremebydesignmovie.com.

## Chapter Seven: The Fertile Zero

1. *Life: Keith Richards*, by Keith Richards, W&N (UK) and Little, Brown & Company (US), 2010.

2. It is not, of course, inevitable that resource richness leads to poor economic performance. There is, conversely, a set of practices, advocated by Stiglitz and other economists, which explore how such resource wealth can in fact be a blessing, rather than a curse. www.project-syndicate.org/commentary/from-resource-curse-to-blessing-by-joseph-e--stiglitz

3. Author's own interview with Marc Priestley May 5, 2014.

4. Author's own interview.

5. Author's own interview.

6. See, for example: Adam Lindgreen and Joëlle Vanhamme, "To Surprise or Not to Surprise Your Customers: The Use of Surprise as a Marketing Tool," *Journal of Customer Behaviour* 2, no. 2 (June 1, 2003): 219–242; Joelle Vanhamme and Dirk Snelders, "What If You Surprise Your Customers … Will They Be More Satisfied? Findings From a Pilot Experiment," in *NA—Advances in Consumer Research* 30, eds. Punam Anand Keller and Dennis W. Rook, Valdosta, GA: Association for Consumer Research, 48–55.

7. Author's own interview.

8. BBC Four, *Beautiful Minds*, May 14, 2012, www.bbc.co.uk/programmes/p00qvql7.

9. Author's own interview.

10. Author's own interview.

11. Author's own interview.

12. Nellie Bowles, "Betabrand Markets with Guy Humor," SF Gate.com, www.sfgate.com/style/article/Betabrand-markets-with-guy-humor-4264294.php.

13. Rachel Wells, "The Man Behind the Aesop Brand," *Sydney Morning Herald* February 23, 2012, www.smh.com.au/small-business/entrepreneur/the-man-behind-the-aesop-brand-20120222-1tntu.html#ixzz30YHgAPyU. "Aesop—Fabled Brand Fabulous Marketing," JP Kuehlwein, wordpress.com, December 3, 2012, http://masstoclass.wordpress.com/2012/12/03/aesop-fabled-brand-fabulous-marketing/.

14. Author's own interview with Ludo Auvray.

15. Sir Lawrence Freedman, *Strategy: A History* (New York: Oxford University Press, 2013).

16. Author's own interview with Ludo Auvray.

17. Author's own interview.

18. Taxi, "Icograda: Saki Mafundikwa and Ravi Naidoo," DesignTaxi.com, http://designtaxi.com/article.php?article_id=193.

19. Wikiquote, http://en.wikiquote.org/wiki/Ernest_Rutherford.

20. Author's own interview with Pier Luigi Sigismondi.

## Chapter Eight: Constraint-Driven Cultures

1. Andy Giegerich, "Ikea Joins Nike in DyeCoo Investment Club," *Portland Business Journal*, April 9, 2013, www.bizjournals.com/portland/blog/sbo/2013/04/ikea-joins-nike-in-dyecoo-investment.html?page=all.

2. Author's own interview.

3. Interviews with Michael Hay. James Thompson, "Record Profits at Ikea after a Year of Global Growth," The Independent, January 23, 2013, www.independent.co.uk/news/business/news/record-profits-at-ikea-after-a-year-ofglobal-growth-8464285.html.

4. HBS Nike case study, June 2013, http://hbr.org/product/Governance-and-Sustainabi/an/313146-PDF-ENG.

5. Ibid.

6. Stanley Holmes, "Nike Goes For The Green," *Bloomberg Businessweek* September 24, 2006, www.businessweek.com/stories/2006-09-24/nike-goes-for-the-green.

7. Ibid.

8. HBS Nike case study, June 2013.

9. Author's own interviews with Nike staff.

10. Nike press release, December 2013, quote from Kuenlin Ho, Nike's contract manufacturer, http://nikeinc.com/news/nike-colordry.

11. Nike, http://nikeinc.com/news/nike-flyknit.

12. Ibid.

13. Author's own interview.

14. This is remarkably similar to the motivational technique Professor Oettingen characterizes as Mental Contrasting.

15. Paul Polman discussing 2013 results and his last five years, www.unilever.com/mediacentre/pressreleases/2014/Unileverreportsgrowthaheadofmarketsin2013.aspx

16. "Future by Airbus: Airbus Unveils Its Vision of "Smarter Skies," http://videos.airbus.com/channel/d8d5814b6ccc.html.

17. Source: Michael Hay.

18. Richard Milne, "Mojang: Smash Hit 'Minecraft' Maker," *Financial Times*, July 22, 2014, www.ft.com/intl/cms/s/2/0283b57c-10ca-11e4-b116-00144feabdc0.html#axzz3D1y767VR.

19. This idea came from Mark Holden of PHD.

20. Author's own interview with Hylton Kallner.

### Chapter Nine: Scarcity and Abundance

1. See, for example, Duncan Green of Oxfam: www.oxfam.org/en/pressroom/pressrelease/2008-06-23/new-deal-needed-to-stop-plunging-millions-into-poverty and Navi Radjou et al. in HBR quoting an *Economist* article: http://blogs.hbr.org/2010/06/ibm-just-released-its-global/.

2. Pip Brooking, "Fixing Capitalism: Paul Polman Interview," *Business Voice*, November 2012, www.cbi.org.uk/media-centre/news-articles/2012/11/fixing-capitalism-paul-polman-interview/

3. Rephrase: Ian Salisbury, "Our Chat with Jeremy Grantham," in *Wall Street Journal* September 20, 2013, http://online.wsj.com/news/articles/SB10001424127887323665504579032934293143524?mg=reno64-wsj&url=http%3A%2F%2Fonline.wsj.com%2Farticle%2FSB10001424127887323665504579032934293143524.html.

4. World Wildlife Foundation, www.worldwildlife.org.

5. Global Water Security, Intelligence Community Assessment, February 2, 2012, www.transboundarywaters.orst.edu/publications/publications/ICA_Global%20Water%20Security[1]%20(1).pdf.

6. Saul Griffith, Long Now Foundation lecture, 2009 http://longnow.org/seminars/02009/jan/16/climate-change-recalculated/.

7. Andrew Zolli and Ann Marie Healy, *Resilience: Why Things Bounce Back* (New York: Business Plus, 2013), http://resiliencethebook.com/.

8. Peter Diamandis and Steven Kotler, *Abundance* (New York: Free Press, 2012).

9. The contents of this table are a synthesis of many books and articles too numerous to list. Some sources are:
   - Diamandis and Kotler, *Abundance*.
   - And this wonderful set of Abundance Infographics: http://discovermagazine.com/galleries/zen-photo/a/age-of-abundance#.UZ-sQusvpXk.
   - Erik Brynjolfsson's TED talk: *Race With the Machines*, www.ted.com/talks/erik_brynjolfsson_the_key_to_growth_race_em_with_em_the_machines.
   - Chris Anderson, *Makers: The New Industrial Revolution* (New York: Crown Business, 2014), www.amazon.com/Makers-The-New-Industrial-Revolution/dp/0307720969/ref=sr_1_3?ie=UTF8&qid=1406783445&sr=8-3&keywords=the+third+industrial+revolution.

- Stewart Brand, *Whole Earth Discipline: Why Dense Cities, Nuclear Power, Transgenic Crops, Restored Wildlands, Radical Science, and Geoengineering are Necessary* (London: Atlantic Books, 2010).
- John Elkington, *The Zeronauts: Breaking the Sustainability Barrier* (New York: Routledge, 2012).
- Tyler Cowen, *The Great Stagnation: How America Ate All The Low-Hanging Fruit of Modern History, Got Sick, and Will (Eventually) Feel Better* (New York: Dutton Adult, 2011).
- The writing of Robert J. Gordon of Northwestern, http://faculty-eb .at.northwestern.edu/economics/gordon/researchhome.html University http://online.wsj.com/news/articles/SB10001424127887324461604578 191781756437940.
- Charles Kenny, "The Age of Scarcity," *BloombergBusinessweek*, July 26, 2012, www.businessweek.com/articles/2012-07-26/the-age-of-scarcity.

10. This is still somewhat speculative, as the ability to manufacture and install at that enormous scale would clearly become a gating item for solar. And none of this addresses climate change already underway.
11. Tonny K. Omwansa, and Nicholas P. Sullivan, *Money, Real Quick: The Story of M-PESA* (London: Guardian Books, 2012).
12. Diamandis and Kotler, *Abundance*, 142.
13. Virgin Atlantic, www.virginatlantic.com.
14. "Farming the Desert," *Time*, July 2013, http://content.time.com/time/magazine/article/0,9171,2146442,00.html.
15. Madeline Levine, *The Price of Privilege* (New York: Harper Perennial, 2008).
16. Alvin Toffler popularized the term back in 1970 in his book *Future Shock*.
17. Mullainathan and Shafer, *Scarcity: Why Having Too Little Means So Much* (New York: Times Books, 2013).
18. Drake Baer, "What Multitasking Does to Your Brain," *Fast Company*, October 9, 2013, www.fastcompany.com/3019659/leadership-now/what -multitasking-does-to-your-brain.
19. Vanessa Loder, "Why Multi-Tasking Is Worse than Marijuana for Your IQ," *Forbes*, November 6, 2014, www.forbes.com/sites/vanessaloder/2014/06/11/ why-multi-tasking-is-worse-than-marijuana-for-your-iq/.

20. Tony Schwartz and Christine Porath, "Why You Hate Work," *New York Times*, May 30, 2014, www.nytimes.com/2014/06/01/opinion/sunday/why-you -hate-work.html.

21. Kevin Kelly, *What Technology Wants* (New York: Viking, 2010), 192.

## Chapter Ten: Making Constraints Beautiful:

1. Sendhil Mullainathan and Eldar Shafir, *Scarcity: Why Having Too Little Means So Much* (New York: Times Books, 2013).

2. Thanks, Rama.

3. Stewart Brand, as quoted in *Whole Earth Discipline. An Ecopragmatist Manifesto*, p. 43, http://discipline.longnow.org/DISCIPLINE_footnotes/2_-_ City_Planet.html.

4. Richard H. Thaler and Cass R. Sunstein, *Nudge: Improving Decisions About Health, Wealth and Happiness* (New York: Penguin, 2009); Mullainathan and Shafir, *Scarcity*.

5. First articulated by Sid Parnes, *Creative Behavior Guidebook* (New York: Charles Scribner's Sons, 1967).

## Chapter Eleven: Leadership and The Future of Constraints

1. Louis Menand, "Cat People. What Dr. Seuss Really Taught Us," *New Yorker*, December 23, 2002, www.newyorker.com/magazine/2002/12/23/cat-people.

2. Kevin Kruse, "What Is Leadership?" *Forbes*, April 9, 2013, www.forbes.com/ sites/kevinkruse/2013/04/09/what-is-leadership/.

3. Robert Blethune, "Self Censorship," *Art Times*, April 2009, www.arttimesjournal .com/theater/April.09_theatre.htm.

4. Professor James Carse, NYU, speech at APG conference, Washington DC, 2001.

5. BBC 2, *Genius of Invention*, Season 1, Episode 4, February 14, 2013, featuring James Dyson, www.imdb.com/title/tt2645332/.

# BIBLIOGRAPHY AND FURTHER READING

Boyd, Drew, and Jacob Goldenberg. *Inside the Box: Why the Best Business Innovations are Right in Front of You.* London: Profile Books, 2013.

Brand, Stewart. *Whole Earth Discipline: An Ecopragmatist Manifesto.* New York: Viking Adult, 2009.

Brown, Tim. *Change by Design: How Design Thinking Transforms Organizations and Inspires Innovation.* New York: HarperBusiness, 2009.

Diamandis, Peter, and Steven Kotler. *Abundance.* New York: Free Press, 2012.

Freedman, Lawrence. *Strategy: A History.* New York: Oxford University Press, 2013.

Gale, Porter. *Your Network Is Your Net Worth.* New York: Atria Books, 2013.

Goldratt, Eliyahu M., and Jeff Cox. *The Goal: A Process of Ongoing Improvement.* Farnham, UK: Gower Publishing Ltd., 2004.

Handy, Charles. *The Age of Unreason.* Boston: Harvard Business School Press, 1989.

Johnson, Steven. *Where Good Ideas Come From.* New York: Riverhead Trade, 2011.

Kelley, David, and Tom Kelley. *Creative Confidence. Unleashing the Creative Potential Within All of Us.* New York: Crown Business, 2013.

Kelly, Kevin. *What Technology Wants.* New York: Viking, 2010.

Levine, Madeline. *The Price of Privilege.* New York: Harper Perennial, 2008.

Leadbeater, Charles. *The Frugal Innovator: Creating Change on a Shoestring Budget.* New York: Macmillan, 2014.

May, Matthew E. *The Laws of Subtraction: 6 Simple Rules for Winning in the Age of Excess Everything.* New York: McGraw-Hill Professional, 2012.

McRaven, William H. *Spec Ops: Case Studies in Special Operations Warfare: Theory and Practice.* New York: Presidio, 2011.

Mullainathan, Sendhil, and Eldar Shafir. *Scarcity: Why Having Too Little Means So Much.* New York: Allen Lane, 2013.

Parnes, S. J. *Creative Behavior Guidebook.* New York: Scribner, 2000.

Poynton, Robert. *Do Improvise.* London: The Do Book Company, 2013.

Radjou, Navi, Jaideep Prabhu, and Simone Ahuja, *Jugaad Innovation: Think Frugal, Be Flexible, Generate Breakthrough Growth.* Hoboken, NJ: John Wiley & Sons, 2012.

Ries, Eric. *The Lean Startup: How Constant Innovation Creates Radically Successful Businesses.* New York: Portfolio Penguin, 2011.

Zolli, Andrew, and Ann Marie Healy. *Resilience: Why Things Bounce Back.* New York: Business Plus, 2013.

# IMAGE CREDITS

1. *Seinfeld:* Jerry Seinfeld—Photo by NBC/NBCU Photo Bank via Getty Images.

2. ExitTicket—with permission of Leadership Public Schools .

3. Visa payWave system on Samsung Galaxy SIII—Photographer: Simon Dawson/Bloomberg via Getty Images.

4. The Audi R10 TDI—Photo by Gavin Lawrence/Getty Images.

5. London 2012 Olympics Volunteers—Photo by Jeff J Mitchell/Getty Images.

6. PHD Source Leaderboard—with permission of PHD.

7. Small Axe Truck, Portland, Maine—Photo by Gordon Chibroski/Portland Press Herald via Getty Images.

8. ColaLife—Photo by Simon Berry.

9. Making app—with permission of Nike.

10. CALVIN AND HOBBES © 1992 Watterson. Reprinted with permission of UNIVERSAL UCLICK. All rights reserved.

11. J D Wetherspoon—Photo by Toby Brown.

12. McLaren F1 pitstop—Photo by Paul Gilham/Getty Images.

13. Never Mind the Anabolics—with permission of BrewDog.

14. Warby Parker Annual Report —with permission of Warby Parker. Photo: Noel Camardo.

15. Smaland stone wall—with permission of IKEA.

16. Nike Air Max 360—with permission of Nike.

17. Dr. Seuss Holds *The Cat in the Hat*—Photo by Gene Lester/Getty Images.

# APPENDIX

---

## The unreasonable challenger

**This appendix contains** a little more detail on BAV's analysis for us of brands whose core offer combines two criteria for choice, historically regarded as trade-offs in the category: "green" and "performance," in cars, for example, being considered two quite separate poles until Tesla united them. We wanted to understand what impact uniting these poles has on what BAV calls energized differentiation or brand energy, that is, a sense of momentum for a brand in the mind of the consumer that is an indicator of their future potential. BAV's work with academics suggests a strong correlation between brand energy and market value (see page 80).

We looked at US examples in three mature, mass-market categories. In quick service restaurants (QSR) we looked at "good value" versus "healthy"; in luxury automobiles we looked at "green" versus "performance;" and in household cleaning products we looked at "efficiency" versus "socially conscious." We looked at category-level data and then drilled down into specific brand cases to illustrate the larger point more clearly.

The two headlines from this analysis are:
- Not surprisingly, given how brands have historically regarded these choice criteria as quite separate poles and rarely, if ever, addressed them both in the core offering, the consumer does indeed see them as distinct and separate. Few brands are seen as offering both polar attributes in their respective categories
- Those brands that do offer both also have a stronger brand energy score than those that don't.

## Quick service restaurants

Figure A-1 shows that while 27% of people strongly associate brands in the QSR category with value, and 12.5% strongly associate them with health, only 6.3% see brands as offering both.

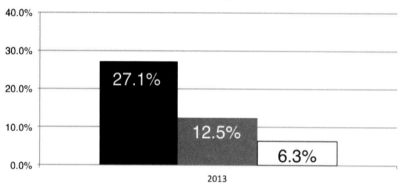

**Brand Perceptions Among QSR Restaurants**

*Figure A-1: Quick service restaurant brands tend to be perceived as good value or healthy, but not both*

Figure A-2 shows the correlation between these attributes and brand differentiation. Brands that score highly on both value and health are more strongly differentiated than brands more strongly associated with just one of these attributes.

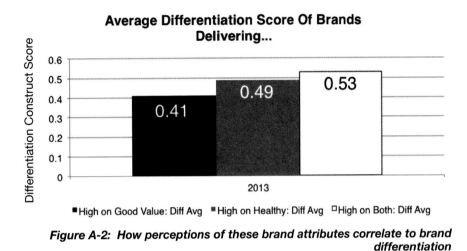

**Figure A-2:** *How perceptions of these brand attributes correlate to brand differentiation*

We looked at two brands in the category a little more closely to assess the differences in their brand energy between 2011 and 2013: Chipotle, who, in addition to a menu oriented around simple, real ingredients, has made extensive efforts to source sustainably and tell the world about it; and Taco Bell, the biggest Mexican–style fast food chain, and a close competitor to Chipotle. We saw that Chipotle is building real brand differentiation and energy based on its perceived ability to offer both health and value, as can be seen in Figure A-3. And Taco Bell, while remaining strong on value is losing brand energy as it loses ground on the health perceptions of its offer.

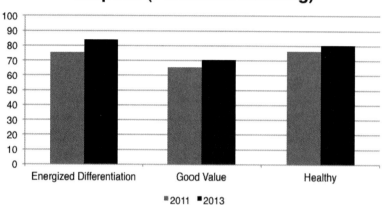

*Figure A-3: How Chipotle's ability to drive both value and healthy perceptions is mirrored in high energized differentiation*

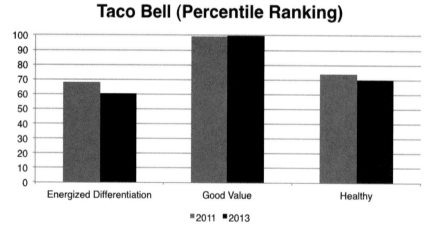

*Figure A-4: How Taco Bell is losing brand energy because of its inability to drive perceptions of healthy along with value*

## Luxury cars

A similar dynamic exists in luxury cars in the US as Figure A-5 shows. In 2013, the latest period for which we have data, only 7.9% of people perceive luxury cars as offering both performance (measured by a basket of attributes including high performance, dynamic, daring) and green credentials (socially-responsible, progressive, innovative). And as Figure A-6 suggests, those brands that do score high on both sets of attributes are more highly differentiated than brands associated with just one set.

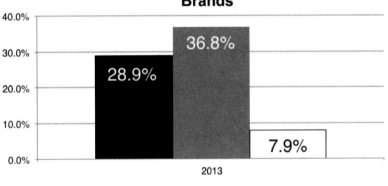

**Brand Perceptions Among Luxury Car Brands**

*Figure A-5: Automotive brands are perceived as green or high performance, but not both*

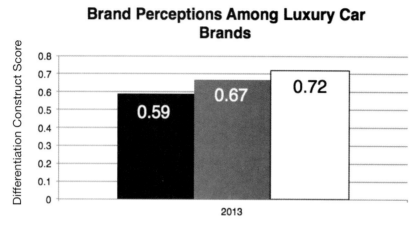

**Figure A-6. Luxury car brands that are perceived as being both green and high performance have higher brand differentiation than those that are "either/or"**

Looking more closely at two brands in the category, Tesla and Mercedes Benz, shows this dynamic playing out even more clearly. Tesla exists to create high performance, battery-powered (hence greener) cars, and it is clearly on the rise as a brand, scoring gains in both attributes and an increase in brand energy. Mercedes Benz on the other hand, though still a very powerful brand, is showing declines in differentiation as its brand loses both green and performance perceptions (see Figure A-7), a pattern seen in some other luxury marques, too. Though it is early in the life of Tesla, and its future is still uncertain, if this kind of dynamic continues, luxury automakers will find themselves more actively de-positioned by this unreasonable challenger, beyond the actual share that its price point enables it to take.

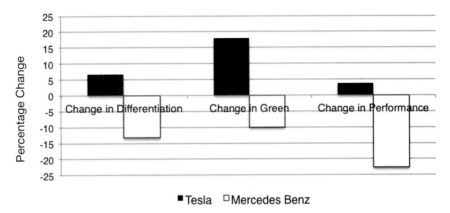

Figure A-7: Increase in perceptions of green and high performance between 2012 and 2013 correlated with higher differentiation for Tesla; decrease in the same correlate with lower differentiation for Mercedes-Benz

### Household cleaning products

And finally, household cleaning products. Figure A-8 shows that an overwhelming majority of brands are seen as efficient cleaners, far fewer are seen as socially conscious, and about the same are seen as both. Household cleaning products are a particularly interesting segment to examine because the notion of being socially conscious is a relatively new one in the category. Due to the newness of this notion along with the extremely high proportion of brands that are perceived as efficient, socially conscious actually tracks very closely with doing both, and is driving some differentiation in the category (see Figure A-9).

# Brand Perceptions among Household Cleaning Product Brands

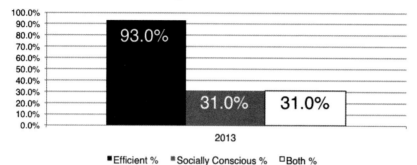

*Figure A-8: Household cleaning brands are perceived as efficient but fewer are seen as socially conscious, or both*

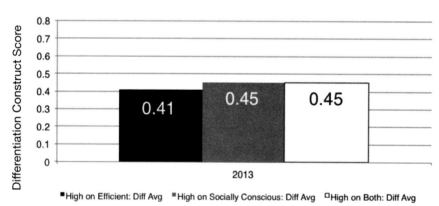

*Figure A-9: Cleaning brands that are perceived as being socially conscious and high performance have higher brand differentiation*

This story is particularly striking when we examine the case of method, a brand that has "unreasonably" united cleaning efficacy with environmentally-friendly credentials. The brand energy average for the household cleaning product category in 2013 was 0.41. For method, brand energy is much higher: 0.52.

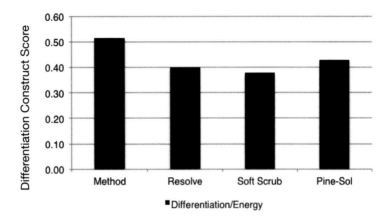

**_Figure A-10: method has higher brand energy/differentiation than conventional brands that have focused only on efficacy_**

# THANKS AND ACKNOWLEDGMENTS

At the heart of this book are the people who gave their time and experiences in the interviews; this is simply a collation of their insights and journeys. We are enormously grateful to:

Sue Allchurch
Rodrigo Arboleda Halaby
Ludo Auvray
Naty Barak
Yves Behar
Michael Bierut
Neil Blumenthal
Tim Brown
Karen Chu
Mike Cooper
Stuart Coulson
Trevor Davis
Porter Gale
John Gerzema
Julian Gorodsky
Katherine Gottlieb
Steven Grasse
Michael Hay
Capt. James Housinger
Martin Huxtable
Rama Iyer
Michael Jordaan
Mary Lou Jepsen
Dr. Caneel Joyce

Hylton Kallner
Geoff Keighley
Colin Kelly
Ben Knelman
Ajoy Krishnamurti
Eric Leininger
Dr. CJ Liu
Janina Marguc
Helen Marriage
Heather McGill
Ravi Naidoo
Professor Gabrielle Oettingen
Professor Jim Patell
Robert Poynton
Marc Priestley
Navi Rajdoo
Dr. Scot Refsland
Paul Seward
Toby Shapshak
Pier Luigi Sigismondi
Dr. Louise Waters and the LPS team
James Watt
Dan Wieden

Behind the scenes, there have also been friends and helpers who introduced us to some of these remarkable people: Richard F. Dallam, Tim Leberecht, George Pereira, Julia Hu, Juan Albanell, Pam Scott and Tim Koogle, Debbe Stern, Richard Hytner, Giles Morgan, Jon Gisby, Trevor Davis, Marcel Corstjens, Jonathan Warburton, Naresh Ramchandani, Norman Adami, John Stenslunde and Robbie Brozin.

And others helped bounce around some of the constituent ideas at an early stage: Jelly Helm, Brian Lanahan, Robin Lanahan, Mark Valentine, Lawrence Wilkinson, Antonio Lucio, Nick Kendall and the BBH London Planning Department, Madeline Levine, Jon Evans, Mark Holden, Bella Acton, Elle Harrison, Peter Field, Giles Elliott, Gayle Harrison, Phil Rumbol, Russell Goldman, Michael Christman, Chris Fitzgerald, and the Opts team. Paul Pendergrass, Chris Fussell, David Smith, Jono Hey, Jeff Bronchick, Stephen Walker, Gareth Kay, Dr. Richard Marks, Chris Riley, Rebecca Armstrong, Kiran Patel, and our friends at Nike pointed us in directions that were as interesting as they suggested they would be.

Clients who have explored putting this approach into practice with us included Marie Chandoha at CSIM, with Jon De St. Paer; and Norman Adami and Mauricio Leyva at SAB, the learnings from which were invaluable. Trevor Cartwright of Coraggio Group helped us road test the work on some of his clients in its early stages.

Special thanks to the team at BAV who have helped us put some substance to the unreasonable thinking within Chapter Three (Propelling Questions): John Gerzema, Will Johnson, Dr. Meredith L. Sadin, Garrett Fonda, Keith Newton, and John Michael Hogan.

Much of this book is, of course, made up of the thinking of others, but two people in particular shared their own IP, along with their experiences and thoughts. Colin Kelly's concept of Can-If is one of the key principles and tools in the book, and Michael Hay contributed significantly to the thinking in Chapters Three and Eight. They have both been remarkably generous and patient with our further explorations of their ideas.

Richard Narramore, our editor at John Wiley & Sons, has been hugely supportive of our desire to find a different way to physically express the book, as well as championing the idea itself. And Tiffany Colon and Deborah Schindlar have patiently helped us navigate the shallows of producing the book in its final form. Our agent Jim Levine has been a generous wellspring of enthusiasm, advice, and resources.

Although there are only two members of eatbigfish with their names on the cover, the reality is that it has been a project that everyone in the company has touched and made better in its gestation. Kathleen Ix and Ruth Morgan helped with much of the early research. Teresa Murphy, Hugh Derrick, Chad Dick, Brett Donahay, Nick Geoghegan, Georgia Craib, Elena Perez, Lucy Taylor, Katy Clift, Peter Fauchon, Samantha Johns, Zoe Zambakides, Kayleigh Peett, Amy Ryles and Rosie Dean contributed research, ideas, challenges, encouragement, constructive criticism, and the space to write a book while being part of a thriving company. Thank you all.

Toby Brown made the tool and map design beautiful and usable, with characteristically self-effacing talent.

Jude Bliss has been at the heart of capturing and editing all our interviews; his suggestions in times of crisis reflect his knowing this material as well as we do. The crisp and elegant film edits you will find on the website www.eatbigfish.com are his work.

And Helen Redstone is the unsung hero of this project. Producer, stylist, cover designer, contributor, art director, she has exemplified at various times almost every principle in this book. She made everything better; without her talent, judgment, and resourcefulness, it would have been a very different thing.

Adam would also like to thank Ruth, for the research, sourcing, proofreading, companionship, and rosé. And his boys, Louis and Will, for their interest, patience, and witty badinage.

Mark would like to thank his parents who made many constraints beautiful in their lives, Oma for her love and support, and Gail Barrie for her insight.

And extra special thanks and love from Mark to Doris Mitsch, wife, co-parent, editor, and proofer, who contributed ideas, suffered all the highs and lows of the process, and somehow makes everything possible.

# INDEX

The page numbers for charts, tables, and illustrations are in italics. The letter *b* following a page number indicates a box on that page. The letter *n* following a page number indicates a note on that page. The figure following the *n* indicates the number of the note.

drip irrigation. *See* Netafim
driverless cars, 238n4
Dr. Seuss and The Cat In the Hat, 226
Duckworth, Angela Lee, 126
Duolingo, 163; can-if and, 89
Dweck, Carol, 243n25
DyeCoo, 181
Dyson, James, 233

## E

eatbigfish, 3–4
Electronic Arts (EA), 29, 88, 101
emotional engagement, 126, 219–20;
    ABC approach and, 219–20;
    challengers and, 133–35; Design
    Indaba and, 137–38; J D Weth-
    erspoon and, 133–34; Leadership
    Public Schools (LPS) and, 131b;
    mental contrasting and, 133–37;
    military special operations and,
    125; narratives and, 141; organiza-
    tional purpose and, 126; positive
    and negative emotions and, 135b;
    propelling questions and, 132–33;
    range of, 139, *140*, 141; South-
    central Foundation and, 127–30,
    131–33; summary of, 145; value
    of, 126–27
ExitTicket. *See under* Leadership Public
    Schools (LPS)
external partners: Brodsky, Norm and,
    107; Lubbe, Frikkie and, 107;
    resourcefulness and, 107

Extreme Affordability. *See* Hasso
    Plattner Institute of Design

## F

4-Hour Workweek, The, 65
Facebook, 191
Farm Input Promotions Africa (FIPS-
    Africa), 9; blue chickens and, 120–21
Ferris, Tim, 65
fertile zero, summary of, 171
Finanzas, Juntos, 84–85, 131b
finite game, 231
First National Bank (FNB), 132
fitness, peaking and, 28
food trucks, can-if and, 94, *94*
Ford, Henry, 161
Formula One, 228
Four Seasons Hotel, 35–36
Freedman, Lawrence, 161
Friedman, Thomas, 81

## G

Gale, Porter, 107, 109
gamesmakers, London, 2012, 86–87,
    *87*
Gates Foundation, 203
Geim, André, *155*
Geisel, Theodore (Dr. Seuss), 225; *Cat
    In the Hat, The* and, 225; *Green
    Eggs and Ham*, 225
Gerzema, John, 73–74; on product
    categories, 75–76

M-PESA, 200–201
Mucci, Henry, 125
Mullainathan, Sendhil, 204; *Scarcity*, 204, 212
Musk, Elon, 201
MyDollarStore, 92–93

## N

Naidoo, Ravi, 137–38, 164
Nakuru, 120
Netafim, 17–19, 51, 205–6
neutralizers, 19, 20, 49, 175, 178, 195, 216–17; ABC approach and, 217–18; stages, strategies and, *32*. *See also* transformers; victims
Nike, 24–26, 31, 177–82, 231; agenda sharing and, 117–18; Air and, 178–79; Air Max 360 and, *180*; Considered Design Ethos and, 179; constraint-driven culture and, 193; Flyknit shoe and, 47, 181; Making app and, *118*, 179; precompetitive spaces and, 118; propelling questions and, 188; resourcefulness and, 108; success factors and, 188, 193

## O

Oettingen, Gabriele, 136–37, 138–39, 231, 245n14
Ogilvy, David, 9, 29
Omidyar Networks, 203

One Laptop Per Child (OLPC), 9, 26–27, 64, 126, 164, 236n5

## P

Page, Larry, 2, 57–58
paradoxical frames, 64b
Parker, Mark, 181
Patell, Jim, 142, 143
path dependence, 36–37, *38*, 217, 237n4; ABC approach and, 217; alcohol marketing and, 50–51; associations and relationships and, 51; beginning assumptions and, 49; constituent parts of, 48–49; development of, *38*; Four Seasons hotel and, 35–36; habits of mind and, 38–39; IDEO and, 41–42; invention of the aircraft carrier and, 53b; KPIs, measures of success and, 51–52; language and, 46–47; Leadership Public Schools (LPS) and, 42–46, 51; limitations and, 40–41; lock-in, success and, 40–41; Moore's Law and, 41b; Netafim and, 51; Nike and, 49; overcoming of, 47–50; repeatability and renewal and, 52, 54; routines, processes and, 49–50; solution sources and, 50–51; Southcentral Foundation and, 46–47; summary of, 55; tendencies and biases, naming of, 48; Unilever and, 47–48, 49–50; Visa and, 51–52. *See also* aircraft carriers, invention of

## X

Xbox, 68

## Y

Yahoo, 191

## Z

Zappos, 7, 68

zero constraint: Aesop and, 159; alliance to scale and, 161; benefits of, 166–67; Betabrand and, 158; citizenM and, 161–62; collaboration and, 161, 161–64; commercial innovation and, 163–66; Design Indaba and, 164–66; fertility and, 171; Formula One and, 147–49; Heineken and, 159–60; industrial theatre and, 150–51; map of, 168; mapping ourselves and, 169; marketing and communications behavior and, *168*, 169, *169*; media and, 159; other peoples' resources and, 162–63; Quaker Mercantile and, 156–58; secondary media and, 159–60; six axes and, 169; truthfulness and, 167. *See also under* drama